THE WORDWORTHY
COMPUTER

The Wordworthy Computer

Classroom and Research Applications
in Language and Literature

Paula R. Feldman
University of South Carolina

Buford Norman
University of South Carolina

RANDOM HOUSE   New York

For Merrill
who taught us about computers

First Edition
987654321
Copyright © 1987 by Random House, Inc.

All rights reserved under International and Pan-American Copyright Conventions.
No part of this book may be reproduced in any form or by any means, electronic or
mechanical, including photocopying, without permission in writing from the pub-
lisher. All inquiries should be addressed to Random House, Inc., 201 East 50th
Street, New York, N.Y. 10022. Published in the United States by Random House,
Inc., and simultaneously in Canada by Random House of Canada Limited, Toronto.

Library of Congress Cataloging-in-Publication Data

Feldman, Paula R.
  The wordworthy computer.

  Bibliography: p.
  Includes index.
    1. Literature—Research—Data processing.
2. Word processing.   3. Literature—Computer-
assisted instruction.   I. Norman, Buford.   II. Title.
PN73.F44   1986   808'.02'0285   86-22000
ISBN 0-394-35623-3

Manufactured in the United States of America

Copyrights and acknowledgments appear on pages 227–228.

Cover design by Katharine Von Urban

PREFACE

We have written the book we wish we had had when we were first starting out with computers. Remembering how frustrating it was to wade through jargon and technical language, we have surveyed the field of computing in the humanities in lay language and have tried to make our discussions easy to understand even for someone with no previous familiarity with computers. Our intended audience consists of teachers, scholars, and administrators curious about how best to take advantage of what the new technology can offer. Because our own academic experience is in English and foreign language departments, the book will be most useful to individuals in those fields. Even so, anyone who works with words will find much that is of interest here. Our discussions put special emphasis on microcomputer applications.

If you have not yet started using a computer, you will discover in this book exciting ways not only to make your work easier and more efficient but also to accomplish tasks impractical by any other means. In fact, once you survey the computer's potential, you may find yourself envisioning applications you never before imagined possible. If you are already a computer user, you will find much new information here.

Our opening section deals with word processing and ways you can use it profitably both for your own academic writing and in the classroom. The book covers topics of interest to any serious writer, such as computer programs that help with taking notes, organizing prose, checking spelling, indexing, footnoting, and creating a bibliography. Many of our colleagues began using computers thinking that word processing would be all that they would need. They soon found to their delight that computers are invaluable for such tasks as storing and updating records (minutes, correspondence, past tests, and syllabi, for example), grading papers, calculating test scores, updating *vitae,* researching literary topics, and exchanging manuscripts with readers at distant locations without waiting for the mail. We discuss these applications along with a number of others.

You will find here a discussion of what features to look for in choosing a word processing program for your own use or for student use, how to select and evaluate software and hardware, how to teach word processing, and how to set up a microcomputer lab. We include a detailed overview of the various types of computer-assisted instruction, including not only drill and practice CAI but also invention and prewriting programs as well as writing analyzers. Many people are misled into thinking it necessary to spend large sums of money for software. We show you how to obtain free or nearly free software from various sources and also include sample exercises you can use with any word processing program to teach students writing or foreign language acquisition skills. Of special interest are discussions of how to print foreign language characters and how to use your computer to help produce a typeset text.

Next we examine the many ways a computer can help with scholarship. You will find a discussion of quantitative techniques that you can use in conjunction with more traditional methods of literary analysis. We take a look at data bases—what they are, what they can contain, how to create or locate them, and how they can help you in your research. We discuss exciting developments in the field of computer-assisted translation. You will also find out how a computer can generate from machine readable literary texts or data bases such things as concordances, statistics, frequency lists, and the uses to which you can put this information. We discuss as well more specific applications, suggested by the nature of individual literary texts, such as analyses of style and identification of authorship. All of these sections include examples of how to proceed and of typical results.

Finally, our appendices include a glossary, which explains unfamiliar computer terms, and an extensive bibliography, which lists the most up-to-date sources of further information. We also provide lists of data bases, networks, professional associations, and journals.

PAULA R. FELDMAN
BUFORD NORMAN

ACKNOWLEDGMENTS

We are grateful to numerous colleagues at the University of South Carolina who encouraged the writing of this book and helped us bring it to fruition. Specifically, Don Edwards helped initiate us into the world of statistical analysis and David Chesnutt read our chapter on computer-assisted editing and shared his knowledge. We owe special thanks to those at the Social and Behavioral Sciences Computer Lab for their help with many aspects of this book. In particular, Homer Steedly, Randy Bullard and Tim White were always willing to provide advice and access to equipment and information, often at a moment's notice. David Cowen, Director, awarded each of us a semester's visiting professorship at the lab, an opportunity which allowed us to keep up with the latest developments in the use of computers in the academic world.

We are also indebted to our graduate assistant, Sheila Toombe, for helping with library research and clerical tasks, and to Bob Stuart for technical advice. The Departments of English and of Foreign Languages and Literatures at the University of South Carolina helped with some clerical costs. Finally, we wish to thank Steve Pensinger, Cynthia Ward, and Fred Burns, our editors at Random House. Steve believed in this project from the very beginning, gave us encouragement, and arranged for a grant to help us write this book. Cynthia gave the first draft of the manuscript a good critical reading and offered valuable suggestions for revision, and Fred saw the project through to completion.

CONTENTS

THE WORDWORTHY
COMPUTER

INTRODUCTION

Word Processing for the Academic Writer and Teacher

WHY USE WORD PROCESSING?

If you've been thinking about trying word processing but are wondering whether it's worth the effort to learn, here's what many academics and professional writers who use it are reporting:

1. *Writing with microcomputer word processing is a faster, more efficient process than writing in the conventional way.* Words, phrases, sentences, and whole paragraphs or blocks of writing can be created and moved around, deleted, added, or altered within a document quickly and easily. Thus word processing can help boost your productivity. But believe it or not, this is the least significant reason for using word processing in your writing. It is merely quantitative.

More important, word processing *qualitatively* alters the writing process. By eliminating considerable drudgery, word processing makes writing a much less menial task. No more writer's cramp. No more retyping. No more erasing or whiting out and waiting for the messy stuff to dry. Word processing streamlines writing. It frees you to concentrate on framing and developing ideas rather than on mechanically recording them. Many people quickly learn to compose directly on the computer without the use of handwritten or typed rough drafts.

2. *Far more than being merely a glorified typewriter, the computer actually becomes an aid to thinking.* Its speed enables it to keep pace with your thoughts in the initial stages of writing, so you can brainstorm freely and follow associations. The computer allows you to capture intermediate ideas that slower writing methods allow to escape.

3. *Word processing enhances creativity because it encourages revision and experimentation with words.* The simplicity of revising takes the pressure off. What does it matter if you write something and then decide against it? With a few keystrokes, you can change it. Polish and precision in writing can be of little concern in the early stages. If the right word doesn't come immediately to mind, almost any word will do for the time being. The computer makes the mechanics of refining your writing so easy that those steps can wait until later instead of interrupting brainstorming.

The result is that your word-processed first drafts tend to be much rougher than what you have become accustomed to producing via conventional methods, but your *final* drafts end up *more* polished. Why? Revising is so much easier that you will create many more drafts on the computer than you do now. You need never retype—even for major organizational changes. And making minor improvements involves so little effort that you suddenly find yourself bothering to make them.

4. *Many people find that word processing relieves writer's block.* The physical process of composing with word processing bears such little resemblance to writing in the conventional way that, often, negative associations formed over the years simply do not carry over. With a computer, there is no intimidatingly blank sheet of paper. True, there is an "empty" monitor screen, but it is never *entirely* empty. It already has writing on it supplied by the word processing program, and you have to press keys to place a few more characters on the screen and ready the computer for writing. Research suggests that this preparatory eye/hand activity is important because it gets you going—it overcomes inertia. Because writers cannot be passive, even in the beginning, they tend not to have so much trouble starting.

5. *Writing becomes an experience that emphasizes the positive and the present.* When you revise with a microcomputer, there are no negative reminders of what did not work out. There are no X's to suggest failure, no crumpled pieces of paper to remind you of how many ideas you discarded. With a few keystrokes, false starts can be made to vanish as quickly as they appeared. Handwritten rough drafts tend to look (and to be) confusing. Pages are cluttered with scratchings out, arrows, and words scrawled in the margins, squeezed between the lines, written on the back, and pasted on the bottom. With a computer, additions can be cleanly integrated into the text. Writing does not seem frustratingly messy or chaotic in the intermediate stages. No longer must you rely on your imagination to visualize the way a change will look. You get the immediate, positive reinforcement of seeing a revision happen almost instantaneously. And seeing the revision in easily readable form enables you to evaluate and to refine it with greater confidence.

WHY HAVE STUDENTS USE WORD PROCESSING?

In addition to the advantages of word processing that we have already listed, there are other incentives for having students use it in any class requiring writing.

1. *Students consider writing with microcomputers fun, and they become more motivated to write.* They really get a kick out of word processing and what they can do with it. Some faculty members fear that students will like the computer at first, just as they would enjoy a new toy, but that they will quickly tire of it when the novelty wears off. We observe precisely the opposite effect. The more proficient students become at composing with word pro-

cessing, the more enthusiastic they grow and, in fact, the more likely they are to use the computer to write essays for other courses.

They do go through a period of doubt about the value of word processing during the first week when they are still in the process of learning the word processing commands. At this stage, students typically get frustrated when they give the wrong command and can't understand why the computer is not doing what they want it to. Sometimes they forget the proper procedure for printing or for saving their files, or they forget which menu they need. These sorts of things lead initially to exasperation, but this stage is short-lived.

And once students begin to feel comfortable with word processing, frustration gives way to a new sense of power and pride. Strikingly, students often describe the experience of writing on a microcomputer in terms of play. One student explained, "I used to *really* dislike writing. Working on a computer makes it a challenging game that is very entertaining and easy enough so I don't become physically exhausted or suffer from writer's cramp." Said a third, "Writing became fun. It wasn't a burden anymore."

Students also take great pride in how impressive their writing looks on the printed page. Even students who protest at the beginning of the course that they cannot type are delighted with the results of their labors. Having clean, printed copy makes life easier for the instructor too. Instead of wasting time deciphering handwriting, you can concentrate on what is being said and how. Everyone benefits.

2. *Microcomputer word processing helps students improve their writing style.* For reasons no one fully understands, the prose of students using microcomputers becomes less stilted, less labored, and more natural. So certain characteristics that one often has difficulty teaching evolve almost spontaneously. Writing well involves communicating ideas not only clearly but also concisely. As it happens, one of the tasks the computer performs especially well is the quick and painless deletion of words. Thus word processing helps fight wordiness. Eliminating an unnecessary word is as easy as pressing a key.

3. *The computer helps the instructor pinpoint students' problems in the writing process itself.* Although specialists in composition have contended for years that writing is a process, monitoring the steps making up that process has been difficult if not impossible. Thus it has been hard to figure out at what stage a particular student runs into trouble. With a computer, you can ask students to do five or six printouts of their assignment at various stages of completion. Such a request involves virtually no extra work for the students —all they have to do is press a few keys—and you can monitor the process of creating an essay as it is being composed. Moreover, the technology allows you to read *clean* rough drafts. You don't have to face the chore of deciphering hurried scrawls and hieroglyphics in the margin, as you would in a conventional class if you asked students to show you their rough drafts.

Students' drafts are every bit as readable as their final essays will be, and this allows you to be a more effective reader.

4. *The computer makes possible certain kinds of assignments that are impracticable or simply not feasible with conventional writing methods.* For example, you can ask students to take a five-page essay, make major organizational changes, and turn the revision in at the very next class meeting. Revising an essay of that length would not be an uncommon task in the working world, but it would be a major, time-consuming assignment in a conventional writing course where typing a clean revision would be necessary. In creating their résumés with a microcomputer, business writing students can try out a number of different formats for the same copy to see which they prefer in terms of its aesthetic impact. They can experiment with the visual effects of boldface, underlining, italics, white space, all caps, and so forth. In fact, they can easily design several résumés with different features for different audiences. Writing is partly a visual art, but students with computers have a much easier time seeing this in their own work than those without computers.

5. *The computer takes what has conventionally been a solitary pursuit and transforms it in the computer lab into a more social activity.* Students get to know one another in the lab. At first they help each other master the word processing commands; later they spontaneously consult each other about writing difficulties. Sometimes they act as critics and sometimes just come to the rescue when someone gets stuck. So it isn't unusual to hear, "Hey Laura, what's another word for *enormous*?" The lab creates the opportunity for this sort of give and take, which usually would not occur if students were spread all over campus, working in their individual rooms or writing in the library. Interestingly, in such classes plagiarism doesn't seem to be the problem it ordinarily is, perhaps because others can see what each student is working on and with what materials.

6. *Microcomputer software can help teach other skills, for example, spelling.* Select a spelling checker program that does not provide the correct spelling but simply goes through the student's text and highlights words that do not match words in its dictionary and that therefore *might be* misspelled. The student must then decide how the word should appear. Often this means that the student has to look up a word in the lab's dictionary and thus learn the correct spelling. You will no longer need to wonder whether an error is typographical or the product of ignorance.

Unfounded Objections

There is some fear that computers are going to make writing teachers obsolete. Hardly. What they will do is free your time for the most important matters.

People ask, "What about students who have no computer background?" Students don't need any computer background. To do word processing, you need no particular mathematical ability or training. You do not even need to know how a computer works, any more than you need to know how an internal combustion engine works to drive a car or to mow the grass.

What about students who can't touch type? There is no need to make touch typing a requirement for a course using word processing. Many students in such classes can't touch type, and these one- and two-fingered typists are among the most enthusiastic fans of word processing. (Many professional programmers, incidentally, don't touch type.) For those who want to learn, we recommend one of the many commercially available and inexpensive self-paced typing programs. (People used to joke that enrolling in certain classes in the novel became a course in speed reading. A class that calls for the use of word processing may end up being a course in speed typing as well!) At any rate, there does not seem to be much correlation between ability to type, prior computer experience, and success in courses using word processing.

What about these computer phobias everyone has been reading about? Is fear a problem? Well, it does exist, but it isn't a serious problem. At the end of the semester, we asked our students on an anonymous questionnaire, "If you had it to do all over again and could choose between two identical writing classes, one with word processing required and one without such a requirement, which would you choose?" Over 90% of our students said they would choose the course with word processing. Interestingly, students make this choice even though many indicate that in doing assignments with the computer, they end up investing more time than they would using conventional methods. Individual revisions can be achieved more quickly on the computer than in longhand, but these students were willing to do more revising and hence often invested a larger total amount of time in an assignment. They could see that the investment paid off in the much improved quality of the final product. And they realized that what they were achieving would have required a considerably longer time had they been using conventional means. "Writing papers on the [computer]," one student noted, "made it easier, more interesting . . . more fun (and more involving)."

In fact, the more serious problem is not cyberphobia (fear of the computer) but cyberphilia (love of the computer). Computer addiction on the part of some students causes them to neglect other aspects of their school work.

Legitimate Concerns

There are, of course, some real drawbacks. At least for the next few years, before the time comes at most colleges when students arrive with their own computers and word processing packages, you will have to spend class time teaching the word processing program. We find, however, that even the more complex programs can be taught in two class sessions, given some opportunity for lab practice in between. And the loss of class time is more than compensated for by the extra work that the computer allows during the semester.

Some researchers are finding that although computers help students polish their writing and catch certain kinds of errors, they also contribute to another sort of error. Helen J. Schwartz notes that "Confusion or inelegances creep into prose when a rewording is not completely accomplished. For example . . . 'the chart on the inside the back cover should help you' is an error caused by an incomplete instantaneous revision of 'on the back cover' to 'inside the back cover.' "[1] Wayne C. Booth, in "Catching the Overflow" (*College English,* 46, February 1984), observes this same propensity. In addition, because it is so easy to revise and edit a text and print a new copy, writers do not have the same sense of finality they once had when they finished a typed draft. Thus it can sometimes be difficult to "let go" and declare the job done.

Students find to their chagrin that they must adjust their writing habits somewhat. For example, if writing must be done at a lab that is not open 24 hours a day, all-nighters are not possible. (This may be a benefit, from the teacher's point of view.) Students can't eat, drink, or smoke while they're writing in a lab. Sometimes others in the lab create distractions. But students seem to think these compromises are worth it. Evaluations by students show that most of them find writing on the computer easier and more pleasurable than conventional methods of composition, and they are willing to make the sacrifice.

There are those who fear the use of computers in instruction. They are afraid computers will depersonalize the classroom and turn learning into an automated, mechanical affair where students have less individual contact with teachers. In our classrooms, computers have had the very opposite effect. In fact, computers help make both teaching and learning an infinitely *more* personal and *more* humane endeavor. You will find you have more time for individual contact with students—not less. And, relieved of much of the drudgery of writing, students have more time for thinking their writing through and refining their ideas.

SELECTING A WORD PROCESSING SYSTEM FOR YOUR OWN USE

Microcomputer or Dedicated Word Processor?

Many academics are tempted to purchase a dedicated word processor rather than a computer because they believe they will be using only word processing. However, the microcomputer costs no more than the dedicated word processor and is much more versatile. You may think you will have no need for the mathematical capabilities of the computer, but few people, when they first start out, are able to imagine the myriad uses to which they will eventually put their micros. With a spreadsheet program, you can figure your students' grades, draft a budget, or compute your income tax deductions. With a modem, you can exchange electronic mail, tap into a data base a thousand miles away, or search your library's holdings. None of these things is possible with a dedicated word processor. It used to be that academics bought dedicated word processors because computer word processing was much more complicated and difficult to learn. However, the new generation of "user friendly" word processing packages and interactive tutorials has made this fear unnecessary. Moreover, computer technology is advancing every day. Who knows what new applications for computers are on the horizon?

Some Tips on Buying Hardware and Software for Instruction

Now that the tremendous educational potential for computers is widely recognized, English and foreign language departments all over the country are buying hardware and software in unprecedented quantity. But the process is fraught with difficulty and danger. All too often, money is appropriated for computer equipment in a lump sum that must be spent quickly or lost. Those responsible for spending funds frequently lack the background required to make the most intelligent decisions about purchases in the highly complex world of computer technology. As a result, too many departments have bought expensive equipment only to discover that it will not run the software most appropriate for the intended instructional use. Or, bewildered by the array of new educational software, departments have been seduced by manufacturers' inflated claims and have spent thousands of dollars before discovering that the computer-assisted instructional programs they now own are pedagogically unsound or ineffective for use with students.

What can be done? Certainly, most English and foreign language faculty members lack the inclination to become computer experts (and, in fact, their doing so would be of no more use than faculty developing expertise in the technology of the ball-point pen). However, departments heeding the following guidelines before making computer-related purchases, can save much energy and pain, not to mention money.

1. *Decide first what you want computers to do.* After settling on your goal, do some research to determine what software is most appropriate for accomplishing it. Then, and only then, select the hardware that will best run that software.

2. *Never purchase software without trying it first.* Much "educational" software is written by people who have little or no knowledge of effective teaching, and their programs are seriously flawed pedagogically. For example, as we discuss in our section on writing analyzers, most of the software

that purports to help students check their writing style provides only negative feedback. Thus students learn what is wrong about their compositions —but not what is right. Instead of being encouraged, they are discouraged. Although the term *artificial intelligence* is bandied about quite a bit, it does not yet exist. It will be some years before computer technology is far enough advanced to make a truly intelligent, sensitive, and complete computer-generated critique of student writing.

3. *Keep in mind the computer's limitations, and don't expect it to work magic on its own.* The computer is only a tool. To be useful, it must be integrated into the larger curriculum. Remember that a computer can have a positive effect only on the delivery or process of learning. It is the teacher's role to provide the content.

For advice about computer purchases, talk to someone who is not trying to sell you something and has nothing to gain. Ask for recommendations from computer people at your school, a paid consultant, or a friend or colleague with computer experience. Sometimes you can learn helpful things from vendors, but when making purchases, never rely solely on what you are told by a single vendor. If you have no one who can serve as an unbiased technical adviser, talk to at least three competing vendors, preferably those who handle more than one brand.

For detailed guidelines on how to evaluate courseware, see pages 45–48.

Word Processing Especially for Scholars and Teachers

The first word processing programs were developed for use by secretaries in business environments. But the writer of a scholarly article has certain needs that go beyond what in necessary for the composition of a sales letter. It was only a matter of time before the commercial market recognized these needs. No doubt there will soon be others, but the first entry in the sweepstakes of word processing created expressly for scholars and teachers in the humanities is Nota Bene. Steven Siebert, a former graduate student in philosophy at Yale, designed Nota Bene by tying together a free-format information storage and retrieval program, FYI 3000, with a word processing program, Xywrite. Nota Bene includes the following special features:

1. *Multilingual word processing*   Special accents and characters for French, Spanish, Portuguese, German, Slavic, and many other languages can be displayed on your monitor. (Other word processing programs that can handle such characters usually do so by displaying special codes or control characters on the screen, making it difficult to read and to edit a foreign language text.) If your printer can handle an accented character for a language that uses the Roman alphabet, Nota Bene will print it and, if you wish,

underline it. It will also allow you to change the keys on your keyboard to foreign language characters and to redefine keys as you wish.

2. *Automatic formatting* In addition to any format you design, you can choose any of five style manuals, including the *Chicago Manual of Style* and the *MLA Style Manual,* and the program will automatically format your text according to its prescriptions. If you then want to submit your article to a journal that specifies one of the other style manuals, the program can automatically reformat the document.

3. *Footnotes, endnotes, and bibliographies* The program automatically numbers footnotes and endnotes. When you insert a note somewhere in the middle, the program automatically renumbers all the others. You can enter bibliographic information anywhere in your text, and the program compiles the information into an alphabetized bibliography. If you wish, the program will compile a primary and a secondary bibliography from the same document.

4. *Table of contents* You can mark chapter and section titles as you write, and the program will compile them into a table of contents, automatically inserting the correct page number. You can mark the titles of illustrations, tables, and charts, and the program will compile them into lists, giving the pages on which they occur.

5. *Indexes* The program can automatically create an index of up to three different levels for your document.

6. *Text-base note system* (like a data base but designed just for text) You can create a text base of notes (interview notes, unconnected sentences containing ideas, critical comments, bibliographic information, free-form notes on an article, and the like). For each record, you can define up to 500 key words of 64 characters each. The program can search this text base without having to display it on your monitor screen and can retrieve items that contain the words you indicate, using Boolean search combinations *(and, or, not).* You can display the retrieved material, transfer it to another file, or insert it in the document you are writing. If yours is a large project, you can spread your text base over 255 floppy disks.

Also included are multiple windows; four-function math operations on columns of numbers; glossaries; an undelete function, a widow and orphan control, automatic date and time functions; automatic printing of form letters; proportional spacing; on-screen formatting without displayed control codes; phrase libraries that store words, phrases, or formatting codes on one key for easy insertion in a document; simultaneous editing of multiple files; and automatic paragraph indenting, if desired. It does not have automatic hyphenation, or spell checking. Nota Bene works on a wide range of microcomputers in conjunction with most printers. It reads *WordStar, Final Word,* and *Perfect Writer* files and can create and read ASCII files.

The Modern Language Association was so impressed that it entered into an unprecedented agreement with the publisher, Dragonfly Software. It not only endorsed the program as a milestone in scholarly writing but also embarked on an aggressive effort to sell it to its membership. However, before you rush out to spend $495 (or $416 for MLA members), be warned of the drawbacks. As Bryan Pfaffenberger notes in a recent review, ". . . all that complexity exacts a price. . . . The program daunts even the experienced personal computer freak. A quick reference guide reveals dozens of keyboard commands, but you have to learn even more: most operations are set in motion by typing a command phrase on the command line. . . . You'll have to memorize two or three dozen cryptic commands such as 'ju,' 'wd,' and 'rha.' . . . Nota Bene is not only the most complex software I've ever reviewed, it's also by far the most aesthetically displeasing." When you are using some of the special features, you will find that "As [the two chunks of the program, Xywrite and FYI 3000] execute, they bewilder the user with a dizzy parade of incomprehensible onscreen messages. And because so much information has to be fetched from disk, the program plods along at an often frustratingly slow pace."[2] However, the day-to-day word processing operations are easy to use and execute extremely quickly. Some users might be bewildered by the amount of technical detail in the manual, but others find it one of the major advantages of the program. For example, the documentation tells you all the codes for the different word processing operations so that you can make up your own macro, a command that tells the computer to execute a predetermined string of commands.

We would agree with Pfaffenberger's recommendation that except for particularly intrepid beginners, only those who already have some experience with other computer programs (such as WordStar, SuperFile, PC-DOS, BASIC, or a spreadsheet program) should try Nota Bene. Those who can master it, though, will find, in Pfaffenberger's words, "the most capable word processing program available for scholarly work."

What to Look for When Selecting Your Own Word Processing Program

The following features are essential:

1. What you see on screen is, for the most part, what is printed out.
2. On-line help.
3. Good documentation.
4. Easy to underline, superscript, subscript, boldface.
5. Block moves and deletes.
6. Easily performs search-and-replace function.
7. Easy to print foreign-language accent marks.
8. Ability to merge two files into one.
9. Document-oriented rather than page-oriented.
10. Document size of at least 40 pages.
11. Edit during print (if memory allows).

12. Allows footnotes and endnotes.
13. Move cursor by word and line.
14. Move cursor by screen.
15. Move cursor quickly to beginning and end of document.
16. Automatic word wrap.
17. Move cursor to beginning and end of screen and to beginning and end of line.
18. Toggle insert/overwrite.
19. At least 80 characters per line.
20. At least 20 lines per screen.
21. Display page number or page break.
22. Delete by word and line.
23. Copy and move columns.
24. Can ignore case in search.
25. Allows you to use the function keys on your computer.
26. Reads standard ASCII files.
27. Allows you easily to control the size of top, bottom, and side margins.
28. Has the ability to send pica, elite, italic, bold, compressed, expanded, and double-strike commands to a dot matrix printer.
29. Automatic page numbering.
30. Compatibility with software used at your educational institution.

The following features are optional:

1. Proportional spacing.
2. Spelling checker.
3. User-definable keyboard table.
4. Ability to handle non-Roman characters (such as Chinese, Hebrew, and Greek character sets).
5. Ability to show foreign-language accent marks on screen.
6. On-screen underlining.
7. Automatic reformatting.
8. Screen tutorial.
9. Password protection for files.
10. Automatic corrections of widows and orphans.
11. Mail merge function (see page 14).
12. Automatic backup copy of files.
13. Windows or split screen (ability to have more than one file open at the same time).
14. Prints labels.
15. Prints multiple copies.
16. Automatic file save.
17. Ability to chain or queue documents for printing.
18. Hard and soft hyphens.
19. Hyphen help.
20. Undelete.
21. Math functions.
22. Ability to place page numbering where you want it on the page.
23. Write block to a separate file.

24. Jump cursor to a specific page.
25. Produces standard ASCII file.

TIME-SAVING APPLICATIONS IN YOUR WORK

Personalizing Form Letters

Personalizing form letters is one of the best ways to increase the efficiency and effectiveness of your correspondence. Many word processing packages come with a software package that, if you use it in conjunction with a letter-quality printer and turn off the tell-tale right-margin justification, enables you to print *en masse* letters that are indistinguishable from typewritten originals. Research shows that a higher percentage of people respond to a letter they believe was written expressly for them than respond to one they perceive as a form letter.

Let us say, for example, that you want to write to 50 different individuals and tell them that you have accepted the paper they have proposed presenting at your conference. Most of the information you must now give each of these 50 people is identical. However, some presentations will be scheduled for 20 minutes, some for 30 minutes, and others for 1 hour. Each recipient must be made aware of how much time will be allotted to her or his paper. Moreover, you have some specific suggestions for a number of the participants. With your file-merging software, in an afternoon you can easily turn out an "original" letter containing all the necessary information to every one of your presenters.

First you create a file containing the name and address of each presenter, along with the title of the paper, the amount of time allotted, and any specific comments you would like to make. Next you write a form letter containing everything each participant will have to know and indicating (for the computer) where in the letter information from the first file should be inserted. The rest is easy. The computer automatically merges the form letter with the personalized information for each participant. Most programs will also print your mailing labels.

Preparing Class Materials

A printer will not cut a mimeograph master, but it will do a fine job with a ditto master. Thus you can easily generate inexpensive handouts. The syllabus for that course you teach every semester can be updated each time you use it simply by entering the new dates and leaving everything else intact. Or perhaps you want to add an extra book to your usual reading list. No problem. Make the addition and do another printout. The days of having to file away old ditto masters are gone. You can keep one hard copy in your file (much less messy) and another on your disk.

In the case of a small seminar or an exercise that only a few students need, you can avoid the duplicating process altogether by simply printing on your dot matrix printer as many copies as you require. (We don't recommend doing this with most letter-quality printers because they are so slow.)

You can also prepare more attractive and effective material for your overhead projector by exploiting the ability of your word processing package to create extra-large letters or boldface type for headings. Moreover, if your computer and printer have graphics capability, with the right software you can generate professional-looking charts, graphs, and illustrations for your lectures.

You can keep a file of exam questions to rearrange and rotate each time you teach a particular course. In fact, by moving blocks of text around on a multiple-choice or true-false test, you can cut down on cheating by creating two versions of the same exam that appear to be entirely different. Another way to accomplish that end is to make some negative statements positive in a second version, thus changing the correct answer. (Your search-and-replace function can help with this.) Or, if you have been teaching a course long enough to have amassed a large number of test questions, you can enter them into a data base program and have the computer randomly generate test questions. That way, you can administer unique exams each semester without having to write all new questions.

In a writing class using word processing, you can make a ditto master of any particular student essay by using the original file. Thus you can run off a copy for every person in the course for an in-class critique.

Recommended reading lists or bibliographies can be updated each year. Moreover, you can tailor material used in the past (and kept on file on disk) to each new group of students. Most word processors provide a way for you to keep certain items in a file from printing. Thus you can make notes to yourself (references, for example, or pedagogical comments) on handout sheets and ensure that they are not printed out for student consumption.

Good News about Your Vita

Imagine never having to retype your vita again! With word processing, all you have to do when there is something to add is insert the new item in the appropriate place and print your revised document. Furthermore, you can create more than one version of your vita with little trouble. Perhaps you want an abbreviated version highlighting only major accomplishments—very different from the detailed version you prepared for your last grant proposal. All you do is copy your vita file and delete unnecessary items. Perhaps you are looking for a new position. With a computer, you can create several different versions of your vita, each emphasizing a particular aspect of your qualifications. In fact, you can tailor your vita for each specific position you are interested in.

Different Versions

Ever have to rewrite a talk for several different audiences? Your computer can simplify the task. Just create an electronic copy of your original talk and make the necessary alterations. The job of turning a conference presentation into a publishable journal article is made easier by the same process.

DISPLAYING AND PRINTING FOREIGN CHARACTERS

Most computers can handle the most common foreign characters quite easily—it depends on the character set in ROM memory, the hardware that drives the monitor, and the software you are using. The full ASCII character set (American Standard Code for Information Interchange, the standard character set for microcomputers; it contains 255 characters, though some computers only use the first 128) contains the necessary characters for most common European languages and a few Greek letters. Almost any combination of hardware and monitor can display them, though some of the older graphics displays only give you a couple of dots above a letter instead of a fully formed accent mark.

Most of the newer word processors allow you to display any character in your computer's memory with one or two keystrokes. They also allow you to customize your keyboard so you can replace a rarely used character ({, for example) with a foreign character you use more often. Older word processors such as WordStar require a special program to display many of the most important foreign characters (ASCII 128–154).

To print the characters on your screen, you are, of course, limited by the characters your printer can print. Daisy wheel printers are quite limited, having only 96 possible characters, which doesn't leave much after upper and lower case letters, numerals, and punctuation marks. Most laser and dot matrix printers can print all ASCII characters, and dot matrix printers have the additional advantage of allowing you to design your own characters. (It's a bit complicated, but most printer manuals explain the process fairly well.)

If you still can't get the characters you need, it's often possible to improvise with backspacing. You can get a theta by printing a hyphen over a zero, or a not-equal sign by printing a slash over an equal sign. Or you can look into the numerous printer-enhancing programs on the market, such as FancyFont, which let you print almost anything with most dot matrix printers and make it easy to print the common characters.

APPLICATIONS INVOLVING MORE THAN A WORD PROCESSING PROGRAM

It is easy to maintain and update mailing lists of any type on your computer by using one of the various file-merging functions.

A data base (see Chapter 4) can hold many more things than a scholarly bibliography. For example, you can put reading lists for your classes into the same data base you use for your bibliography, update them from semester to semester, and print out all or part of them at any time, depending on the needs of your students.

You can also keep your notes in one of the data bases that allows for long entries. When it is time to teach a class on Keats, for example, you can search the data base for all entries concerning Keats, or just those concerning specific works you're teaching that day. No more searching through piles of files and notebooks to find that elusive bit of information you need immediately.

If you do a lot of committee work, data bases are great for keeping up with minutes. You can type them on your word processor, distribute them to colleagues, and then transfer them directly from the word processor to the data base. That way you can easily call up the minutes from a certain date, or those from any meeting where a certain subject was discussed.

You can also store student scores in a data base, since most programs can perform simple calculations. If you give a test that has several parts and need to add up the scores for each part and then prepare a report that lists the results for each student on each part and her total score, just type the names and numbers into a data base. You can then generate a report with all the details, with students arranged alphabetically, by score, Social Security number, or any way you like. There are some specialized programs designed just for this application; an example is Ron Ellis's Papergrader, which calculates grade distributions. (For more information, write to Ellis in care of the Department of English, The University of Wisconsin at Whitewater, Whitewater, WI 53190.)

For more complicated scores, you can use what is called a spreadsheet. This is basically a grid of cells labeled A1, A2, B1, B2, and so forth into which you can put numbers and words. You can set up a column for each student, and in the rows enter the grade for each assignment—homework, quizzes, exams, papers, and so forth. You can then perform almost any kind of calculation. For example, you could calculate an average for each category (homework, quizzes, exams, and term paper, for example), give each category a weight (say, 15% for homework, 20% for quizzes, 40% for exams, 25% for term paper), and then combine each weighted category into a final grade. This can take forever, even with a calculator, if you have 30 students and some kind of grade for almost every class meeting, but the computer does it at the touch of a key.

One great thing about a spreadsheet is that you can change a number or a formula (average or weight, for example) and recalculate the grades immediately. You can try a different grading formula, or you can give a student a hypothetical grade for the final exam and show him what he would have as a grade for the term if that were indeed his grade on the final.

Spreadsheets are handy for budgets, too, for your grants or administrative work. Their main advantage is that you can make changes, either real or hypothetical, and see the new result immediately. This way you can see what would happen if you spent more in a certain category, or if a source of funds were cut 10 percent. Another nice feature is the ability to link one category to another. For example, you could define your "miscellaneous" category as your available funds minus whatever you spent in the other categories, and the computer would automatically calculate how much was left for miscellaneous expenses each time you made a change in some other category.

Electronic filing systems enable you to keep and easily access all your letters to any given correspondent. In fact, if you keep backup copies of your disks, you could theoretically eliminate the need to fill file cabinets with hard copies.

Indexing programs (some of which come with the more sophisticated word processing packages) let you not only create finished indexes of reports or scholarly editions but also search large documents for ideas or particular passages of interest.

Idea organizers help you store notes and later assemble them into a coherent structure or write with the aid of an outline. (Imagine life free of index cards.) Maxthink, Ready!, Framework, PC-OUTLINE, and Thinktank are popular idea organizers, but word processing programs are increasingly coming equipped with their own. For example, Microsoft Word 3.0 successfully integrates word processing and outlining functions.

There are other programs designed for specialized purposes. For example, William Dennis Horn's The Proposal Writer helps users organize and write grants and proposals by leading them through the process via a series of prompts. Menus enable you to write different parts of the proposal at different times and save sections on disk, to later compile them into the full proposal. (For more information, write to Horn at 25 Hamilton Street, Potsdam, NY 13676.)

Communications packages (along with a modem) enable you to hook into a mainframe computer or to "network" with other micros. In the not-too-distant future, much of our mail will arrive in this way. Each office in a department will be linked to a central computer, and most information that needs to be sent back and forth will be sent electronically. You will check your computer for messages and memos and decide which ones you need to save on disk, or print. Probably, though, most of it will be read and then erased, saving a lot of paper and storage space. The Travelers Insurance Company saves the equivalent of 32 railroad boxcars of paper each year by doing most of its "paperwork" electronically!) With the same equipment, you can tie into a distant data base or search your library's holdings. In the future, when many books will be available online, you will be able to look up a particular passage, save it, and insert it as a quotation into the article on which you are working!

SELECTING A WORD PROCESSING SYSTEM FOR YOUR STUDENTS' USE

Setting Up Your Microcomputer Lab or Classroom

If you plan to have students use word processing in class, you will need a classroom with a microcomputer for each student and another for the instructor. In addition, you should have a large demonstration screen on which the instructor can project what appears on her or his monitor, and you should consider networking the microcomputers so that students and teacher can communicate with each other electronically. Computers should be positioned so that each student can easily see the instructor.

If you plan to have students do their writing outside of class, two computers will support 20–25 students. One printer for every two computers is comfortable. One for every four is adequate. If you don't have a printer for every computer, you must make it a rule of the lab that students writing at one of the microcomputers hooked up to a printer must let someone who wants to print interrupt them.

Dot-matrix printers are the most practical choice for labs; they are less expensive and faster than daisy wheel or laser printers and can produce either high-speed, draft-quality copies or slower, almost letter-quality final drafts. If you can afford it, though, include one letter-quality printer in the lab. (Students take tremendous pride in seeing their work look as good as the version a letter-quality printer produces.) Some printers are extremely noisy and potentially distracting to users. Unfortunately, the quietest printers are generally the most expensive. If your printers are noisy, equip them with one of the sound-proofing devices now on the market or move them away from areas where students are composing.

Before you purchase hardware, decide what software you will need. *Then* select the hardware that will run that software. If you make your decisions the other way around, you may find that the software program that is just what you need won't run on your system. Most educational software is being written for IBM or Apple computers. You may want to consider hardware that is compatible with (and often less expensive than) these two brands. However, bear in mind that many computers calling themselves compatible are not 100% compatible. And remember to think of the future. You want to be able to use new software as it is developed. What is compatible today may not be compatible tomorrow.

When negotiating contracts for the purchase of hardware and software, you should expect to be offered a sizable educational discount. Moreover, volume discounts are customary. The amount of price reduction varies greatly, however, so be sure to shop around. If you do not have staff or facilities for repairing hardware in-house, you should buy a service contract. One of the provisions of that contract should be same-day service. You can reduce the need for servicing by cleaning the disk drive heads regularly (a simple operation) and by purchasing power-surge protectors.

Your lab should be staffed at all times by either a knowledgeable student or a faculty member who not only checks users in and out of the lab but also monitors use, makes sure rules are observed, answers questions about hardware and software, and provides help for students who run into trouble. You may be able to obtain release time for faculty members. Try to keep the lab open for at least *some* time at nights and on weekends.

You will also need technical support staff in charge of keeping hardware and software in good working order. At some institutions, such staff members also offer workshops on how to use the equipment and software programs.

For security reasons, some facilities ask students to relinquish their ID's when they check out software to be used in the lab. Others require each student to purchase a copy of the software. (Inexpensive educational versions of major word processing packages are available.) Either of these policies will help protect you against the loss of software. Obtaining a site license for a software package is another way to avoid the problem of unauthorized copying, which constitutes copyright infringement.

Well before opening a lab, you need to plan for the physical security of hardware. All equipment should be labeled and inventoried. Hardware can be physically bolted to less movable objects such as desks. Campus police should be apprised of your lab's operating hours and should know what equipment you have. Take out insurance to cover any thefts. Many policies specifically exclude computer equipment. If that is the case with your present policy, you may need to purchase a rider or an independent policy. You may find that windows and doors need new alarm systems or locks and that access to the building after regular working hours needs to be controlled.

Take into consideration the electrical requirements of the lab when selecting the lab site. Especially if the building is an older one, grounding (which is necessary) may be missing. Furthermore, you may need to have the wiring modified so that it can handle the heavier load. Because computers generate heat but need to be kept cool, your air conditioning system will probably need upgrading, and you will have to take measures to cut down on dust in the lab.

If you have a shortage of computers on your campus, you might want to take the precaution of limiting lab access to students enrolled in writing courses. Otherwise you could well find your facility monopolized by students from computer science, business, and engineering. You can limit access effectively by requiring students to present an ID to gain entrance to the lab. The name on the ID should match a name on one of the class rolls left on file by the professor. Some labs operate well on a drop-in basis. Where there is higher demand, you may need to have students sign up in advance to reserve blocks of time on the computer.

Make sure that each workstation includes work space for a student to spread out books, notes, or other research materials. Try to avoid putting too many computers together in one large space. Such arrangements tend to be noisy and distracting. Much more satisfactory are small clusters of two or three computers separated by some sort of visual and noise barrier. Each workstation should be provided with a dictionary (or you have only yourself to blame for misspellings). Also, keep several copies of the user's manual to your word processing package available to students.

Because eyestrain can be a problem, place your overhead lighting in such a way as to avoid glare on monitor screens. If you can't get rid of the glare any other way, you can buy inexpensive, glare-reducing screen covers. When purchasing monitors, get the highest-resolution monitors you can afford.

Decide on lab rules well in advance, and post them in a conspicuous place. The following rules are standard:

1. No eating, drinking, or smoking in the lab.
2. Please keep the lab tidy by cleaning up after yourself.
3. Be considerate of other users and try to keep the noise level down.

Post procedures for operating the printer(s) and a list of commands for the word processing package.

What to look for When Selecting Your Students' Word Processing Program

The following features are essential:

1. What you see on screen is, for the most part, what is printed out.
2. On-line help.
3. Good documentation.
4. Easy to underline.
5. Block moves and deletes.
6. Easily performs search-and-replace function.
7. Ability to merge two files into one.
8. Document-oriented rather than page-oriented.
9. Document size of at least 5 pages.
10. Move cursor by word and line.
11. Move cursor by screen.
12. Move cursor quickly to beginning and end of document.
13. Automatic word wrap.
14. Move cursor to beginning and end of screen and beginning and end of line.
15. Toggle insert/overwrite.
16. At least 80 characters per line.
17. At least 20 lines per screen.
18. Display page number or page break.
19. Delete by word and line.
20. Allows students to use the function keys on the computer.

The following features are optional:

1. On-screen underlining.
2. Automatic reformatting.
3. Screen tutorial.
4. Automatic backup copy of files.
5. Windows or split screen (ability to have more than one file open at the same time).
6. Undelete.
7. Hard and soft hyphens and hyphen help.

Spelling Aids

If your school has the resources, go ahead and let your students take advantage of one of the spelling checkers on the market. Many instructors fear that such aids will keep students from ever having to learn to make their own judgments about spelling, but if you select your software carefully, such a tool can be a powerful learning aid. After all, having a computer program indicate words in a student's document that *might* be misspelled will send students to the dictionary. (It is helpful to keep a college dictionary by every computer station.)

Some of the least expensive spelling checkers simply identify words that do not match a list and ask the user whether the words should be corrected. Beware, however, of the more sophisticated spelling checkers that suggest correct spellings. These can indeed encourage laziness. Warn students, too, that spelling checkers will ignore words that are misused, such as "lose" in a context requiring "loose." Pick a spelling checker with a dictionary of at least 40 to 50 thousand words. If you don't, you will be harassed by software that questions such things as plurals and gerunds.

Free or Nearly Free Software

Although many of the most popular software packages sell for between $300 and $500, there are some good products that users may freely copy and share, sometimes for little more than the cost of a disk. Shareware and public-domain software (also known as freeware) are available directly from the developer or through user groups, software libraries, or electronic bulletin boards.

For example, PC-Write, a fairly sophisticated word processing package for the IBM-PC and compatible computers, sells for $10 (including a manual on the disk), and you may make as many copies as you wish for free. It is available from Quicksoft, 219 First N. #224, Seattle, WA 98109. If you like the program, you may register your copy for $70 and receive two free updates, a printed manual, and telephone support. Printed manuals in quantities over 50 may be purchased for $10.

This sort of arrangement solves a sticky problem for institutions on a tight budget. Copyright laws dictate that you must have a separate legal copy of your software program for every computer in your lab. At even $300 a copy, a lab with 20 computers is going to run up a $6,000 software bill. With "shareware" such as PC-Write, the same lab may legally be equipped with a word processing package on each computer for $70 plus the cost of 19 blank disks, or less than $100. Furthermore, the institution is relieved of another worry—the problem of students pirating copies. With shareware you can, in good conscience, encourage them to make as many copies as they like. To find out about other free or nearly free software programs, consult the following publications:

The PC-SIG Library, 1030 E. Duane Ave., Suite J, Sunnyvale, CA 94086; (408)-730-9291. $8.95

How to Get Free Software by Alfred Glossbrenner (1984). St. Martin's Press, New York, NY.

Apple Software for Pennies by Bertram Gader and Manuel Nodar (1984). Warner Books, 666 Fifth Avenue, New York, NY 10103. $10.95

Free Software for the IBM PC by Bertram Gader and Manuel Nodar (1984). Warner Books, 666 Fifth Avenue, New York, NY 10103. $10.95

Several companies distribute shareware, including: Expressware (call 1-800-321-4331, or write P.O. Box 230, Redmond, WA 98073), which handles File Express, ExpressCalc, and ExpressGraph, each available for $10; Soft Works Development (415-962-1279; 750 Steirlin Road, Suite 142, Mountain View, CA 94043), which produces an outlining program called PC-Outline; and ButtonWare, Inc. (206-454-0479; P.O. Box 5786, Bellevue, WA 98006), which publishes PC-File III, a database program rated by readers of *Consumer Reports* as the best filing program, even though some of its competitors cost $600, and PC-Type, a word processor.

Moreover, some companies offer software to educational institutions at deep discounts. Chambers International Corporation's (305-997-9444; 5499 North Federal Highway, Suite A, Boca Raton, FL 33431) Special Offers Program makes many of the most popular commercial software products available for a fraction of the usual cost. For example, they sell Word Perfect 4.1 (retail price $595) for $125; Norton Utilities (retail price $99.50) for $37.50; Easy Filer (retail price $195) for $59, and Volkswriter Scientific (retail price $495) for $75. Micro Pro's Software Endowment Program (Educational Sales, P.O. Box 2246, 15 Loudoun Street, S.W., Leesburg, VA 22075) makes WordStar (retail price $495) available for $70 for PC-DOS or MS-DOS and $40 for Apple. They also offer MailMerge, CorrectStar, and Star Index together in a package for $80 for PC-DOS or MS-DOS and $60 for Apple. The Spanish and French Canadian versions of WordStar and MailMerge are $90. Prentice-Hall offers specially altered educational versions of software, but the alterations often make the product less powerful or useful than the commercially sold version.

What You Need to Know about Copyright Laws

Copyright laws dealing with software are somewhat different from those governing books. In general, unless you make some other arrangement with the software company, you must purchase a separate copy of a software package for each computer on which it will be used. Recently, software companies have begun filing suit against institutions and companies that violate copyright law by allowing people to make unauthorized copies of their programs.

Multiple copies can, of course, end up being quite costly. If you discover a product you like but find that it would be prohibitively expensive to buy for your institution or department, inquire about a site license. Many companies are willing to allow you to make as many copies as you like (with some restrictions) for use at one site for a set fee. This fee is usually considerably less than it would cost to equip each machine separately.

SUGGESTIONS FOR TEACHING WORD PROCESSING

1. Be enthusiastic. Some students will be skeptical or afraid in the beginning. Your attitude can either reinforce their fears or motivate them to succeed.

2. Use word processing for your own writing before you try to teach it. Your familiarity with the commands and procedures will make your class presentation run more smoothly and will help you deal with student questions and problems.

3. Avoid telling students anything about computers that they don't *have* to know to do the word processing. Too much information will confuse or overwhelm them. You don't need to understand about bits and bytes to do word processing. As one instructor put it, "I no more want students to become computer experts than I want them to become fascinated with their pencils."

4. Assure them that there is practically nothing they can do to damage the equipment (assuming they don't eat, drink, smoke, or get violent in the computer room).

5. The analogy between a data disk and a file cabinet is helpful in teaching students word processing. Reading the directory of a disk is like looking at the labels of all the file folders in a cabinet at once; opening a file is like taking a file folder, opening it, and examining the contents; editing a file is like working on the papers in a file folder; saving a file is like putting the papers safely back in the folder; abandoning a file is like throwing the folder and its contents in the waste basket; and so on.

6. Handouts summarizing commands are often helpful to students in the initial stages of mastering word processing. Most find they don't need them after a very short time, but they appreciate having the security of a sheet to which they may refer. It is useful to do print screens of all menus and duplicate them, or have students do their own so that they can take them home and learn them at leisure.

USING WORD PROCESSING TO RESPOND TO STUDENT WRITING

Giving Students Feedback before They Print

Some instructors prefer to read students' homework assignments on disk rather than on paper. One advantage to this arrangement (in addition to sparing trees, wear and tear on your printers, and your supplies budget) is that you can advise students about their work before they have a sense of its being "finished"—that is, committed to paper. Thus it is easier to ask them to make revisions. You can write your comments and recommendations (as well as your grade) directly into the student's file.

If students are using floppy disks, have them keep their disks in a box at the lab. When you are ready to look at their assignments, you simply drop by the lab and do your reading right there. This system allows students always to have access to their disks (except when you are actually reading). It also reduces risk to the disks, which do not need to be transported back and forth from lab to home to class. If students' computers are electronically linked (or networked), they can all store their writing on a central hard disk, the contents of which are accessible to you. The next time they go to the lab, they can read your comments in their file.

If you ask students to turn in hard copies of their first drafts, take advantage of the easy formatting capabilities of your word processor. Ask students not only to double-space but also to leave a wide right margin (3 or 4 inches) for your comments.

Computerizing Your Comments

Do you find yourself using the same comments over and over again on student papers? Or do you ever find you can't remember what recommendation you made to a student on her last paper or whether you have already told her to work on a particular problem? Bradford Morgan, a professor at the South Dakota School of Mines and Technology, has come up with a system to avoid repetition, to keep a record of comments, and to give students more detailed information on evaluations of their papers.

A particular comment can be written once and then saved. According to Morgan, "It can be recalled again and again . . . and delivered as needed to various students who deserve the same comment. . . . With the word processor, an extended comment can be called up with a keystroke or two, inserted into an evaluative commentary, and then printed automatically." An advantage is that the instructor can give the student a detailed comment instead of one or two cryptic words in the margin. Morgan keeps a catalogue of comments and inserts them in a boilerplate personalized with each student's name and the title of the essay. Reference to particular aspects of the paper can be keyed in manually and interspersed with comments on file to make the comment sheet seem quite personal.

You can also record a student's progress from assignment to assignment by saving copies of completed comment sheets on disk. Thus, when a student does not do what you recommended in your last assessment, you can write a more emphatic follow-up. And when a student does show improvement, you are more likely to remember to provide positive feedback.

Morgan says everyone benefits. Having a catalogue of comments makes his job easier and more efficient, and students receive more in-depth assessment. They are pleased with a full page of typed commentary and never suspect the role the computer played.

For more detailed information on Morgan's system and on how to go about setting up one for yourself, see his article "Evaluating Student Papers with a Word Processor" in *Collected Essays on The Written Word and the Word Processor,* ed. Thomas E. Martinez (Villanova, PA: Villanova University Press, 1984) pp. 233–242. Another version of his report appeared in the *Research in Word Processing Newsletter* for September 1984. It includes examples of student comment sheets.

DISK CARE

Like cassette tapes and phonograph records, diskettes can be damaged if they are not cared for properly. They can get so warped, scratched, or dirty that the computer will be unable to read them, just as a cassette player might be unable to play a damaged cassette. The jackets of many brands of disks warn users not to touch the magnetic tape or bend the disk and to keep the disk protected from dust, magnets, and extremes of heat and cold.

You will want to elaborate somewhat on these instructions. Point out to students that most machinery generates a magnetic field. Thus it is foolhardy to place a disk on a printer, a photocopying machine, or a microwave oven while it is in use. Similarly, the dashboard of a car on a sunny day can be dangerous. One colleague unintentionally destroyed all the data on a disk by absentmindedly brushing the disk against his wool sweater on a cold day. To protect against damage from static electricity students should touch something metal before reaching for their disks when they sit down at their computers.

Take care when labeling disks. Write on a sticky label first and *then* affix the label to the disk. If it is necessary to write something on a label that is already attached, use a felt-tip pen. *Never* write directly on a disk in ballpoint pen. Don't attach a disk to anything with a rubber band or paper clip. Never set anything heavy on top of a disk. Keep disks away from food, beverages, and cigarette smoke. A convenient, safe, and inexpensive way for students to carry a disk is to tape the disk jacket to the inside of a hardcover textbook.

Unintentionally overloading a disk can also make a mess of your files. Be sure students know what the capacity of their disks is and how to check periodically to determine how much space is left.

Protecting Files

Students have all heard their share of catastrophe stories about lost computer data, and they already have some fear of trusting their work to an electronic medium. In your discussion of disk care, you will find yourself reinforcing their apprehension. It is healthy for them to realize the vulnerability of electronic files so that they will take adequate precautions. However, you can reassure those who are skeptical about trusting their work to the computer by pointing out that their bank accounts, car payments, and the mortgage on the family house are all recorded electronically (not to mention most of the world's financial transactions). They can use the same method that financial institutions use to make sure data are not lost. They can back up their files! Advise them to copy files onto another diskette at frequent intervals and to store that diskette in a separate place.

NOTES

1. Helen J. Schwartz, *Instructor's Manual for Interactive Writing: Composing with a Word Processor* (New York: Holt, Rinehart and Winston, 1985), p. 73.
2. Bryan Pfaffenberger, "The Scholar's Software Library—Nota Bene," *Research in Word Processing Newsletter* 4.1 (January 1986):10.

PART ONE

Classroom Applications

CHAPTER 1

Computer-Aided Instruction

COMPUTER-AIDED INSTRUCTION

The computer has many uses in teaching language and literature. "Drill-and-practice" computer-aided instruction (CAI) can help students learn the fundamentals of vocabulary, grammar, and mechanics, and it is especially useful in foreign-language applications. Other programs that can help teach writing are of several types: prewriting, writing strategy, invention, and writing analysis. There are also applications in teaching literature.

DRILL-AND-PRACTICE CAI

You can buy drill-and-practice CAI programs or create them yourself with an "authoring" system; we'll talk more about that later. In either case, you need to keep in mind the strengths and limitations of the computer as well as the particular needs of your students.

The basic idea behind drill-and-practice CAI is to help students learn fundamental information and concepts at their own pace, so that class time can be devoted to more creative activities. Good CAI does not replace instructors; it enables them to help students apply what they have learned and spares them having to lead students through explanations and drills that the student does not require the special talents of the instructor to master. It takes much of the drudgery out of the classroom and prepares students for real learning by providing individualized instruction through activities that students enjoy.[1]

Advantages

Perhaps the main pedagogical advantage of drill-and-practice CAI is that students can learn at their own pace. The teacher decides what they should learn, and the computer presents the information and gives students as much time as they need to assimilate it. They can skip over topics they already understand or repeat ones with which they have trouble, and they can ask for more information and examples. The computer doesn't mind repeating information or answering questions at any hour of the day, and students don't have to wait for slower classmates or fall behind faster ones.

Drill-and-practice CAI usually runs on a microcomputer (some CAI programs run on mainframe computers, but for the moment let's limit the discussion to micros). The student inserts a floppy disk in the computer, turns it on, and follows the instructions on the screen. The program usually asks for the student's name and then describes the activities that will follow and gives some instructions. The activities normally include the presentation of material, examples, sample exercises, and a test.

Explanatory text and examples appear on the screen, sometimes accompanied by graphics (computer-generated illustrations) and sound. Students can spend as much time as they like on each screen and then move on to the next screen or skip to the next activity. If they don't need to review the material, they can go straight to the exercises and the test. In most programs, they can return to the presentation of material, or to briefer "help screens," at any time while working on exercises (and on tests, if the instructor desires).

The exercises and tests consist of questions on the screen and a place to supply an answer. The student types in a response and usually has a simple editor (that is, a word processor) with which to make changes. (Instructions for using the editor are often displayed at the bottom of the screen.) The computer analyzes the student's answer and tells whether it is right or wrong and, in a good program, why. It can indicate how to go about correcting the answer and suggest which help screens may be useful. After the student gives two or three incorrect answers, the program usually supplies the correct answer and then asks another question. While all this is going on, the computer records the number of correct responses, the number of incorrect responses, and (if you like) how long it took the student to answer each question.

The computer's graphics and sound capabilities can liven up a presentation or, more important, illustrate terms or show geographic locations. With graphics CAI programs you can create charts and graphs, have parts of the screen in different colors or enclosed in boxes, move words from one place to another (to teach word order or verb endings, for example), and so forth. The computer's ability to imitate the human voice is still limited, but it can create an accurate reproduction of a small number of words or control a tape recorder. It can also play quite complex music, which makes certain programs much more interesting.

Once a CAI program has presented information, it can ask sample questions to determine whether the students have understood and then give them a test. It is here that the computer's flexibility is especially valuable. It can choose any number of questions, give students any number of chances to get them right (and some hints along the way), repeat questions if necessary, and continue the process until the student has answered a certain number of questions, or a certain percentage of them, correctly. Students can take as long as they like (or as long as the teacher decides the computer should allow) to answer the questions, and they have an opportunity to find out immediately whether their answer was right or wrong, and why. When they reach the end of a lesson, they feel confident that they have mastered the material.

This combination of presentation and testing of material is an excellent way of ensuring that students are prepared before they come to class. Using more traditional methods, you can never be sure how well they have read an assignment or how well they understand it. With drill-and-practice CAI, however, the computer records whether students have completed a lesson successfully, how many mistakes they made, and how long it took them. If the CAI program has been well designed, the instructor can be sure that the students who have completed the lesson have attained at least a minimal level of understanding and can structure the following class accordingly.

Limitations

There are, of course, some limitations to this sort of computer-assisted instruction; most involve the need to predict what responses a student might make.[2] A computer cannot realize that an unusual answer is as good as the expected one unless it has been programmed to accept that very answer, nor can it have all the information in just the right form to meet the needs of every student. A computer is best at matching an answer to a question that has only one correct answer, though with foresight and good programming you can make it extremely flexible. For example, it is easy to have a computer ask an ESL (English as a second language) student for a specific form of a verb in English and check her answer against the correct form. It is much more complicated to have it ask "How are you?" and be prepared to accept "Fine," "Very well," "OK," "Not too bad," "So-so," "Lousy," "Rotten," "Not too good," or dozens of other possible acceptable answers. Good programming can solve most of these problems, but for simple applications, it is best to stick to questions that have fairly predictable, right-or-wrong answers.

Another limitation is access to a computer or terminal, though this becomes less of a problem all the time. Many colleges and universities are making microcomputers available to students at most hours of the day, and technical advances in telephone connections to computers and in joining several computers in a network are making it easier to offer access to a central CAI program from a dorm room or office. Do keep in mind your campus's constraints on access to physical hardware, though, as you do your course planning; the best program in the world does very little good if students can't get to it.

Applications

Let's look at some particular applications of computer-assisted instruction to the teaching of a foreign language or literature. We can't mention all the possibilities here, but the following examples should give you a good idea of what can be done both with commercially available programs and with those you write yourself.

The most obvious and immediate application is in the mastery of vocabulary. You can buy programs that present the most frequently used vocabulary items or programs that go along with the textbook you're using. Such a program typically prints a word on the screen in English and prompts the student for an equivalent in the foreign language, or vice versa. There are usually very few possible correct answers, and the computer can easily be programmed to accept any answer the instructor or program designer finds acceptable. (It is of course essential that the authors have thought of all possible correct answers in designing a program; the computer is only as smart as the person who gives it instructions.)

With careful programming, the computer can recognize that an answer is almost right and can suggest what changes to make. For example, if the student is to supply the French equivalent for "dog," the correct answer is "chien." The student's answer should be considered correct, however, if it gives the feminine form "chienne" (unless the masculine was specifically called for). Moreover, if the response is "chiem" or "chiene," for example, the answer should not be rejected as hopelessly wrong. The student should be told that the answer is almost correct and that she should check her spelling carefully. (A really good program can suggest why the answer is wrong. In the case of "chiene," it can point out that "ene" is not a normal combination of letters in French and refer the student to a help screen with rules about accent marks and double consonants.) She would then have a chance to edit her answer (a good program allows editing, rather than requiring that the entire answer be retyped) and try again. The computer can keep up with how many tries it took and grade her accordingly, but she should have the opportunity to figure out what is wrong and to arrive at the correct answer herself.

You can use similar approaches to teach grammar. It is easy to have the computer ask students for the forms of regular and of common irregular verbs, for example, and then match the students' answers with the correct forms.[3] There would usually be only one correct answer, and if a student's answer doesn't match the correct one, the computer can find out where the problem is. It can determine whether there is a mistake in the stem or in the ending (or both) and then offer the student the rules for stem changes or a chance to review the endings.

A good drill-and-practice CAI program can teach almost any aspect of grammar that lends itself to questions eliciting right-or-wrong answers: correct forms, when to use them, and where to place them in the sentence. You can simply ask students to supply the correct form of a verb or pronoun, or you can give them a sentence with a missing word that they have to fill in with the proper form. A program with simple editing capabilities can teach word order by presenting students either with a sentence containing words in the wrong order or with words that they have to combine into a sentence. (They mark each word as one marks a block of text in a word processor and then put it in the proper place.) You can also ask students to generate or translate simple sentences, but you must be sure that you have told the computer how to recognize all possible correct answers.

Plenty of programs that are on the market provide this kind of instruction for your students, but you need to evaluate them carefully. Many of them offer no flexibility at all and may tell students they have made an error when in fact they have given a response that is correct but is not what the computer expected. For example, a French program asks for the compound past tense of the verb *partir,* and expects the answer "je suis parti." If the student happens to be female, or just adventurous, and responds "je suis partie," the computer greets a perfectly correct response with "Sorry; try again." No encouragement, no suggestion of why the response isn't acceptable. A similar program asks students to combine two sentences using a relative pronoun, but it accepts the clauses in only one of two possible orders and does not accept a legitimate alternative form of the pronoun *(duquel* for *dont).*

Most CAI designers avoid such mistakes. Try to test a program before purchasing it, though, and give it some wrong answers to see what happens. The computer's responses should be encouraging and indicative of what is wrong, and there should be some variety. It is particularly helpful to have a large number of interesting messages in response to correct answers—and to have them in the target language. Students try hard to figure out what the messages mean, and because they know they are being congratulated, they can usually figure out the meaning even if they don't know all the words. For example, a little imagination reveals that a mysterious message is the French equivalent of "Pass GO and collect $200," and students can have fun learning to translate the pat on the back.

There should be a large number of varied exercises and questions so that students don't get the same questions every time they repeat part of the program. A good program lets you move easily from one part to another so that you don't have to answer 20 questions about something you've already mastered just to get to the next topic. Any program gets boring under these circumstances.

You need to be sure that all the questions can be answered with the information presented in the program, and that, while trying to answer a question, students can get to the explanations and then back to the question. Be sure the computer allows them enough time to answer and that it gives them at least one or two chances to correct an error before providing the correct answer (ideally, with an explanation of why it is correct) and moving on to the next question. Check the editing capabilities of the program—you should be able to make corrections without retyping the complete answer, and you should be able to enter accent marks easily and see them clearly on the screen.

Do It Yourself!

If you can't find a program that meets your students' needs, consider creating your own. There are several excellent "authoring systems" on the market that enable you to create your own questions, answers, and explanations. You can allow for errors in spelling and capitalization, accept alternative answers, specify words to be ignored in judging whether an answer is correct, and designate certain words as equivalents of others in an answer ("sea" and "ocean," for example, or "voiture," "auto," and "automobile" in French). You have control over the screen, so you can use different colors and sizes of letters or have a message stay on the screen while different questions are displayed. Most authoring programs let you embellish your presentation with sounds and graphics, though too many graphics slow the program down and use up memory that could be better devoted to such things as error analysis.

Authoring programs also give you control over how many times students can get a question wrong before being given the right answer and over how long they have to begin typing in an answer. Such programs keep up with the number of right and wrong answers and with the types of mistakes made, and they provide you with a detailed progress report and grade.

Some of these authoring systems are easier to use than others. If you just want to set up questions that have straightforward answers, you can get a program that demands no more than that you type in the questions and answers and then answer a few questions yourself (How many incorrect answers are allowed? How many questions per exercise?). If you want sophisticated error analysis and screen formatting, though, you will have to be willing to learn a little about how the program works. (Some of the programs are authoring *languages* rather than systems.) This amounts to learning some simple programming, usually in BASIC. If you decide it's not worth your time, you may be able to get someone in your department or in your school's computer lab to do it for you. There are numerous grant possibilities to support such projects.

The future is especially bright for drill-and-practice CAI. New technology (such as videodisks that allow storage of large amounts of audio and video information) shows students accurate reproductions of scenes from the countries in which the target language is spoken. Thanks to developments in artificial intelligence (AI), computers are increasingly able to understand "natural" human language. In one system being designed at MIT, a "Poltergeist" talks with the student and "uses natural discourse: he requests clarification if unable to understand the student's command, suggests grammatical or spelling repairs, and gives listener feedback. The student learns to take the computer seriously and enters into negotiation whenever a communication difficulty arises" (*NE Newsletter* 18 (1985), p. 47). With programs such as this, students will be able to interact directly and more naturally with a computer and to rely on its "knowledge" to answer their questions rather than on the instructor's ability to foresee every possible question.

PREWRITING, INVENTION, AND WRITING STRATEGY SOFTWARE

In general, the application of drill-and-practice software to writing instruction has proved far less satisfactory than its application to foreign-language acquisition. Kathleen Kiefer notes,

As recently as 1980, educators discovered that most software purportedly teaching writing actually drills for spelling, comma placement, and other mechanics of proofreading. Most of the programs are so boring, moreover, that students who might benefit from review learn only that "writing" is tedious. If the lockstep review alone were not condemnation enough, most of these programs do not require students to write at all. At most, students press one or two keys to indicate the correct answer to the question posed by the computer.[4]

Programs that take advantage of word processing and work with what students themselves compose have proved of much more value in writing instruction. In 1977 at the University of Texas, Hugh Burns and George Culp developed a primitive invention program called TOPOI to help students with the prewriting stage of persuasive writing. A student answers a series of questions posed by the computer and derived from the 28 enthymeme topics Aristotle set forth in his *Rhetoric.* Responses to questions about reasons, consequences, opinions, and the like must be brief—a word or at most a few sentences. The program is one cut above a mimeographed sheet of questions in that it scans responses for key words and branches when a particular word suggests a new direction for inquiry. It is also personalized, integrating key words from a student's answer into follow-up questions and creating the illusion of dialogue. However, students soon discover to their amusement that the program isn't really very smart. They can key in nonsense in answer to questions and receive responses that repeat the nonsense and appear to take it seriously.

Burns went on to create two other programs: BURKE, to aid in the invention and prewriting of journalistic or informative essays; and TAGI, to aid in the invention and prewriting of informative and exploratory prose. A student who is considering an essay topic can explore it, narrow its focus, and finally create text to fit into the paper. All three of these programs—TOPOI, BURKE, and TAGI—are available at no cost. Send a floppy disk along with a stamped, self-addressed mailer to George H. Culp, Computation Center, University of Texas, Austin, TX 78712.

Burns and Culp's early pioneering work inspired a number of other writing teachers to develop more sophisticated prewriting programs that ask students the individualized questions an instructor might pose in a conference. Valarie Arms and Jim Gibson of Drexel University designed Create/Recreate for technical writing classes. Students with a topic in mind may use the questions in the prewriting program Create to shape their material and consider matters such as purpose and audience. Then Recreate directs their attention toward global revision rather than superficial revision of mechanics. Helen J. Schwartz designed her Seen program to help students develop and support their ideas about literary characters in a nonthreatening milieu. Her Organize program prompts students via questions and explanations to think about topic, thesis, audience, and rhetorical purpose in planning their composition.

Arthur Winterbauer's Writeaid, still being tested at the University of Denver, conducts an in-depth interview with students after an initial "consultation." The program probes for details on the basis of the student's responses to questions posed earlier in the session and then builds further probes based on these answers. Writeaid inquires recursively for increasing amounts of detail until the student has nothing more to say. During this process, the program has been building a sample outline for the student to critique. Most interestingly, with a separate interface program, an instructor can customize Writeaid by altering its vocabulary and manipulating the question pool.

James Strickland's Free was inspired by Peter Elbow's free-writing strategy in *Writing Without Teachers.* The program not only helps a student explore a topic via a series of free-writings interspersed with periods in which the student focuses on a "center of gravity"; it also stores the student's writing for later use. Strickland's Quest asks students prewriting questions based on the systemic heuristic found in Patrick Hartwell's *Open to Language* (New York: Oxford University Press, 1982) and stores for further revision the text that students generate. Both of these programs are available to educators from the author at no charge. To receive a copy, send a floppy disk and a self-addressed, stamped mailer to him at 313 Eisenberg Hall, Slippery Rock University, Slippery Rock, PA 16057.

Creative Problem Solving, by Raymond and Dawn Rodrigues, was designed to help students think about their topics in creative and non-stereotypical ways by forcing them to draw analogies, which often result in new insights. Their program is also available at no charge. Send a formatted disk and a stamped, self-addressed mailer to them in care of the Department of Curriculum and Instruction, Box 3AC, New Mexico State University, Las Cruces, NM 88003.

For business writing students, David Byrd, Paula Feldman, and Phyllis Fleishel at the University of South Carolina have created *The Microcomputer and Business Writing* to be used in conjunction with any of a number of word processing programs. Disks contain the texts of business documents to be revised and edited. Because they do not have to type and then retype the texts, this package saves students time and makes it possible for them to concentrate on revision and on the visual, aesthetic impact of their documents.

Of interest to those researching the writing process is Robert Connors and Mark Haselkorn's program Recomp, which monitors students as they compose. It gathers the following potentially useful data: how many times the student reviewed a sentence; how many times she began a period of review; what sentences she reviewed during each period; the duration of each period of review; what new sentences she composed during each period; how long it took to complete each sentence; how much of that time she spent drafting the sentence; whether she inserted a sentence or wrote it at the end of existing text; whether she deleted a sentence; how many times she edited each sentence; what changes she made each time; what new sentence she was writing at the time of each change; what sentences she reviewed at the time of each change; and what percent of the total composing time she spent reviewing previously written text, writing sentences at the end of previously written text, and inserting sentences in previously written text.

These are just a sampling of the process-oriented programs that writing teachers have developed. (For a more thorough listing, see the end of this chapter.) More comprehensive programs intended to help students with prewriting, drafting, revising, and proofreading include HBJ Writer (formerly WANDAH), developed at UCLA; Wordswork (formerly Wordsworth II), developed at Michigan Technological University; and one so-far-unnamed program under development at Carnegie–Mellon University. From what we have seen of these programs, the prewriting, drafting, and revising sections are more useful than the proofreading sections, which suffer from the problems of writing analyzers in general (see the following section). Until the technology improves, you will do far better (and spend a great deal less money) to find a prewriting program you like and combine it with a word processing program.

WRITING ANALYZERS

Imagine the day when writing students will no longer turn in compositions filled with dangling modifiers, comma splices, trite expressions, wordiness, faulty parallelism, subject/verb disagreement, sentence fragments, and overused passive voice. When that day comes, you as a writing teacher will be free to devote most of your time with students to discussing rhetorical strategies and ways of polishing prose. You will be reading essays to help students strengthen them conceptually, confident that they are getting intelligent, effective, and sensitive individualized assistance outside of class on the mechanics of writing.

Computer programs will one day be able to help students recognize their strengths and weaknesses as writers and give them instant feedback whenever they want it during the act of composition. These writing analyzers will not only help students catch outright errors before you ever see their writing but will also give each student the immediate instruction in usage and mechanics that he or she needs to understand specific problems and avoid them in the future. How much more satisfying our jobs will be when that glorious day arrives, as it surely will. But don't get too excited about this prospect yet. Such writing analyzers are not currently available and will not be for some years. Researchers have been making impressive progress, but the field is still in its infancy.

What about the computer programs now on the market that bill themselves as text analyzers able to comment on everything from grammar to style? Although many of them will serve useful purposes in writing research, even the best is still too crude to be of much use to undergraduate students in composition classes. In fact, some of them can be downright destructive in such a setting. Why? Computer technology is not yet sophisticated enough to provide the level of artificial intelligence required for that kind of writing analyzer. Computers can match words or phrases against dictionaries, recognize punctuation, count words, and sometimes even determine parts of speech, but they cannot yet—and this is the crucial point—*understand meaning*. For example, even a simple word such as *cat* can mean many different things. People who speak English easily differentiate among the various meanings, using context and parts of speech as cues. But text analyzers now commercially available cannot with a high degree of accuracy tell the difference among the following types of *cat:*

> He's a cool cat.
> At the hospital, they gave me a CAT scan.
> A cat says "meow."
> He put a cat rig on his sailboat.
> I'm going to cat around tonight.
> He made his living as a cat burglar.
> The tractor I like best is a Cat.

Without the ability to understand meaning, text analyzers cannot be effective or even useful critics of student writing. If we try to thrust them into that role before artificial intelligence has advanced to the necessary degree, we risk doing our students more harm than good.

Claims for so-called writing analyzers or "style checkers" now on the market make them sound quite appealing. Let us examine what they really offer. Recently our university purchased The Quintilian Analysis, which claims to analyze writing style in essays of up to 10,000 words using an IBM-PC or TRS-80, and which costs $995 for a site license. Much of the feedback the student receives has its basis in various word-counting processes. For example, a typical comment sheet begins with a count of the total number of words in the essay and concludes with the following:

SOME DATA ABOUT THIS COMPOSITION

1. Number of sentences—26
2. Average sentence length—15.73 words
3. Number of paragraphs—5
4. Average paragraph length in words—81.80 words
5. MOST ACTIVE WORDS-
   22 - i   16 - the
   18 - to   15 - and

How valuable is such information to an undergraduate writer? It clutters students' minds and doesn't help them improve their writing. Instead it tends to divert students from the true task at hand and encourages them to feel that writing is too complicated to be enjoyable or done well.

Quintilian's creators have attempted to take numerical results and translate them into interpretive prose feedback. However, these comments prove less than satisfactory, because, again, without the ability to understand the meaning of what a student has written, any commentary must necessarily be generalized and based strictly on numerical data. Here is an example of the first part of a typical comment sheet (furnished by the publishers for illustration):

> You are writing with above-average word repetition. This suggests, in the essay, a primer-like effect or sometimes even an incantatory effect, depending upon the particular vocabulary involved. In information-oriented texts, e.g. academic or technical, such 'redundancy' may create a strongly emphatic or 'insistent' tone.
>
> You would seem to be writing in a fairly strong monosyllabic style. Are you deliberately striving for simplicity, for the colloquial?
>
> Your vocabulary has a certain simple, common, even elementary aspect to it. Are you trying to be very simple? Are you writing for children? For an audience with limited vocabulary? Indeed, given your high monosyllabic count, you seem to be aiming for an extremely plain, simplistic style. . . .
>
> Your sentences run to the short side, typical of popular journalism or writing for audiences unwilling to cope with longer sentence constructions. Are you using such short sentences for some particular effect? Are you trying to outdo Hemingway? Of course, sometimes 'poetic' styles also have this characteristic. . . .

Despite the designers' intention to make the prose commentary non-judgmental or, in their words, "obviously, quite objective," it clearly does not have that effect. Consider what a student would sense upon reading the paragraph beginning "Your vocabulary has a certain simple, common, even elementary aspect to it." We cannot help wondering how Hemingway himself would have felt with feedback such as "Are you trying to be very simple? Are you writing for children? For an audience with limited vocabulary?"

But this is a difficulty shared even by the best text analyzer now on the market, Writer's Workbench. Because computer technology is not yet sophisticated enough to enable software to comprehend meaning and therefore to make truly intelligent judgments, text analyzers by their very nature cannot recognize good writing. Thus they cannot give students genuinely positive feedback. Even the best of these writing analyzers tend to focus on error identification—on what students *may* be doing wrong rather than on what they *are* doing right. Thus students get plenty of negative feedback (much of it inaccurate) and virtually no positive feedback. And, far from being reassured by such qualifiers as "might be" in the feedback sheets the computer generates, students tend to be dismayed and discouraged by the number of things they are asked to check to make sure they are correct. Their suspicion that revision consists mainly of correcting "errors" gets confirmed. It is astonishing to us how many educators, in adopting these text analyzer programs for their students, seem to have forgotten the pedagogical need for positive reinforcement to facilitate learning.

Writer's Workbench consists of 32 separate style, diction, and organization programs and uses a function word and verb dictionary, along with some rules concerning phrase structure, to generate reports on a text.

Among other writing faults, it identifies possible spelling and punctuation errors, wordiness, split infinitives, passive constructions, and sentences it judges overly long. It will also assess the text according to four readability indexes.

Because a computer program cannot understand the content of what it is reading, and often cannot even identify a word's grammatical function in a sentence, what gets marked as an error or possible weakness may or may not be a real problem in the essay. Moreover, it may entirely ignore a serious error. For example, Writer's Workbench generated 6 pages of feedback concerning our keyed-in version of the first 3 paragraphs (395 words) of George Orwell's essay "Politics and the English Language." On one sheet it printed the following feedback on style:

    style -mm -li usc readability grades:
       (Kincaid) 12.6 (auto) 12.9 (Coleman-Liau) 10.5
    (Flesch) 13.2 (48.3)

    sentence info:
                no. sent 16 no. wds 395
                av sent leng 24.7 av word leng 4.66
                no. questions 0 no. imperatives 0
                no. content wds 197 49.9% av leng 6.39
                short sent (<20) 31% (5) long sent (>35) 13% (2)
                longest sent 43 wds at sent 12; shortest sent 8
    wds at sent 10

    sentence types:
                simple 6% (1) complex 38% (6)
                compound 13% (2) compound-complex 44% (7)

    word usage:
                verb types as % of total verbs
                tobe 46% (25) aux 22% (12) inf 9% (5)
                passive as % of non-inf verbs 8% (4)
                types as % of total
                prep 8.4% (33) conj 4.6% (18) adv 7.6% (30)
                noun 18.7% (74) adj 14.2% (56) pron 9.6% (38)
                nominalizations 1% (5)

    sentence beginnings:
                subject opener: noun (2) pron (4) pos (1) adj (3)
    art (2) tot 75%
                prep 0% (0) adv 6% (1)
                verb 0% (0) subÇconj 6% (1) conj 6% (1)
                expletives 6% (1)

Furthermore, the program flagged all occurrences of *which,* marked words spelled according to proper British usage as "possible spelling errors," noted that there was too much variation in sentence length, and advised Orwell to break at least 22% of his compound and compound–complex sentences up into simple sentences. Yet, apart from spelling, it made no comment whatsoever about the following "sentence," which was mistyped: "It follows that any struggle against the abuse of language is a sentimental archaism, like pe is a sentimental archaism, like preferring candles to electric light or hansom cabs to aeroplanes." The program was perfectly indifferent to this nonsense, clearly the most egregious error in the writing sample. According to Donald Ross, Jr. and Lillian S. Bridwell, "It is not uncommon for [Writer's Workbench] programs to produce five pages of commentary for a two-page freshman text, comments that range in 'heinousness' from the mildly questionable to the unpardonable."[5]

What constitutes good writing is in some cases a legitimate matter for debate. The subjective criteria of Writer's Workbench would not be appropriate for the writing classes of those whose opinions happen to differ from those of Writer's Workbench's linguists. For example, the program is designed so that a nonrestrictive clause beginning with *that* gets flagged as an error. It is true that many writing teachers subscribe to this view, but others disagree. And, as Ross and Bridewell point out, instructors who have been working with students on sentence-combining skills will be dismayed to have their students scolded by the program for using words and sentences it deems too long.

Writing analysis programs often perform rather pointless functions. For example, the ALPS Writing Lab program will go through a student's essay and highlight all forms of the verb *to be*. Students can then review their marked essays, looking for the passive voice. Because the verb *to be* occurs in good writing all the time, and because there are some legitimate reasons for using the passive voice on occasion, what has the student gained? She will still need to be able to look at the highlighted words to differentiate passive constructions from other uses of the verb *to be* and will also need to be able to judge whether the passive construction is called for when it appears. The student who has attained that level of knowledge doesn't need a computer to point out forms of the verb. A student who does not have that knowledge will not be helped either. What good is a list of *to be* verb forms if you don't know what to do with them?

One of the ALPS programs highlights words that are commonly confused, such as *lie* and *lay, like* and *as, effect* and *affect*. The problem, though, is that it highlights these words whether they are used incorrectly or not. Thus, in our 395-word sample from George Orwell, it flagged 37 words (almost 10% of the total), all of them used correctly. Consider the unnecessary extra work such a program would ask a student to do. Consider the way a student's essay looks with 10% of the words marked up! The name of the program may well describe the feeling it could be expected to induce in students: "Confused."

Even sophisticated users sometimes have trouble interpreting information provided by a text analysis program. For example, not too long ago we received a call from an anthropologist friend of ours who had been using Grammatik to check a review she had written for a professional journal. "The program tells me that my average sentence length is 17.3 words. Should I be worried?" she inquired. What good is such raw data without an intelligent way to interpret it?

Recently, as an experiment, we keyed into five different text analyzers, including Writer's Workbench, the texts of essays by half a dozen writers widely admired for their prose style. The programs chided these writers for everything from excessively low readability scores to overuse of nominalizations to wordiness. Had these authors created their works with the "help" of these text analyzers, they probably would have given up writing in despair, for they would have been presented with pages and pages of possible "problems." Recently, *Wall Street Journal* staff reporter David Wessel keyed the Gettysburg Address into a style checker called Right Writer. According to Wessel, "On an index of the strength of delivery, the software rates the Gettysburg Address an even zero, indicating 'a weak, wordy writing style.'" The software, which dislikes negative constructions, suggests rephrasing one of the most admired sentences in the language, "The world will little note nor long remember what we say here, but it can never forget what they did here." It suggests that Virginia Woolf use simpler sentences and, according to Wessel, makes "snide remarks about Mark Twain's *The Adventures of Tom Sawyer.*"[6] You might try this test with a writing analysis program that looks appealing to you. Key in an essay by an author whose work you admire and see what feedback the program provides. You will find out (1) how accurate the program is, (2) whether a student is likely to receive genuinely helpful comments, and (3) whether you agree with the program's subjective criteria for good writing.

Until text analyzers can recognize good writing—that is, can intelligently parse a text and tell students what they are doing well, not just what they are doing wrong—this software has no place in any undergraduate writing classroom. Even under the best of circumstances, such "error checking" software discourages the creative use of language and the development of a personal style and encourages students to focus undue attention on superficial cosmetic revision of their writing.

There is no doubt, however, that even now these "text analyzers" can help researchers study various features of students' writing. What we learn may well help us develop the kind of intelligent computer text critiquing we can only dream about today.

APPLICATIONS FOR CAI IN LITERATURE CLASSES

You can use CAI in literature classes too. For example, the computer's ability to scan poetry (see pp. 110–112) can give students a chance to practice scansion outside of class. The computer can give a student a line to scan and can check the results against the rules for scansion that are programmed in (rather than storing in memory the correct scansion for each line). You can have a tremendous variety of lines to scan, the entire text of the *Illiad* or the *Aeneid,* for example, and have the computer choose lines at random for practice in scansion. Another advantage is that, with the "rule-oriented" approach developed by David J. Zhu and Joel Farber, the computer keeps up with which rules were necessary to scan the line. Thus it can let students know where they went wrong by printing an error message reporting in which part of the line the mistake was made (which rules were improperly used). The computer can also record these errors and types of errors for the instructor to examine later.

Another possibility for literature classes is to have students use a computer in preparing assignments and papers. Many of the programs described in the chapters on data bases, concordances, and stylistic analysis can be used after a few minutes of instruction, especially some recent ones designed for microcomputers. For example, students could save much time by searching the *MLA Bibliography* with the help of the computer. The BYU concordance program, or an even simpler one called FATRAS developed at the University of Montreal, can help your students find out what the key words are in a text or can search the text for occurrences of words they have already noted as important. When they are preparing an assignment on a passage from a longer work, for example, they can use the computer to find out whether any words in the passage are used in a similar context in any other parts of the text—and thus get a better understanding of the passage they are studying.

You can also use CAI to teach any kind of factual material you would include in a literature class. For example, in a survey class the computer could make sure the students know who wrote the major works you're teaching. You can also use the computer to present the proper format for footnotes and bibliographies and then to quiz students until they have mastered it. The quiz could consist of questions and answers, or it could require the student to create a footnote or a bibliographic entry from raw data.

EVALUATING COURSEWARE

The Educational Products Information Exchange (EPIE), a nonprofit, consumer-supported organization founded at Columbia University in 1981, recommends that you follow seven steps when acquiring software.

1. *Conduct a needs analysis.* What are your instructional goals and priorities? What resources do you already have on hand? Which students might benefit from using a computer—developmental, honors, etc.? What kind of instruction is needed?

2. *Write specifications for the courseware.* Rank the needs you identified. You may very well find that no existing programs address your highest-priority needs or that none of high enough quality have yet been developed. At this point, you may need to decide whether to rethink your priorities and adapt them to what is available, to switch to some other sort of instructional medium, or to develop the computer-assisted instructional courseware yourself.

3. *Identify the courseware.* Consult professional journals and newsletters, trade magazines, reviews by professional associations, and directories such as *The Educational Software Selector (T.E.S.S.),* which lists nearly 7,000 educational software programs of all types.

4. *Evaluate the courseware.* The most reliable sources of reviews are professional journals and newsletters (see Appendix II), because their evaluations are written by teaching professionals rather than by programmers, systems analysts, or (as is sometimes the case) interested but naive amateurs. This is not to say that popular magazines do not offer valuable information, but professional journals contain articles whose conclusions rest upon evidence gleaned from well-conceived and focused research. Courseware testing tends to be more sophisticated in such publications.

Nonprofit professional organizations that solicit and compile evaluations from individuals can also be useful sources. MicroSIFT, an organization sponsored by the Northwest Regional Educational Laboratory, publishes an *Evaluator's Guide* that describes and reviews instructional material. EPIE also provides information on educational software. However, most of the evaluations by these two groups focus on materials outside of the humanities and are designed for elementary and secondary school students rather than for students at institutions of higher education. (That emphasis simply reflects the current educational software market.)

T.E.S.S. is published by Columbia University, EPIE, and Teachers College Press. It includes an evaluation of each piece of software it lists, along with the names of individuals and institutions that have purchased it. *T.E.S.S.* can be accessed on line through the CompuServe Information Service network. (See p. 142.)

The CALICO Journal contains reviews of many of the programs listed in the CALICO data base (see pp. 143 and 146). Language teachers should also find useful Gerald R. Culley and George W. Mulford's *Foreign Language Teaching Programs for Microcomputers: A Volume of Reviews.* This volume grew out of a summer institute in computer-based education for foreign-language teachers that the National Endowment for the Humanities and the University of Delaware sponsored in 1982.

If you cannot find an in-depth evaluation in a source you respect, you will need to evaluate the courseware yourself. EPIE suggests that you consider the following questions (our elaboration is in parentheses):

a. Who are the users?
b. What is the program supposed to do?
c. Is the program appropriate for intended users? (Is it on an appropriate level and does it address student needs?)
d. Is the program accurate and fair?
e. How effective is the presentation of directions and content? (Is the screen easy to read?)
f. Is the program well designed technically? (Can you find any bugs?)
g. How effective is the program's approach? (Is the program pedagogically sound? Does it take advantage of the computing medium?)
h. Are the documentation and teacher's guide well designed and useful? (Reviewers usually find that the quality of the documentation is a good indication of the quality of the software.)
i. How much control does the program give the students?
j. Can the teacher alter the program?
k. How does the program use feedback? (Is it given in a clear and nonthreatening way?)
l. How does the program use graphics? (Are they appropriate and well integrated?)
m. Is there an audio component to the program? (If so, does it enhance feedback?)
n. Is random generation used? (Random generation is better because it allows the program to change.)
o. Does the program include tests?
p. Does the program include branching?
q. What kind of record-keeping and management systems does the program have? (Do students get a report?)

Other organizations that have developed evaluation procedures for courseware include CONDUIT, SOFTSWAP, and the Minnesota Educational Computing Consortium.

5. *Preview the courseware.* Even if you have read favorable reviews, *never* purchase software without trying it yourself. Many of those who have disregarded this advice have lived to regret it. Your priorities, goals, needs, pedagogy, and educational values may differ from the reviewer's and from the developer's. It is even more hazardous to buy software just on the basis of the manufacturer's or developer's claims. Sad to say, much promotional literature consists of wishful thinking and unsubstantiated claims. In examining the courseware, pay particular attention to the documentation—the teacher's guide or user's manual. Most responsible vendors will allow you a 30-day trial period or a money-back guarantee.

6. *Draw up recommendations on purchase and potential use.* You can have the most wonderful courseware in the world, but if other faculty members do not know it is available or how it can be used, it will simply gather dust. You might want to schedule workshops to introduce it and demonstrate its use. Or you can send out a flyer with suggestions on integrating it into courses. Make sure, too, that you have the peripherals to support it—that is, that your

computers are equipped with enough memory or, if required, with boards, light pens, mice, or graphics printers.

7. *Obtain feedback from faculty and students.* Unfortunately, much software makes it to the market with little or no field testing. Check to be sure that those who are using it believe their needs are being met.

INVENTION, PREWRITING, AND WRITING STRATEGY PROGRAMS

Brainstorm, Michael Spitzer, Dept. of English, New York Institute of
Technology
BURKE, TAGI, TOPOI* Computation Center/HRC, University of Texas
Composition Strategy, Behavioral Engineering
Create/Recreate, Drexel University
Creative Problem Solving*, Raymond Rodrigues, New Mexico State
University
Free*, James Strickland, Slippery Rock University
Holtcomp, Holt, Rinehart and Winston
Organize, Helen J. Schwartz, Dept. of English, Oakland University
The Microcomputer and Business Writing, Random House
The Paragraphing Program, Holt, Rinehart and Winston
Prewrite, Boynton/Cook Publishers
Quest*, James Strickland, Slippery Rock University
Seen, Helen J. Schwartz, Dept. of English, Oakland University
Wordswork (formerly Wordsworth II), Michigan Tech Software
Writeaid, Denver Research Institute
Writer*, Richard Elias, Ohio Wesleyan University
Writer's Helper, CONDUIT
Writing is Thinking, Kapstrom, Inc.

Text Analysis Programs

The following software programs consist in whole or in large part of text analyzers.

COMMERCIALLY AVAILABLE THROUGH A PUBLISHER OR DISTRIBUTOR

ALPS Writing Lab, Automated Language Processing Systems
Analysis of Writing (also called Anandam), Miami–Dade Community
College
Comment (works in conjunction with Grammatik), Texas Tech University
Eyeball: A Program for Stylistic Descriptions, University of Minnesota
Grammatik, Digital Marketing
HBJ Writer (formerly WANDAH), Harcourt Brace Jovanovich

*These programs are available free of charge.

Homer: A Computerized Revision Program, Scribner's Sons
Lancelot, Clarkson Software
The Quintilian Analysis, Joseph Nichols Publisher
Writer's Helper, CONDUIT
UNIX* Writer's Workbench† Software, AT&T Technologies

AVAILABLE AT NO CHARGE

Writer, Department of English, Ohio Wesleyan University

UNDER DEVELOPMENT

CRITIQUE (formerly EPISTLE), IBM (When completed, this program may be a great deal more sophisticated than any of the foregoing.)

Mechanics Programs

English: Basic Mechanics, Educulture, Inc.
Grammarlab, Little, Brown & Co.
Socrates 2000, Thomas Bacig, Duluth, MN
TICCIT English Course, Computer Teaching Services
The Write Well Tutorial Series, CONDUIT

Foreign-Language Drill and Practice

It is nearly impossible to give any kind of representative list of the wide variety of CAI software for foreign languages. A complete list is available from the CALICO (Computer-Assisted Language Learning and Instruction Consortium) data base:

CALICO 3078 JKHB
Brigham Young University
Provo, Utah 84602.

The *CALICO Journal,* available from the same address, contains reviews of some of the software and articles on computer-assisted language instruction.

NOTES

1. The novelty may fade as we all get more and more used to computers, but studies show that computer-assisted learning is fun for most foreign-language students. It will be a while before we know for sure whether they enjoy it because it's new and different and seems like a game or because it really helps them learn in an efficient and individualized way.
2. To recognize a correct response, the computer must be able to match it letter for letter with a response the instructor has given it. Some flexibility is possible,

*Trademark of AT&T Bell Laboratories
†Trademark of AT&T Technologies

though, because you can tell the computer to ignore upper and lower case or misspellings of words that aren't essential to the answer.

3. The computer can "learn" the rules for conjugating regular verbs, so it doesn't have to store every possible form in its memory. And once it knows the rules, students can ask it for any form of any regular verb and practice conjugation by comparing their answers to those the computer furnishes.

4. Kathleen E. Kiefer, "Writing Using the Computer as Tool," *Computer-Aided Instruction in the Humanities,* ed. Solveig Olsen (New York: Modern Language Association of America, 1985), p. 91.

5. Donald Ross, Jr. and Lillian S. Bridwell, "Computer-Aided Composing: Gaps in the Software," *Computer-Aided Instruction in the Humanities,* ed. Solveig Olsen (New York: Modern Language Association of America, 1985), p. 107.

6. David Wessel, "Computer Software for Writers: Helping the Bad, Hurting the Good," *The Wall Street Journal* (July 7, 1986):17.

CHAPTER 2

Writing Activities Your Students Can Do Using Any Word Processing Program

Chapter 1 gave you an idea of the many types of CAI software packages now available. Already it is difficult to keep track of all the products competing for our dollars. And more are coming out all the time. But word processing is still the single most valuable contribution of computers to the writing classroom. You can provide your students with numerous useful writing activities that require nothing more than a word processing program. Some examples follow. To find out about others, make a habit of consulting the journals and periodicals listed in Appendix II at the end of this book. The bibliography (Appendix III) also lists articles on using computers in the classroom.

Getting Comfortable with Word Processing: The Computer Conversation

This exercise enables students to have fun and to practice the rudiments of word processing at the same time. It's a great ice breaker at the beginning of the semester.

It requires a lab situation in which pairs of computers can be situated in such a way that their monitors can be exchanged. That is to say, with student X and student Y each seated at a computer, student X can see the monitor screen connected to student Y's computer but not the screen connected to his own. Similarly, student Y can see only the monitor screen connected to student X's computer. Thus student X can send a message to student Y by typing text into a file. Student Y can answer student X in the same way, and so on.

This exercise is a good one to use when students are just beginning to learn about word processing. They need not even know how to save or print a file to carry on a "computer conversation." All they have to do is open a file and start typing. You might give students an introductory demonstration of word processing and then ask them to "converse" with a partner for 20 or 30 minutes.

You will find that in the course of their "conversations," students spontaneously coach each other on word processing functions. They not only enjoy such a social approach to writing but also find that it makes the whole process of learning to use the computer less intimidating. If you don't have enough computers in your lab for every student to sit at a keyboard, have students team up to take turns carrying on group conversations. If exchanging monitors is not practical in your lab, you can have students exchange keyboards.

A Brainstorming Technique:
How to Quiet the Critic Inside

Some students find it difficult to resist revising and editing a free-write or a first draft as they are initially composing. Yet such a tendency can get in the way of brainstorming. The following technique allows such inveterate self-critics to relax and forget about perfection for the time being. For a full discussion, see "Not Seeing Is Relieving: Invisible Writing with Computers," by Stephen Marcus and Sheridan Blau, in *Educational Technology,* 23 (April 1983), 12–15).

Simply ask students to turn the brightness control on the monitor all the way down so they can't see what they are writing. That's all there is to it. They can't revise or edit what they can't see. Warn students not to turn up the brightness until they have gotten all their ideas down. At that point they can save and print the file and look at it with a critical eye.

Collaborative Narration

Have students break up into small groups clustered around a micro. Assign a topic for a narrative and ask students to take turns, each writing one sentence or one paragraph, until the group decides the narrative is completed. (You might want to set a required length.) Some instructors also like to specify that each person revise and polish the contribution of the student who went immediately before.

Students can write an essay, a journal, a news story, a novel, a short story, a play, a poem, or any other narrative collaboratively. For the longer projects, you will probably want to have a traveling disk so that students can contribute outside of class. Brian Gallagher ("Computers, Word Processing, and the Teaching of Writing," *Research in Word Processing Newsletter,* April 1985, p. 3) points out that such an exercise works particularly well when you use microcomputer word processing, because this method "gives more substance to the effort by displaying the results on a screen, by focusing the single writer's and several onlookers' attention on the display where the evolving text is being recorded, and by providing multiple copies for further group analysis and amendment."

Collaborative Writing and Critiquing in Class

Computers make collaborative writing projects much easier for large groups. You will need equipment that projects what appears on your monitor onto a large screen everyone in the class can see. (Such equipment is now made by a number of companies, including NV Barco Electronic (Noordiaan 5-B8720 Kuurne, Belgium), Electrohome Limited (809 Wellington Street

North, Kitchener, Ontario, Canada N2G 4J6), Hughes Aircraft Company (6155 El Camino Real, Carlsbad, CA 92008), Vivid Systems Inc. (41752 Christy Street, Fremont, CA 94538), and SONY (P.O. Box 6185, Department MS, Union, NJ 07083).

Select a student's composition (preferably an anonymous one from another class), and enter it on disk outside of class. You might want to choose the composition on the basis of the kinds of writing problems it demonstrates or the sort of writing assignment it tackles.

In class, project the composition onto the large screen. (Some find it helpful to have printed the composition onto a ditto master and to have run off a hard copy for each student to refer to.) Ask students to read the essay through once. Then have them offer their comments, criticisms, and suggestions. Right in front of students' eyes, make actual revisions based on this running critique. Sometimes after a suggested change is made, students are able to see on screen that it still needs improvement. You can all work on the revision together until it seems satisfactory.

This technique can be used with other sorts of writing exercises. For example, if you want to work on sentence combining, you can enter on disk several sets of short, related sentences. The class as a whole can then work on combining each set by moving words around to make a more interesting and complicated sentence. In fact, if you make several copies of each set of short sentences, students can create several different sentences, each of which would serve well as the revision.

With a microcomputer, you can show students revision strategies individually *as they are writing.* And the computer enables you to preserve a copy of the student's original so the student does not feel her own work is being desecrated and so she will have the drafts to compare after the session.

Learning to Critique Writing More Objectively

Here's a technique to help students hone their revision skills and learn to be their own best critics.

Ask students to come to class on the date a writing assignment is due with two printouts of their completed homework assignment and the floppy disk on which it was written.

Have students hand one of the printouts in to you and exchange the other with that of a partner. Now ask each student to write a critique of her or his partner's essay. The critique should include constructive advice about how to revise the essay to make it more effective. It usually works best to ask students to do the critique in class and to tell them that they will be graded on its quality.

After they have finished (allow 30 to 45 minutes), ask students to borrow from their partners the floppy disk with the original file of the essay they have critiqued. Now assign the critiquing students to follow their own advice and revise *their classmate's* essay! They may either work directly on their classmate's disk or copy the file onto their own disk.

Students will moan and groan, but after the fact, most find this an extremely useful assignment. They get experience in improving a piece of writing plagued by many of the same problems as their own, but they bring more objectivity to the task. Students say they find it easier, after completing such an exercise, to spot and correct problems in their own work.

Monitoring the Process of Composition

Try this technique for any essay-writing assignment. It will allow you to observe stages in the thinking and writing process. You will be able to pinpoint at just what stage difficulties occur. For example, an instructor discovered that one student who tried this exercise was throwing out some of his best ideas and choosing to develop the less creative but less risky ones. Had the instructor had only the student's final draft to consider, she would not have been able to help him overcome what turned out to be a lack of self-confidence.

Hand out a sheet with the following procedure on it. (You might want to revise it somewhat, depending on your purposes.) Make sure your students know that, although you will require them to turn in all stages of the procedure, they will not be graded on this preliminary work.

1. Brainstorm. Type into a file all your ideas, reflections, observations, and possible strategies, or approaches to the material you need to consider for the assignment. Relax. Don't evaluate your ideas. Forget about complete sentences. Don't worry about writing style or logical order. Just get your ideas down any way you can.

PRINT

2. Look through your list of ideas. Which are the best ones? Underline them on your printout. Separate any ideas on strategy and any notes to yourself and put them at the end of your file. Place the ideas you think need to be in your essay at the beginning of your file.

PRINT

3. Delete all your strategy ideas from the file. (You have them on your printout for reference.) Now survey the material left in your file. Can you see which idea should be the main one in your essay? Move this idea to the very top. Delete all ideas or statements that are not related to or do not support this main idea.

PRINT

4. Arrange the remaining ideas in a logical order and add any others that might be necessary. You now have a working outline.

PRINT

5. Flesh out the outline by expanding each entry into a full sentence, elaborating on your ideas, explaining them, and adding supporting evidence where appropriate. You now have a first draft.

PRINT

6. Revise this first draft. Are your introduction and conclusion adequate? Is the tone effective? Is your writing style interesting and energetic? Polish your prose. Proofread for punctuation, spelling, and grammar. Have you been as concise as possible? Is your writing clear and easy to understand? Have you achieved your purpose? Finally, when you are satisfied . . .

PRINT!

Have students turn in all six versions, identifying them by number and arranging them in order of composition.

The beauty of this method is that students can make printouts at various stages in the evolution of their essay without much trouble, but you end up with much more information than usual.

You will probably want to require students to use this procedure only for one or two assignments—enough to use for diagnostic purposes. Some students, however, find it so helpful that they adopt it for later assignments.

Understanding the Importance of Person

This exercise can help students learn how important, in the overall success of the work, is the decision a writer makes about person. Enter a piece of prose on disk. (It can be an essay or a work of fiction.) Ask students to change the person in which the work is written. If it is written in the third person, for example, ask them to change it to a first-person narrative. Initially, have them use search-and-replace commands to substitute pronouns. What students quickly discover with this exercise is that person involves tone, style, and perspective—much more than just pronouns. When they alter only pronouns, the result is generally unsatisfactory because other elements are "out of kilter."

Search-and-Replace Exercises

The search function on your word processing program can be used to give students practice in working on particular writing problems. Let us say, for example, that you would like to help students learn to avoid sexist language. Give students a list of potentially troublesome forms, such as *man, he, him, his, brother, father,* and so on. Ask them to have the computer perform global searches of an essay for these terms. Once the terms are found and called to the student's attention, it is up to the student to review each case and decide whether the usage is sexist or not. There is no need to have students search specifically for longer forms that contain shorter ones, such as *mankind* and *brotherhood,* because the computer finds these when looking for the shorter ones. (Warn students, though, that the computer will also alert them to words such as "manage.") Of course, the success of this exercise depends on your having explained in class the concepts behind sexist language.

Similarly, you can devise individualized drill-and-practice exercises for particular students, using their own essays for text. For example, students who tend to overuse the passive voice can be asked to search for the various forms of the verb *to be* in their essays. (There are a number of expensive software programs that will do this, but a list of the forms to search for works just as well, and students learn more in directing such a search than they learn when the computer finds *to be* verbs automatically. Besides, once a student learns what the passive voice is and how to recognize it, such software is unnecessary.) When the computer finds a *to be* verb, the student must decide whether it represents use of the passive voice and, if so, must substitute a verb in the active voice. Ask students to hand in "before-and-after" printouts.

Synonyms, Antonyms, and Homonyms

To practice the use of synonyms, antonyms, or homonyms, have students select an essay that they completed earlier in the semester and still have on disk. (You might want to specify a particular assignment.) Ask students to go through the essay and, wherever possible, substitute an appropriate synonym. This exercise is also effective, and works to particularly comic effect, for practicing the use of antonyms and homonyms. In fact, you can have students edit the same essay three different times—once to substitute synonyms, once antonyms, and once homonyms.

Working on Organization

You can help students work on organization skills by taking advantage of the computer's ability to perform block moves quickly and easily. Enter a well-organized essay on disk (or simply copy one that you already have on disk). Be sure to choose an essay whose original your students cannot look up. Next scramble the order of the paragraphs so that the essay becomes quite disorganized and illogical. Keep this master disk in a central location, so that students can copy the file onto their own disks. Their assignment is to take the scrambled essay and reorder the paragraphs until they end up with an example of well-organized prose. This assignment permits students to concentrate their energies on organization without being distracted by other writing difficulties. Furthermore, because they already have the text on disk, you can ask them to turn in the completed assignment at the very next class meeting, even if the essay is five pages long!

You can also design an exercise that will help students concentrate on organization at the paragraph level. Give them ten different paragraphs, each scrambled internally. Have them work out an effective organization of the sentences in each scrambled paragraph. (*Note:* These two exercises should not be combined. Students find it too confusing to reorganize both sentences and paragraphs at the same time.)

Finally, you can use this principle to work with students on problems at the sentence level. For example, you can give the students sentences with misplaced modifiers and ask them to move the words around to place the modifiers in the correct position. (*Hint:* Throw in a sentence or two in which the modifiers are correctly placed.)

Learning to Paragraph Effectively

This exercise enables students to work on developing effective paragraphing skills. Enter in a file on a master disk the text of an essay by a professional writer, and leave out all paragraph indentation or spacing. (Choose an essay that students would have difficulty looking up.) Ask students to copy this file onto their own disks. The students will initially confront at least several pages of paragraphs all run together. (Just having to look at such a forbidding thing as text unrelieved by intermittent white space may in itself be a lesson to students who have not taken paragraphing seriously enough!) Their assignment is to insert effective paragraph spacing.

In the next class, distribute or display a copy of the essay as the author originally published it and ask students to compare their paragraphing with the author's. No doubt they will discover some interesting discrepancies that can provide material for class discussion. Invariably there are some student decisions that, though they differ from the author's, are justifiable. (Be sure to acknowlege this when it occurs.) But comparing their own paragraphing with a professional's helps students grasp the rationale for decisions about paragraphing.

Using Windows for Imitation

The capacity of many word processing programs to provide "windows" is useful in "writing by imitation" exercises. Windows make it possible to view material from one text file on the screen while editing another file. Simply have the student enter the text to be imitated in one file. Then, as Brian Gallagher suggests (see "Computers, Word Processing and the Teaching of Writing," *Research in Word Processing Newsletter* April 1985, p. 3), "the text to be imitated can be put in one window and scrolled up as the student writes his or her imitation of it in the other window."

Helping Students Assess Their Progress

One of the best things about having students do their writing on a computer is that they amass a portfolio of the semester's work. (A student who uses a computer throughout college can keep a copy of all four years' worth of written work!) It is useful to encourage students to look back at their early output to get a sense of their progress.

The following exercise not only helps students develop critiquing ability but also offers useful feedback about progress in writing skills and is generally good for class morale. About two-thirds or three-quarters of the way through the semester, ask students to print out an anonymous copy of (1) one of their earliest writing assignments in the course and (2) one of their most recent. Assign each student a number to write on the top of the first page, and have each person staple the two essays together. Collect the stapled sets, shuffle them, and hand them back so that everyone gets someone else's work.

Ask students to read over the essays they have received and note what differences they see in the writing. Has it improved over the course of the semester? If so, how? If not, why not? Has the style changed in any way? Is the prose more technically proficient? Is the language clearer and more precise? Make up your own list of questions to direct students in critiquing the essays. In classes where essays are not easily identifiable with a particular assignment, you can ask students to decide which essay was written early in the semester and which more recently—and to justify their decision on the basis of evidence gleaned from the essays. (If you plan to do this, have the students staple their essays together in random order.) Encourage students to give feedback that is detailed and precise. If you are teaching more than one section of the same course, you can exchange essays from one class with those from another.

The peer feedback students glean from this assignment helps to reinforce (and sometimes to elaborate on or supplement) your own comments. It also generally gives students positive reinforcement at a crucial time in the semester. It is useful to find a way to remind students that their hard work is paying off and that an unbiased reader can see the difference!

Speech Synthesizers

Speech synthesizers promise to be increasingly useful in the years to come for ESL and foreign-language students. Though applications are still extremely limited, in the not-too-distant future it will be possible for students to type into the computer words they have trouble pronouncing—and to hear, on command, the correct pronunciation. Students will also be able to enter words with similar pronunciations and hear the difference. The sort of listen-and-repeat drills now done in class or on tape will be augmented by computer practice with the speech synthesizer.

Speech synthesizers can also help blind students and those with lesser visual impairments.

Adventure Games for ESL and Foreign-Language Students

ESL teachers have had great success having students use adventure games to increase their English-language skills. Adventure games are interactive, and students must give directions in English to play. To win, they must respond quickly to what they have read in English. You can also incorporate the *speaking* of English by having students play the game in teams of two or three. To win, they are forced to talk to each other in English. There are many commercial products on the market (Zork, Amazon, and Castle are but a few of the most popular). Most of this software is quite inexpensive.

Many games are available in foreign languages, especially Spanish and French. These editions are excellent tools for introductory to intermediate foreign-language classes.

Some games—for example, Farenheit 451—are based on a book. Students quickly discover that they can get clues for winning the game by reading the book. This is a subtle way to encourage outside reading in the language being learned.

All of these games force students to take care with spelling, because the computer steadfastly refuses to respond to incorrectly spelled commands.

Self-Generated Drill and Practice
for Developmental or ESL Students

Ask students to take one of their own stories or a piece of their own written work and edit it to practice a particular language element such as verb tenses or the use of pronouns, apostrophes, the possessive, the plural, or the negative. For example, a piece of text written in the present tense can be changed to past tense or future tense. Or a student can be asked to make all statements negative or into questions or to replace nouns with pronouns, wherever possible. Ask students for before-and-after printouts. If your word processing program permits windows or a split screen, you might want to ask students to copy helpful rules (for example, how to make a declarative sentence into an interrogatory one, or how to form the negative or the possessive in English). Thus they can have the rule in front of them for reference as they work on the exercise.

PART TWO

Research Applications

CHAPTER 3

Why Use a Computer for Literary Research?

THE COMPUTER'S ROLE IN LITERARY RESEARCH

According to a survey of 443 MLA members completed in the spring of 1985,[1] literary scholars who don't use a computer for word processing are now in the minority. Word processing is only one of the many things a computer can do, however, as more and more of our colleagues are finding out.

Seeking Information

Even the smallest micro or personal computer can provide instant access to vast amounts of information. One can search bibliographies and library catalogues thoroughly and quickly, go straight to a specific passage in a long novel without flipping through hundreds of pages, or send a draft of an essay to colleagues electronically and receive their comments without waiting for the mail.

Preparing for Publication

A computer can also perform many of the tasks involved in preparing a critical text for publication. It can read texts, compare several texts and prepare a list of variants, help find the relationships between manuscripts, keep up with notes and bibliographic entries, and prepare a table of contents or an index. A computer can also take all this information and produce a version for a typesetting machine to use to set the type for a journal article or book, thus reducing time, expense, and errors. We will devote a whole section to textual editing later, but just think how nice it would be to avoid the errors that are introduced when type is set by hand—to go straight from the document you create with your computer to page proofs! A good editor may still make a contribution, but the whole stage of proofreading can be eliminated.

Quantifying Textual Data

The computer can also be a powerful tool in literary criticism, providing scholars with all sorts of important information. Of course, the computer cannot *replace* the scholar, whose presence is necessary at each stage of the analytical and interpretive process, who asks the initial questions, and who evaluates the answers. As a tool, however, a computer can do tasks that would take years or even lifetimes by traditional methods, and can turn up material that suggests additional questions to the scholar. (One advantage of a computer is that, unlike humans, it will always come up with the right answer when it is asked the right question and given the right information; and computers are fast "learning" to ask the right questions.)

Although literary criticism will always depend on the somewhat subjective views of human beings, it can be based on certain quantitative procedures. A literary text is made up of a finite number of words, and a computer can help you be sure you have not neglected any of them. It is probably no coincidence that recent developments in literary criticism that emphasize the text and its workings took place during the same time that computers were becoming more powerful and more readily available. A similar frame of mind underlies developments in both domains. A critic who responds to a text in a certain way can now use a computer to help analyze an interpretation, isolate the parts of the text that support it, compare those parts to the rest of the text, and show how the text as a whole supports that interpretation. Nathan Edelman put quite aptly his notion of the literary critic in his essay "Criticism in a Thousand Hard Lessons," published posthumously:

> You critics and professors, you have a perfect right to read as Tom, Dick and Harry; you have a perfect right to close a book and dash off snappy or vague words—but keep your impressions for your admiring relatives and your good friends; don't feed our public, all too anemic, with watered blood. Young critic, be a real teacher, analyze. Beauty is not so low that it need not be understood. Analyze. If you are a critic, analyze; that is your role.[2]

Analysis is where a computer can help us most in literary criticism.

Given the right data and the right programs, you can easily find out how and where a certain word, phrase, theme, or structure is used; look at every utterance by certain characters; trace the usage of certain sounds and rhythms; or study the use of certain parts of speech or of punctuation. The possibilities are almost endless—as endless as the elements of literature. The great advantage of the computer is that it can keep up with many of these elements no matter how large the corpus or how many times they occur, and it can provide all sorts of information about where they occur, in what context, and how they are distributed and grouped. You can thus make sure you are basing an analysis of a work on opinions that have real, often quantitative support in the text.

All of these possibilities for using a computer, and more, will be discussed in detail in the following chapters. First of all, however, we need to look at what is involved in using a computer and at just how easy using it can be.

ALLIES IN YOUR USE OF THE COMPUTER FOR LITERARY ANALYSIS

Using a computer does not have to be mysterious or difficult. In many cases you know exactly what you want to do, there is a program designed to do it, and all you have to do is read the instructions. (In the past, manuals were notoriously technical and difficult to understand, but this is rarely the case anymore.) In addition, most computer software developers offer support by telephone, often at no extra cost.

The Software Is on Your Side

In some cases it is not even necessary to read the manual, because much software is extremely "user friendly" and "menu driven" (that is, you have only to answer a series of questions and then wait for the results). Take the example of a data base package for a microcomputer that has already been set up to produce mailing labels. There is little to do but decide whether you want to add new names and addresses or delete existing ones, and then print the labels.[3] When you insert the program disk in the computer and turn it on, you soon see something like

1 Add a record
2 Modify a record
3 Delete a record
4 Display a record
5 Print records
6 Sort records
7 Quit

A *record* is simply one name and address. If you want to add a record, you type '1' and then see something like

NAME . . . .
STREET . . . .
CITY . . . .
STATE . . . .
ZIP . . . .

You type in the information on the first line, up to the maximal length shown, and then hit the return key and type in the information for the next line, etc. When you have entered the information on the last line, you can go on to the next record or stop.

If you want to print the labels you've typed in, you type '5' and then choose a format from the ones available. Next you answer some questions about how many labels you want to print (all of them, or those with zip codes greater than 30000, for example), and the printer starts to work. When it has finished, you type '7' to leave the program, or you just turn the computer off.

Be assured that almost any task on the computer is well within the capacities of the average academic. Say you may have to adapt a program to a specific task, such as printing a message along with your mailing labels or storing certain information about each person on your list. You would then need to read part of the manual (rarely more than a few pages), follow instructions, and hope it works; if it doesn't, it is usually easy to spot the error and correct it. Or you may need to use a program that asks you to make some choices and supply some information before you can use it. In that case you simply read the manual to find out what difference your choice will make and then answer the questions as they appear on the screen.

More and more users in the humanities are learning to design their own programs. This is not so difficult as it sounds, but you must be willing to look at a problem in a logical, step-by-step way—that is, to "think like a computer." A computer can do nothing but make yes–no decisions one at a time. To program, you need to conceive of solving a problem in this way and design a series of questions that will lead to the final answer. It is not much different from writing a recipe that will enable anyone to take the necessary steps to prepare a dish.

It is by no means demeaning or antihumanistic to "think like a computer," though it is rather Cartesian. It is basically a matter of taking things one step at a time and of not neglecting any steps—of taking nothing for granted. It is excellent mental exercise and a way of thinking that is applicable to many different problems, from the origins of the universe to the flaws in one's tennis game.

The Flowchart

People who work with computers normally develop a flowchart to record each step of the problem-solving process. Such a chart takes the form of a series of procedures and questions, and paths lead from each question to a new question or back to a previous step, depending on whether the answer to the question was positive or negative. For example, if you were intrigued by the way Dante uses the word *stars (stelle)* as the last word of each part of the *Divine Comedy* and wanted the computer to find all the other occurrences of the word and list the lines in which it is found, along with their line numbers, you would develop a flowchart like this one:

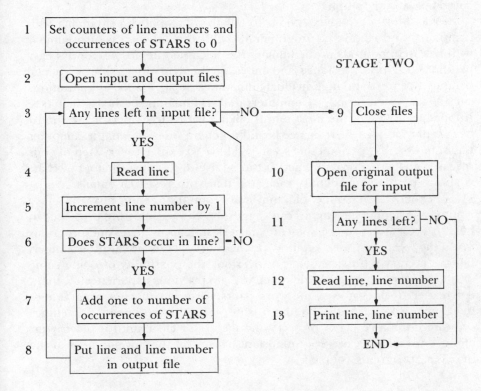

START
STAGE ONE

1   Set counters of line numbers and occurrences of STARS to 0

STAGE TWO

2   Open input and output files

3   Any lines left in input file? —NO— → 9   Close files

    YES

4   Read line

10   Open original output file for input

5   Increment line number by 1

11   Any lines left? —NO—

6   Does STARS occur in line? —NO

    YES

    YES

12   Read line, line number

7   Add one to number of occurrences of STARS

13   Print line, line number

8   Put line and line number in output file

    END ◄

Step 1 gets the computer ready to count line numbers and occurrences of *stars;* each time it reads a new line or finds an occurrence, it increases the corresponding number by one. Step 2 tells the computer where to find the text (input file) and where to store the results (output file), whereas steps 9 and 10 make the original output file the input file so the next stage of the program can print out the results stored in that output file. The real work starts in steps 3 and 11, as the computer looks at one line at a time until there aren't any left. In the first stage it gives each line a number and checks to determine whether *stars* occurs in the line. If so, it increments the number of occurrences by one and stores the line and its number in the output file. It then goes back to step 3 and repeats the process until there aren't any lines left. In the second stage, the program simply prints out the lines it found to contain *stars,* and their numbers, all of which information was stored in the output file.

"Resource Persons" and Colleagues

This is a rather simple example, but it indicates how to go about deciding whether—and how—a computer can be useful in your own literary research.

Can you make use of information about how words, phrases, and/or grammatical structures are used in a text? Can you use help in editing or in compiling a bibliography?

If you think so, the next step is to talk to someone who is familiar with computers and computer programming and who (ideally) is also familiar with research methods in the humanities. Such people are not always easy to find, but there are more and more of them in university or college computer centers and in individual humanities departments. Organizations such as the Association for Computers in the Humanities can also help (see Appendix I). To get the most out of talking with such a person, you must have a precise idea of your needs and a general idea of what a computer might be able to do. Sometimes you will have to explain every step of your research goals to a programmer. It can be useful to know what a flowchart is and to be ready to identify each step that your research entails.

If neither the personnel of a university computer center nor your more computer-oriented colleagues can suggest how to use existing programs to help in a research project, someone must design approaches and programs to do the job. This often requires the help of a professional programmer, but the literary scholar should not overlook the possibility of doing some of the programming personally, even with no previous experience. At times it is easier to do some of the work yourself than to have a programmer develop a program and then find it isn't quite what you need. Sometimes the directions a research project will take aren't clear until it is fairly far along, and in such cases it is important to control the development of the necessary programs yourself.

Your Own Resourcefulness

Programming is not difficult, especially in a language such as BASIC, which resembles English. In particular, scholars who have extensive experience in working with "natural" languages (English or Spanish, for example, as opposed to computer languages such as BASIC and PASCAL) should not find it difficult to pick up a bit of new vocabulary and syntax. If you are willing to adapt somewhat to the computer's way of doing things and to be specific with instructions and with their format, the rest is fairly easy.

For example, a BASIC program to implement the flowchart on page 67 and find occurrences of the word *stars* in Dante's *Divine Comedy* could read the following extracts from John Ciardi's translation:[4]

Midway in our life's journey, I went astray (I, 1)
From the straight road and woke to find myself
Alone in a dark wood.
. . .
This fell at the first widening of the dawn (I, 37)
As the sun was climbing aries with those stars
That rode with him to light the new creation.

. . .
And we walked out once more beneath the stars. (XXXIV, 142)

with these results:

2 lines contain STARS:
  5   As the sun was climbing aries with those stars
  7   And we walked out once more beneath the stars.

Such a program is quite simple to understand, especially when it includes, as any good program does, remarks (lines introduced by "REM") to explain what sections of the program code are for. Here is the program:

```
10    LINENO = 0
20    STARCOUNT = 0
30    '
99    REM        Open files for input and output
100   OPEN "INFERNO" FOR INPUT AS #1
110   OPEN "STARLINE" FOR OUTPUT AS #2
115   '
119   REM        Check for end of input file
120   IF EOF(1) THEN PRINT STARCOUNT "lines contain
      STARS:" : CLOSE : GOTO 1000
128   '
129   REM        Read one line of file unless no text
130   LINE INPUT #1, LINES$
135   IF LINES$= ". . ." THEN GOTO 130
139   REM        Give each line a number
140   LINENO=LINENO | 1
148   '
149   REM        Look for STARS
150   X = INSTR(1, LINES$, "stars")
160   IF X > 0 THEN STARCOUNT = STARCOUNT + 1: PRINT
      #2, LINENO, LINES$
170   GOTO 120
998   '
999   REM        Print line number and text where STARS occurs
1000  OPEN "STARLINE" FOR INPUT AS #3
1010  IF EOF(3) THEN END
1020  INPUT #3, LINENO, LINES$
1030  PRINT TAB(5); LINENO, LINES$
1040  GOTO 1010[5]
```

File #1 (line 100) contains the extracts of the text of the *Divine Comedy*, and file #2 (line 110) contains the lines and line numbers that contain *stars*. Line 120 checks for the end of the input file (EOF) and, when it is found, prints the message about how many lines with *stars* were found; it then closes the input and output files and goes to line 1000 to print the results contained in the output file. Line 130 reads one line of the text at a time and assigns it to the variable LINES$ (The $ indicates a variable made up of letters rather than numbers). Line 150 checks the variable LINES$, starting with the first letter, for occurrences of *stars* and makes the value of X the value of the place in the line of text where the first letter of *stars* occurs. Thus, in line 160, whenever X has a value greater than 0, an occurrence of *stars* has been found, and the program adds one to the number of times *stars* has occurred (increments the variable STARCOUNT by one; it was originally 0) and puts the line number and the text into a file, which can be read by the part of the program beginning with line 1000. All that is left, then, is for line 170 to send the processing back to line 120 in order to repeat the process over and over until all lines of text have been read. This last operation is perhaps the most important, for it allows the computer to repeat an operation continually, rapidly, and accurately for as long as necessary; a computer is definitely better at this than a person is.

Doing all of this may seem like taking many very small steps to achieve a fairly simple result, but a language like BASIC has to sacrifice some efficiency to remain simple and express its commands in something like normal English. More highly structured languages such as SNOBOL and PL-1 can perform the same operations with fewer instructions, and thus more quickly, but their instructions are harder to understand unless you have considerable experience. (This BASIC program could have been more succinct too, but it would have been less clear to an inexperienced user.) There are many techniques that can be learned quite quickly, and the literary scholar who learns them will be rewarded, will save much time, and will accomplish things otherwise beyond his or her scope. There is no need to be afraid of using a computer, and there are many reasons to seize the opportunity gladly. The following chapters will examine many of these opportunities in more detail.

NOTES

1. Virginia M. Doland, "Computer Utilization in the Profession of Literature: A Systems Theory Analysis of a Revolution." Paper at the Seventh International Conference on Computers and the Humanities, 1985.
2. *The Eye of the Beholder: Essays in French Literature,* ed. Jules Brody (Baltimore: Johns Hopkins University Press, 1974), 164–165.
3. Of course, you have to set up your format for the mailing label the first time you use it, but this takes only half an hour or so with the manual and five minutes at the keyboard.
4. Extracts are used here only to make the example short; the computer could search the entire *Divine Comedy* in a matter of seconds.
5. This program would find all occurrences of "stars" but not of "Stars"; a simple subroutine could allow the program to find either.

CHAPTER 4

Data Bases

UNDERSTANDING DATA BASES

The finest computer and the best software are useless without something to work on—that is, data. It may seem cold and "scientific" to refer to *Hamlet* or *Paradise Lost* as data, but they and other texts are the raw material of the literary enterprise, the obligatory starting point of any literary research. Of course, they are a different kind of data from the numbers of mathematicians or the vital statistics of social scientists, and literary scholars do different things with their raw materials. Still, without a careful treatment of a text, literary scholarship has no foundation.

A collection of data forms what computer people call a data *base,* another reminder that data are the obligatory starting point. For most computer users in the past, a data base has consisted of mathematical data derived from observations and experiments, of statistics taken from censuses and surveys, or of mailing lists and other information about business customers. However, the main type of data base for a literary scholar is simply a collection of texts—anywhere from bibliographic items through an individual work to a huge corpus drawn from all aspects of a national literature. Working with such a data base, scholars can do anything they would normally do with a text, but in many instances they can do it faster and more thoroughly.

The "Mailing-List" Data Base in Academia

Before going into such possibilities, however, let's take a brief look at more traditional, nontextual data bases to get an idea how all data bases are set up and used. Of the three types of traditional data bases mentioned in the preceding paragraph—mathematical data, statistics, and mailing lists—the latter is the most common and the most applicable to work in literature and language. We have all received mailings generated by a computer, which means that someone typed our name and address (often misspelled—another reminder of the importance of accurate data) into a data base.

You put information into a data base by fields and records. A *record* is all the information about one person or topic (the name and address of one person, or census information about one household, for example), and a *field* is each individual bit of information in that record (name, address, or zip code in a mailing list; age, sex, or marital status in a census). When you create a mailing list, the computer gives you a screen with room for each field in a record, and you type in the information, one field at a time, until you have finished with the record. (You can skip any field that isn't necessary for a particular record.) You would see something like this:

```
LAST NAME   ....................
FIRST NAME(S)   ..........................
STREET   .......................
CITY   ..........................
STATE   ..
ZIP CODE   .....-.....
```

The cursor would be at the beginning of the first input line, and you would type the name, up to the maximal length indicated by the line. (You sometimes have to abbreviate the information in a field, because fields are normally set up with a fixed length.) Then you hit 'return,' the cursor moves to the beginning of the next input line, and you repeat the process. When you have typed the zip code, a new record appears and you start over with the new name. And so on, until you decide to stop.

Each time the user types a name and address into the data base, the computer stores the information in its memory or on some medium such as a disk or magnetic tape. It will be available for a myriad of uses—after all, getting the information out is really what you're after, not putting it in. With the data arranged this way, you can ask the computer for all the information from one or more records or for the information from one or more fields from some or all of the records. Thus you could find out the complete name and address (entire record) of certain people or the last name (one field) of all the people (records) in the data base or of the members of some subgroup.

This ability to get the information out in any form and about any group of people is one of the greatest advantages that using a data base offers. The computer can print mailing labels for each person in the data base, following a specified format, or you can generate a selected list by telling the computer to include only residents of certain cities or states or to print labels only for certain zip codes. If more information had been put into the data base, such as income or special interests, the computer could select only residents of certain states who were interested in cooking and who had an income of more than $30,000.

Such a data base can be useful for the faculty member who is interested in mailing out information about conferences, publications, or degree programs. For example, you could easily select all teachers in the state with a M.A. but no Ph.D. and an interest in German. The literary scholar could create a data base of bibliographic data in order to produce footnotes and bibliographies automatically formatted in accordance with specific manuals of style. To take a simple example, instead of answering questions about name and address, you could respond to the following screen:

```
AUTHOR  . . . . . . . . . . . . . . . . . . . . . . . . . . . . . .
TITLE  . . . . . . . . . . . . . . . . . . . . . . . . . . . . . . . . . . . . . . . .
PUBLISHER  . . . . . . . . . . . . . . . . . . . . . . . . . . . . .
PLACE OF PUBLICATION  . . . . . . . . . . . . . . . . . .
DATE OF PUBLICATION  . . . . . . . . .
```

You could later ask for a printout of books by a certain author, listed in the proper form and complete with commas, colons, italics, and all the other details most of us tend to forget when going back and forth from one format to another.

You would probably want to include more information about the work (editor, translator, language, series, number of volumes) and appropriate information about journal articles. In addition, you could enter a few key words, such as the subject of the work, the time period it covers, and perhaps an evaluation of its importance (1, 2, or 3, for example). Such a data base could be quite useful. You could ask the computer for a printout, in alphabetical order by author, of all books and/or articles on Cervantes that were published in English after 1950 and to which you have assigned a rating of at least 2.

The more you think about data bases, the more uses for them you will discover. It might be helpful to have information about which historical or mythological characters occur in certain works or about literary characters depicted in works of art. This would be more like the census type of data base mentioned earlier; indeed, it could be useful to have a sort of census of the characters in a large-scale work such as Balzac's *La Comédie humaine.*

The University of Iowa has created an extensive data base of William Blake's work, complete with video. You can ask the computer to display all of Blake's graphic designs depicting lillies, or the character Los as a blacksmith, or figures in chains, and so on. If you want, you can limit your search to a specific work, to material published after 1805, or to the later prophetic books.

The Numerical Data Base in Literary Research

Data bases composed of mathematical data derived from experiments or observations are less common in literary research, but they too have their place, especially in stylistic studies (discussed in more detail in Chapter 7). Rather than conduct an experiment, the literary scholar can gather information about phonemes, words, or parts of speech in a text, put it in a data base, and then obtain information about how frequently and where those elements are used. Such a project is a good example of how various capabilities of a computer can be combined. One can obtain information about words or parts of speech directly from a concordance program or from some sort of stylistic analysis program, avoiding the tedious task of entering the data manually.

Indeed, it is becoming unnecessary to create your own data base. Just as one company can share its mailing list with another, deluging you with magazine offers, so one scholar or group of scholars can create a data base that many others can share. You can already consult the *MLA Bibliography*, and many others, through a telecommunications network called Dialog. You can subscribe to Dialog and use your own computer to get information from its data bases, but it is generally cheaper to use it at a library. Most research libraries now subscribe to Dialog and to other, similar services, and most have someone who can help you ask for a printout containing works by or about certain authors, about certain subjects, written at a certain time, or whatever. For example, if you are working on the passage in *Madame Bovary* where Emma and Leon go to hear Donizetti's *Lucia di Lammermoor,* you can search the *MLA Bibliography* (from 1968 to the present) for all works containing *Flaubert* and *Lucia* or *Flaubert* and *opera.* You find there are two works meeting these criteria, one on an operatic version of another Flaubert novel and one on the theme of the evening at the opera, which is just what you are looking for!

It takes about a minute or two to do this. You have to establish connection with Dialog, enter your search criteria, and than wait a few seconds for a printout. The results of the complete procedure look like this:

File71:MLA International Bibliography—1970 thru 1982
    Set Items Descriptions

--- ----- ------------

? ss flaubert/de and (lucia or opera)
    1   796 FLAUBERT/DE
    2   45   LUCIA
    3   762 OPERA
    4   2   1 AND (2 OR 3)
? T 4/7/1–2

4/7/1
    8219151   82-2-001653
    Salammbo de Reyer: Du roman à l'opera
    Bailbe, Joseph-Marc
    Romantisme: Revue du Dix-Neuvième Siècle, ISSN 0048-8593,
        75005 Paris, France 1982; 12(38): 93-103 1982
    Languages: French
    Document Type: journal article

4/7/2
    8208985   82-2-001001

La Soirée à l'opéra: Etude d'un thème littéraire
Actes du Colloque organise à Aix-en-Provence par le Centre
    Aixois d'Etudes et de Recherches sur le XVIIIe siècle, les 29,
    30 avril et 1er mai 1977

Michot, Pierre
550-578 IN, Bourde, André, foreword, L'Opera au XVIIIe siècle
Aix-en-Provence: Univ. de Provence; 1982. 578 pp.
Languages: French
Document Type: book article

The question marks indicate where the user supplies information. In response to the first one, you tell the computer that you want it to find works that contain *Flaubert* and either *Lucia* or *opera* in the title or among the key words that describe the work. The computer replies by revealing how many works it found in each of the three categories and then how many meet all the criteria. After the next question mark, you tell it to print information on both of the works that meet all the criteria. The computer responds with identification numbers, bibliographic information, and descriptions of the two works.

The only difficult part about such a search is choosing your criteria. In the case of the foregoing example, a search for *Donizetti, Lucia, Lucie,* and *opera* yielded only articles about Donizetti that had nothing to do with Flaubert (though it did find general works about Donizetti as a dramatist) and articles about Lucie Pellegrin and Edward Lucie-Smith. Basing the search on Flaubert rather than on Donizetti turned out to be the better choice, but it was impossible to know this without trying both. The two searches together, along with a similar search of a music bibliography, cost eight tax-deductible dollars.

Computerized Indexes and Catalogues

There are many other types of data bases you can consult to obtain bibliographic information. The Institute for Scientific Information provides access to the *Arts & Humanities Citation Index.* The OCLC system, available in many libraries, contains most of the entries from the Library of Congress catalogue, and there are more specialized library catalogues that you can search, such as collections of rare books. Services such as CompuServe provide access to the EPIE data bases for software, hardware, news, and events related to education, and you can also search the ERIC data base (or, for $7.50, buy a disk with the entries from the last 5 years). One can search listings of grant possibilities and even listings of new software.

The day is not far off when the catalogues of most libraries will be "on line"—that is, searchable by a computer rather than by cards. A computer screen may not have the charm of a card catalogue, but it is certainly faster and more accurate than the human hand and eye, and it can be available via direct telephone hookup so that you can find out right away what is in a distant library (or in your own, without having to walk across campus). Some people argue that computerized catalogues will minimize the chance of stumbling on an interesting reference while looking for something else in a card catalogue, but this need not be true. You can look through a catalogue entry by entry with a computer as well as by hand, and you can search just as "randomly." Moreover, you can print a hard copy with much less trouble!

Data bases don't have to consist of brief fields and records but can contain segments of data of almost any length. For example, there are programs for microcomputers that enable you to store annotations with your bibliographic entries and others that can take letters and other documents up to several pages in length. In addition, some programs are designed so you can use your word processor to incorporate all or some of these comments directly into a text you are writing; some word processors, such as NotaBene, even include such a text-searching system.

In data bases with long entries, you retrieve information by searching for important words, which can be either words that are actually in the document or key words that you have entered along with the document as identifiers. If you were working with Boswell's comments on the theater in his *London Journal,* you could have in your data base an entry corresponding to each entry in the journal. You could have the computer show you every entry that contains the name Garrick, but you wouldn't find any references to Farquhar unless you had entered his name as a key word to two entries where his works are mentioned but his name isn't. You could of course use your own correspondence or notes to create such a data base.

There is also a growing number of textual data bases. The major works of most western literatures are now available in some sort of machine-readable form (usually on magnetic tape), and you can either obtain a copy of a text for use on your own computer or retrieve information from a distant data base through an individual telephone hookup or through a network. Networks such as BITNET and EDUNET link hundreds of universities and research centers all over the world, giving you access to many data bases through a computer at your own university. There are extensive data bases of American, English, French, Greek, Italian, and Norwegian literatures, for example, and many others. Some of the most important of these data bases are listed in Appendix I.

PUTTING DATA BASES TO USE

The chapters on concordances and on stylistic analysis offer many examples of how to put a data base to good use. A few examples will suffice here. You might want material from a data base just to read it, if it is a rare text that is difficult to obtain or copy. More frequently, you would want a machine-readable text so that you could run some sort of program on it—for example, one that would generate a concordance. In many cases, the data bases are set up so that you can retrieve the information you want directly, rather than having to run your own programs on the text itself. For example, you can obtain word counts, rhyming words, lists of important words or themes (individually or in groups), or the text of speeches by a certain character simply by specifying what you want and from what texts. The information can be generated instantly and either viewed directly on a local computer or printed and mailed to the user.

If you need to create your own data base and can't find the texts in machine-readable form, the most common way to enter the data is to type them at a computer or terminal. (Microcomputers can handle the complete works of many authors, but for a really large corpus you would have to use a mainframe computer.) There is no longer any reason to use punch cards or paper tape, which are cumbersome and have to be read by another machine. Whether you work at a microcomputer or a mainframe terminal, and whether you respond to questions on the screen or enter text freely, you simply type at a keyboard just as you do using a word processing package. In fact, you can often use the word processor you are familiar with to type a text into a data base.

The format is the main consideration in creating a data base: The data must be put into a data base in such a way that any user can retrieve all or some of them easily. In particular, if a user is likely to want information that a computer cannot find easily, you will have to "tag" certain parts of the text —that is, insert special characters at key places. For example, a computer can find a proper noun like *Milton* easily, but if you want it to find all proper nouns, you have to give it a list of every proper noun in the text. It is usually easier to identify each proper noun either as you put it into the text (by placing a $ or a # in front of it, for example), or with the search-and-replace function of your word processor, than to create a list (which may have errors or omissions) against which the computer will have to check each word in the text.[1]

As you set up your data base, you also need to consider how you will mark off different sections of your text. For example, you may need to insert markers to indicate divisions between paragraphs, pages, or chapters or where characters in a play begin and end their speeches. There may also be foreign phrases that should be separated from the principal language of the text, because the computer doesn't know the difference between French and English. Such distinctions may not be important to you, but they may be to other users of your data base, and it is important to think them through before you begin to create a data base.

The drawbacks to entering long texts at a computer keyboard include time, money, fatigue, and tedium, but optical character scanners are changing all that. They are like copying machines that make electronic files from printed text; they produce machine-readable characters instead of paper copies. Such machines vary in price, accuracy, and speed, but at this writing the best of them, the Kurzweil 4000, has what its inventor calls "intelligent character recognition" and can recognize the characteristics of a letter rather than simply match it against a pattern. In this way it can handle different type faces, proportional spacing, accent marks, and even kerns and ligatures. It can read a normal page of text in about 1½ minutes and make fewer than one error per line on a clearly printed page; the user generally has time to correct the errors as the machine finishes scanning the page. The scanner works best on typed manuscripts, but it can read almost anything with a bit of "training" (if it does not recognize a letter, it can ask the operator for help and then remember the answer for future reference). It also has a 33,000-word lexicon against which it can check letters and words that it has a hard time recognizing.[2]

One problem with large data bases has always been that they are cumbersome and expensive to use, unless you are at the same institution that houses them. This situation is about to change, and these large reference data bases, which are currently housed on mainframe computers or sold on magnetic tape for use on other mainframes, are now being replaced by new technology that stores the same information on CD-ROM (Compact Disk Read Only Memory), the same type of disk used in stereos. You should soon be able to get, for about $200, a disk drive for your microcomputer that can search the equivalent of more than 1,500 floppy disks in about 10 seconds!

You can already get the entire ERIC data base on three disks, and Brown University has the *Thesaurus Linguae Graecae* (TLG) almost ready for distribution on one disk to individual scholars who do not want to pay access fees or whose universities do not have the funds or computer storage to provide local access to the data base. You can also get the full text of Grolier's *Academic American Encyclopedia* on such a disk for $199, and search the *whole* encyclopedia—not just an index—in a few seconds.

Scholars are finding that data bases not only can assist them in their normal work but are also helping them develop new methods of literary research. The following chapters look at some examples of what you can do once you have access to a literary data base.

NOTES

1. A more complex problem is how to lemmatize a text and identify parts of speech; even the most advanced lemmatization and parsing programs are still far from perfect. For more details, see Chapter 5 on concordances and especially Chapter 7 on stylistic analysis.
2. The Kurzweil 4000 costs $36,500 but can be well worth it if you and your colleagues need to scan large quantities of text; you can save $36,500 in typists' salaries and in time rather quickly. Other types of scanners are considerably cheaper ($6,000–$8,000) and two or three times faster, but they do not work on anything except typewritten text. There is even a hand-held scanner for $500, but it is no faster than a good typist.

CHAPTER 5

Concordances in Literary Research

One of the most exciting aspects of computer use in literary research is its potential for assisting scholars in the study and analysis of texts. The computer can make the job of analysis easier, faster, and less tedious for many types of literary criticism, and it also opens up many ways of looking at a text that were not feasible before.

The oldest and most obvious computer tool for literary analysis is the concordance. Concordances of the Bible have existed in English since the seventeenth century; Alexander Cruden's 1769 concordance was perhaps the most important. Computerized projects go back as far 1949 when Father Roberto Busa, with the support of IBM, began planning his *Index Thomisticus* (published in 1974). The Cornell University Press began its series of computer-generated concordances in 1959 with a concordance to the poetry of Matthew Arnold. Hundreds of concordances are available now, and more are appearing all the time, although there is some debate about just what form they should take and whether it is worth the expense to print a full concordance, including the context of every word.

Concordances have several important uses, and scholars are constantly finding new applications. You can use them to find a particular passage in a text or to find all passages that include certain words. You can also find out what the most frequently used words are in a text, and where and in what context they appear. These results can point the way to other important words and passages, can reveal the influence of other writers, and can suggest formal structures that might otherwise have gone unnoticed. We will examine these and other uses later in this chapter, but let's look first at exactly what a concordance is and, briefly, how to produce one.

WHAT IS A CONCORDANCE?

A standard concordance is an index of each occurrence of every word in a text; the word's location is noted, along with the context of its occurrence.[1] Each word (usually called a "key word") is listed in alphabetical order, or according to frequency or length, and then all its occurrences are given. The reference to location provides the number of the chapter, act, scene, page, paragraph, line, or other appropriate division of the text; when the source is the text of a play, the reference can include the speaker as well. You can

ERR
Some few in *that*, but Numbers err in *this*, ... 1.EOC.5.239.
The *Vulgar* thus through *Imitation* err; .... 1.EOC.424.288.
To Err is *Humane*; to Forgive, *Divine*. .... 1.EOC.525.297.
Nor err from me, since I deserve it all: .... 1.TrSt.773.442.
Born but to die, and reas'ning but to err; .... 3.EOM2.10.55.
And, lest we err by Wit's wild, dancing light, ... 5.DunA1.153.82.
And lest we err by Wit's wild dancing light, ... 5.DunB1.175.283.
To tempt my Youth, for apt is Youth to err: .... II.24.530.558.
But re-consider, since the wisest err, ... Od.16.334.122.

ERR'D
Nature in her then err'd not, but forgot. .... 3.Ep2.158.64.
Thy Dart has err'd, and now my Spear be try'd: .... II.5.348.283.
Fain wou'd my Heart, which err'd thro' frantic Rage, ... II.9.153.439.
Which willful err'd, and o'er his Shoulder past; .... II.10.442.23.
The Javelin err'd, but held its Course along, ... II.13.656.137.
Then mildly thus: Excuse, if Youth have err'd; .... II.23.668.516.
Err'd from the Dove, yet cut the Cord that ty'd: .... II.23.1025.529.
Nor err'd this hand unfaithful to its aim; .... Od.21.466.282.
I thoughtless err'd in) well secure that door: .... Od.22.173.295.

ERRANT
In errant Pride continue stiff, and burn? .... 4.HAdv.152.87.

Example 5.1   Concordance to the poetry of Alexander Pope.

thus find a passage easily and can see at a glance where a word occurs most often.

The context is usually a line of poetry or, in the case of prose, as much as will fit on one line (about 100 letters). The most popular format is the key word-in-context (KWIC) format. Here the keyword appears (often in boldface) in the middle of the line, surrounded by the words immediately leading up to and following it—that is, its context. Poetry can also be handled in this way, so that the key word is identifiable at a glance, but it is often printed with every line beginning in the same column. This gives a neater appearance, and in a line of normal length the key word isn't hard to find. The occurrences of each key word can be listed either in the order in which they occur in the text or alphabetically according to the word immediately preceding or following. These alphabetical arrangements allow one to see all occurrences of a particular phrase at a glance. Let's consider some examples.

Examples of Printed Concordances

Bedford and Dilligan's concordance of Pope's poetry (Example 5.1) is quite basic. It gives the key word, line, and reference (work, line, page) in a condensed format. On the other hand, Misek's concordance to *Paradise Lost* (Example 5.2) gives more information than most scholars would need. The columns after the context give the place of the word in the line, line number, book number, scene, speaker, audience, speaker number in the work as a whole and the specific book, and speech number in the book and work.

Crosland's concordance to *The Great Gatsby* (Example 5.3) is a good example of a concordance to a work of prose that locates the key word in

vantage then • To union, and firm	faith	, and firm accord, • More than can	5	36	2.PAND	SATAN	TO	COUNCL	7	1	2	20
first broke peace in Heaven, and	faith	, till then • Unbroken; and in pro	8	690	2.H—GT	DEATH	TO	SATAN	1	1	18	36
re • Of true allegiance, constant	faith	or love, • Where only what they n	5	104	3.THRN	GOD	TO	SON	1	1	3	56
roof of their obedience and their	faith	? • O fair foundation laid whereon	8	520	4.EDEN	SATAN	TO	SELF/3	16	3	16	95
d. • Was this your discipline and	faith	engaged†, • Your military obedien	6	954	4.EDEN	GBRIEL	TO	SATAN	7	7	58	137
ighest • Should yet remain, where	faith	and realty[3 • Remain not: Where	5	115	6.NRTH	ABD/RL	TO	SELF/1	3	1	4	210
e not of thy train; there be, who	faith	• Prefer, and piety to God, thou	10	143	6.NRTH	ABD/RL	TO	SATAN	4	2	6	212
e pledge of thy obedience and thy	faith	, •'' Amid the garden by the tree	8	325	8.EDEN	GOD/A	TO	ADAM	25	3	19	305
rs • Thy equal fear, that my firm	faith	and love • Can by his fraud be sh	7	286	9.EDEN	EVE	TO	ADAM	12	2	9	340
supposed† • Not incorruptible of	faith	, not proof • Against temptation:	4	298	9.EDEN	ADAM	TO	EVE	41	2	11	342
hought • Less attributed/1 to her	faith	sincere, • Thus her reply with ac	5	320	9.NARR	EP.VCE	TO	READER	106	6	12	343
ss, from the event. • And what is	faith	, love, virtue, unassayed† • Alone	4	335	9.EDEN	EVE	TO	ADAM	13	3	13	344
ack • Despoiled† of innocence, of	faith	, of bliss! • For now, and since f	5	411	9.NARR	EP.VCE	TO	READER	109	9	18	349
f honour void, • Of innocence, of	faith	, of purity, • Our wonted ornament	4	1075	9.EDEN	ADAM	TO	EVE	47	8	56	387
k needless cause to approve • The	faith	they owe; when earnestly they see	2	1141	9.EDEN	ADAM	TO	EVE	48	9	58	389
life; • Whose failing, while her	faith	to me remains, • I should conceal	5	129	10.EDN	ADAM	TO	GOD	51	2	12	406
rp tribulation, and refined† • By	faith	and faithful works, to second lif	2	64	11.THR	GOD	TO	SON	39	1	4	461
• Eve, easily my	faith	admit, that all • The good which	4	141	11.EDN	ADAM	TO	EVE	58	1	9	466
will be avenged†; and the other's	faith	, approved†, • Lose no reward; tho	7	458	11.HIL	MCHAEL	TO	ADAM	6	5	35	492
justice and temperance, truth and	faith	, forgot; • One man except, the on	6	807	11.HIL	MCHAEL	TO	ADAM	17	16	71	528
im, but thou canst not, with what	faith	• He leaves his Gods, his friend	10	128	12.HIL	MCHAEL	TO	ADAM	20	2	6	538
randchild‡, leaves; • Like him in	faith	, in wisdom, and renown: • The gra	4	154	12.HIL	MCHAEL	TO	ADAM	20	2	6	538
n such righteousness • To them by	faith	imputed, they may find • Justific	4	295	12.HIL	MCHAEL	TO	ADAM	22	4	12	544
filial; works of law to works of	faith	. • And therefore shall not Moses	9	306	12.HIL	MCHAEL	TO	ADAM	22	4	12	544
nce, • Imputed, becomes theirs by	faith	; his merits • To save them, not t	5	409	12.HIL	MCHAEL	TO	ADAM	23	5	16	548
not, and the benefit embrace • By	faith	not void of works: This God—lik	2	427	12.HIL	MCHAEL	TO	ADAM	23	5	16	548
, but to the sons • Of Abraham's	faith	wherever through the world; • So	3	449	12.HIL	MCHAEL	TO	ADAM	23	5	16	548
pirit within them; and the law of	faith	, • Working through love, upon the	9	488	12.HIL	MCHAEL	TO	ADAM	25	7	21	553
ld • His living temples, built by	faith	to stand, • Their own faith, not	6	527	12.HIL	MCHAEL	TO	ADAM	25	7	21	553
lt by faith to stand, • Their own	faith	, not another's? for, on earth, •	3	528	12.HIL	MCHAEL	TO	ADAM	25	7	21	553
r's? for, on earth, • Who against	faith	and conscience can be heard • Inf	3	529	12.HIL	MCHAEL	TO	ADAM	25	7	21	553
th slanderous darts, and works of	faith	• Rarely be found: So shall the	8	536	12.HIL	MCHAEL	TO	ADAM	25	7	21	553
to thy knowledge answerable; add	faith	, • Add virtue, patience, temperan	7	582	12.HIL	MCHAEL	TO	ADAM	26	8	25	557
d; • Chiefly what may concern her	faith	to know, • The great deliverance	6	599	12.HIL	MCHAEL	TO	ADAM	26	8	25	557
will be many days, • Both in one	faith	unanimous, though sad, • With cau	4	603	12.HIL	MCHAEL	TO	ADAM	26	8	25	557

occurrences = 35 , .0438%

Example 5.2 Concordance to *Paradise Lost.*

DIVAN (1)
to me. She was extended full length at her end of the divan, completely motionless, and with her chin raised a   10.19

DIVERGENCE (1)
this was because she felt safer on a plane where any divergence from a code would be thought impossible. She was   71.6

DIVINE (1)
you God's truth." His right hand suddenly ordered divine retribution to stand by. "I am the son of some   78.7

DIVING (1)
it high tide in the afternoon I watched his guests diving from the tower of his raft, or taking the sun on the   47.6

DIVISION (1)
he said, politely. "Weren't you in the Third Division during the war?" "Why, yes. I was in the Ninth   57.18

DIVISIONAL (1)
battle be got his majority and the command of the divisional machine-guns. After the Aristice he tried   180.24

DIVISIONS (1)
up at last they found the insignia of three German divisions among the piles of dead. I was promoted to be a   79.23

DIVORCE (2)
if they can't stand them? If I was then I'd get a divorce and get married to each other right away." "Doesn't   40.11
apart. She's a Catholic, and they don't believe in divorce." Daisy was not a Catholic, and I was a little shocked   40.20

DIVORCED (1)
S. W. Belcher and the Smirkes and the young Quinns, divorced now, and Henry L. Palmetto, who killed himself by   75.15

DIVOT (1)
over the wire as something fresh and cool, as if a divot from a green golf-links had come sailing in at the   186.2

DIZZY (1)
it was a new experience for me, and I felt a little dizzy for a while." We shook hands. "Oh, and do you   214.6

DO (85)   Also see "DYOU"
PAGE REFERENCES: 2,4,7,12,14,15,16,17,25,26,28,32,38,39,40,44,52,53,55,56,59,66,71,81,82,83,86,88,92,94,96,99,100,102,
104,108,109,114,119,124,128,136,141,145,146,147,148,152,157,158,169,171,177,180,182,184,199,203,206,209,214,215

Example 5.3 Concordance to *The Great Gatsby*.

A KWIC (keyword-in-context) concordance with the keyword **GO** (sorted on the following words "TO HEAVEN" / "TO HELL"):

MRS I (195)	A HIGHER DEGREE THAN YOU DID; SO WHY SHOULD SHE	GO	TO HEAR YOU PREACH? /REV. S./ DONT BE DISRESPECTFUL,
SUPR III (101)	ARE INVIDIOUSLY CALLED THE BLEST. /ANA/ I SHALL	GO	TO HEAVEN AT ONCE. /THE STATUE/ MY CHILD: ONE WORD OF
CAPT III (294)	[illegible]	GO	TO HEAVEN FOR IT. I WAS READY TO GO TO HELL FOR MINE.
CAPT III (231)	SAILORS THATLL DO NOTHING FOR THEIR CREED BUT	GO	TO HEAVEN IF HE KILLS AN UNBELIEVER. /LADY CICELY/ BLESS
SUPR III (125)	OWN GOOD. BUT EVERY MAN OF THEM BELIEVES HE WILL	GO	TO HEAVEN IF HE WANTS TO? /THE DEVIL/ WHATS TO PREVENT
LION I (99)	AND ME. I REALLY DONT THINK I COULD CONSENT TO	GO	TO HEAVEN IF I THOUGHT THERE WERE TO BE NO ANIMALS THERE.
SUPR III (231)	WHATS TO PREVENT HIM? /ANA/ CAN ANYBODY-- CAN I	GO	TO HEAVEN IF I WANT TO? /THE DEVIL/ (RATHER
CAPT I (125)	THE PEOPLE IN ENGLAND BELIEVE THAT THEY WILL	GO	TO HEAVEN IF THEY GIVE ALL THEIR PROPERTY TO THE POOR.
LION I (101)	/FERROVIUS/ (CLENCHING HIS FIST) DO ANIMALS	GO	TO HEAVEN OR NOT? /SPINTHO/ I NEVER SAID THEY DIDNT.
SUPR III	/THE STATUE/ IN SHORT, MY DAUGHTER, IF YOU	GO	TO HEAVEN WITHOUT BEING NATURALLY QUALIFIED FOR IT, YOU
LION III (129)	MEAN TO DIE IN THE ARENA: ILL DIE A MARTYR AND	GO	TO HEAVEN; BUT NOT THIS TIME, NOT NOW, NOT UNTIL MY
SUPR III (101)	ARE HERE-- PRINCES OF THE CHURCH AND ALL. SO FEW	GO	TO HEAVEN, AND SO MANY COME HERE, THAT THE BLEST, ONCE
SUPR I (38)	FRIGHTFULLY SELF-CONSCIOUS. /TANER/ WHEN YOU	GO	TO HEAVEN, ANN, YOU WILL BE FRIGHTFULLY CONSCIOUS OF YOUR
LION I (123)	IN THE ARENA, YOULL BE A MARTYR; AND ALL MARTYRS	GO	TO HEAVEN, NO MATTER WHAT THEY HAVE DONE. THATS SO, ISNT
LION I (124)	THE GOOD OF PRAYING? IF WE'RE MARTYRED WE SHALL	GO	TO HEAVEN, SHANT WE, WHETHER WE PRAY OR NOT? /FERROVIUS/
SUPR III (99)	LIES THAT MAY. /ANA/ BUT WHY DOESNT EVERYBODY	GO	TO HEAVEN, THEN? /THE STATUE/ (CHUCKLING) I CAN TELL
GENV III (72)	WOULD ALLOW SUCH AN INFAMY. THEY WILL ALL	GO	TO HELL FOR IT. AS TO MY LOVING THIS MAN, I HATE, LOATHE,
CAPT III (294)	BUT EQUALLY DISHONEST PEOPLE TOLD ME I SHOULD	GO	TO HELL FOR MINE. PERHAPS YOU DONT UNDERSTAND THAT. /LADY
MIS. PREFACE (9)	DO THIS," AND " YOU MUSTNT DO THAT," AND " YOULL	GO	TO HELL IF I DID NOT MAKE MYSELF AGREEABLE TO THEM.
POSN (444)	DO THIS," AND " YOU MUSTNT DO THAT," AND " YOULL	GO	TO HELL IF YOU DO THE OTHER." I GAVE HIM THE GO-BYE AND
ROCK II (275)	ELSE TIL DEATH DO YOU PART. IF HE TELLS YOU TO	GO	TO HELL TODAY INSTEAD OF TRYING TO ARGUE WITH YOU, HE
ROCK II (278)	DAVID HAS RATHER A HABIT OF TELLING PEOPLE TO	GO	TO HELL WHEN HE IS TOO LAZY TO THINK OF ANYTHING BETTER
PRES (151)	TO BY A SERGEANT THAN BY YOU. HE TELLS ME TO	GO	TO HELL WHEN I CHALLENGE HIM TO ARGUE IT OUT LIKE A MAN.
ROCK PREFACE (173)	ABSOLUTELY CONVINCED THAT ALL ROMAN CATHOLICS	GO	TO HELL WHEN THEY DIE, A CONVICTION WHICH INVOLVED ALL
GENV PREFACE (15)	CATHOLICS WERE AN INFERIOR SPECIES WHO WOULD ALL	GO	TO HELL WHEN THEY DIED: AND I DARESAY THE ROMAN CATHOLIC
SIM PREFACE (15)	PIOUS WILL DRAW IS THAT I, AT ALL EVENTS, WILL	GO	TO HELL. AS TO THE INDIFFERENT AND THE SCEPTICAL, I MAY
ROCK II (275)	WHAT DID HE SAY TO THAT? /ALOYSIA/ HE TOLD ME TO	GO	TO HELL. HE'S LIKE THAT, YOU KNOW. /SIR ARTHUR/ YES, A
ROCK II (278)	TO HIM? /SIR ARTHUR/ YES. HE TOLD HER TO	GO	TO HELL. /LADY CHAVENDER/ DAVID HAS RATHER A HABIT OF
LION I (124)	MARTYRED TODAY, NO4. I SHALL DIE IN THE NIGHT AND	GO	TO HELL; YOURE A SORCERER: YOUVE PUT DEATH INTO MY MIND.
MIS. PREFACE (93)	SCHOOL THAT IF YOU BECOME A DISSENTER YOU WILL	GO	TO HELL FOR HELL IS PRESENTED AS THE INSTRUMENT OF
ROCK PREFACE (171)	NEIGHBORS WHO BELIEVE THAT ALL EVOLUTIONISTS	GO	TO HELL; THAT CHILDREN LANGUISH AND DIE WITHOUT
POSN (463)	MY FELLOWMAN STRAIGHT IN THE EYE AND TELL HIM TO	GO	TO HELL, THAT FETCHED ME. /THE BOYS/ QUITE RIGHT. GOOD.

Example 5.4   Concordance to Shaw's theater.

ni (104 fois)
THEBAIDE 21,48,120,720,990,1059,1089,1089v,1188,v,ALEXANDRE 185,773,795,1147,
ANDROMAQUE 1285,1285v,1317,v,v,PLAIDEURS 242,356,483,599,BRITANNICU 361,551,610,1497,
BERENICE 587,1229,1229v,1485,BAJAZET 126,551,981,1142,1267,1554,MITHRIDATE 182,270,
425,473,533,533v,688,975,976,977,978,1369,1660,IPHIGENIE 426,1191,1311,1399,1475,
1517,PHEDRE 675,868,1126,1536,ESTHER 178,200,215,346,561,839,1018,1090,1127,
ATHALIE 466,475,918,1092,1485,Convalescence 61,89,Sign du Formulaire 58,216,
Le Clerc IPHIGENIE 8,Portrait d'Arnauld 10

nids (1 fois)

	On les voit suspendre ces nids,	Pt-Royal III	32

nie (1 fois)

	Mais qu'on l'accorde ou qu'on le nie,	Sign du Formulaire	239

nièce (3 fois)

Burrhu:	Qu'on disposât sans lui de la nièce d'Auguste.	BRITANNICU I 2	244
Agripp:	Prit insensiblement dans les yeux de sa nièce	BRITANNICU IV 2	1131
Acomat:	Du père d'Amurat Atalide est la nièce;	BAJAZET I 1	169
Acomat:	Du père d'Amurat Atalide la nièce,	BAJAZET I 1	169v

nier (4 fois)

Roxane:	Me nier un mépris que tu crois que j'ignore?	BAJAZET V 4	1482
Monime:	Mais vous-même, Seigneur, pouvez-vous le nier?	MITHRIDATE I 3	278
Monime:	Mais il feignoit peut-être: il falloit tout nier.	MITHRIDATE IV 1	1134
Aricie:	Seigneur, je ne vous puis nier la vérité:	PHEDRE V 3	1419

nierai, voir nirai

Example 5.5　　Concordance to Racine's poetry.

the center of the page. Crosland includes references to page and line and
gives the number of times the key word occurs. This last information, which
is simple to provide but missing from many concordances, keeps you from
having either to count by hand or to look the word up in a frequency list.
Bevan's concordance to Shaw's theater (Example 5.4) arranges the occurrences in alphabetical order according to the words after the key word.

The size of such a concordance can get out of hand quickly. For example,
Hugh Davidson and Pierre Dubé's concordance to Pascal's *Pensées,* a fairly
short text of just over 100,000 words (plus variants and Latin quotations),
takes up 1,458 pages of small print (92 lines per page). Davidson and Dubé
decided to list every occurrence of every word with its context, but other
editors have chosen to shorten the concordance considerably by omitting
function words such as articles and common prepositions. (The preposition
de alone takes up 48 pages in the concordance to the *Pensées,* and this does
not include *d'* or contractions with the definite article; all these forms together occur 7,079 times and take up 77 pages!)

Freeman and Batson's approach in their concordance to the theater and
poetry of Racine represents an excellent compromise. They printed only the
raw number of occurrences for the most common function words (articles,
de, à, and *et*) but listed in an appendix the line numbers where they occur.[2]
For other extremely frequent words, they printed the location in the main
body of the concordance, but not the context. Crosland also adapted this
procedure for his concordance to *The Great Gatsby* (see Example 5.3). Examples 5.5 and 5.6 give some excerpts from the Racine concordance. Note that
Freeman included the speaker of each line when the occurrence was in a play
and that he included variants (marked with a *v* after the line number).

Most concordances also include a frequency list: a list of the words in

```
AUX  (356 FOIS)
THEBAIDE 3,7,13,v,v,147,166,180,193,229,247,413,v,v,484,503,544,552,564,602,686,716,
813,972,1208,1238,1362,1388,1486,1516,ALEXANDRE 11,259,292,328,328v,350,376,477,511,
644,706,742,755,770,870,912,971,1017,1040,1238,1248,1390,v,1414,1428,1436,1464,1508,
ANDROMAQUE 6,12,12v,77,213,248,249,260,288,358,444,449,449v,661,785,844,900,989,1003,
1102,1209,1259,1305,1322,1334,1339,1385,1430,1587,1613,PLAIDEURS 22,42,72,247,348,
640,v,682,815,816,BRITANNICU 322v,373,561,568,581,592,616,706,v,v,840,974,1074,1153,
1304,1474,1513,1515,1532,1552,1592,1692,1768,BERENICE 57,68,68v,122,157,257,322v,
325,426,600v,790,1007,1223,v,1272,1406,1434,BAJAZET 60,112,122,185,197,219,533,591,
644,687,698,699,796,874,895,952,1094,1100,1286,1304,1422,1434,1549,v,1559,1711,
MITHRIDATE 28,62,65,76,142,196,281,616,628,726,798,832,887,898v,909,921,986,1088,
1197,1296,1337,1430,1478,1488,1578,1628,1641,1692,IPHIGENIE 20,163,224,266,276,293,
298,382,390,401,534,629,874,894,954,988,1112,1219,1310,1358,1371,1378,1537,1556,1649,
1658,1695,1766,PHEDRE 7,11,54,89,222,254,384,386,422,456,532,600,736,767,798,
857,875,929,1060,1158,1280,1284,1290,1301,1326,1392,1394,1532,1506,1588,
ESTHER P5,P65,ESTHER 28,68,80,109,137,179,192,214,267,282,345,459,464,476,486,560,
597,604,618,678,739,843,888,898,925,1104,1118,1177,1198,1212,1269,
ATHALIE 12,18,121,137,155,195,262,323,331,336,343,376,397,400,432,443,444,454,472,
567,572,647,734,090,891,950,1058,1255,1336,1368,1385,1392,1395,1405,1415,1532,1552,
1600,1608,1645,1,79,A VITART I 37,41,PT.ROYAL II 2,60,PT.ROYAL III 58,
PT.ROYAL VI 34,PT.ROYAL VII 69,77,86,MADRIGAL 7,NYMPHE SEINE 53,140,v,178,190,
CORRES 11.11.61 15,CORRES 31.1.62 21,CORRES 4.7.62 93,CONVALESCENCE 44,
RENOMMEE MUSES 13,22,23,55,67,91,SIGN DU FUMULAIRE 88,ASPAR FONTENELLE 5,
IDYLLE PAIX 24,25,51,62,LUN LAUDES 27,JEU LAUDES 12,SAM LAUDES 3,LUN VEPRES 7,
MER VEPRES 15,CANTIQUE I 23,26,29,40,49,CANTIQUE IV 22,PORTRAIT D"ARNAULD 6,
SUR LE PORT.ROYAL 1
```

Example 5.6   Concordance to Racine's poetry, Appendix I.

WASTED	10	EMERGING	9
WEEDS	10	ENRICH	9
WEIGHS	10	ENRICH'D	9
WHIG	10	ENTRANCE	9
WILES	10	ERR	9
WONDRING	10	ERR'D	9
WOODLAND	10	ESCAPE	9
YOU'D	10	EUROPE	9
ABELARD	9	EURYALUS	9
ACCESS	9	EURYLOCHUS	9
ACQUIR'D	9	EXCEED	9
ADMIT	9	EXCLAIMS	9

Example 5.7   List of words in Pope's poetry in order of occurrence.

the text arranged in decreasing order of occurrence. Example 5.7, which is taken from the concordance to Pope's poetry (see Example 5.1), is part of such a frequency list. Note that, within the body of words that appear the same number of times (9, in this case), the words are listed alphabetically. It is also useful to have a list of all the words in alphabetical order, followed by their frequency of occurrence (Example 5.8), though one should be able to find this information in the main body of the concordance as well. You can use the frequency list to compare the frequency of one word to that of another or to see which words are used the most frequently and which the least. Some lists also tell you what percentage of the entire text is accounted for by words up to a certain frequency. Example 5.9 reveals that the five most common words in Pope's poetry account for 16% of all the occurrences.[3]

Another useful type of frequency list has the words in reverse alphabetical order (starting from the end of the word) to facilitate the study of rhyme or word endings. For example, Wisbey's concordance of the Old High German *Alexander* contains such a list (Example 5.10), in addition to a standard concordance. It also includes a list of rhyming words (Example 5.11).

ERMIN'D	1
ERR	9
ERR'D	9
ERRANT	1
ERRATIC	1
ERRING	23
ERRONEOUS	4
ERROR	10
ERRORS	10
ERRS	2
ERSE	1
ERST	3
ERYALUS	1

Example 5.8   List of words in Pope's poetry in alphabetical order, with their frequency of occurrence.

Definition of Symbols Used in Table				
	X	Frequency of occurrence	$FX.X = fxX$	Number of tokens accounted for by types of frequency X
	$FX = fx$	Number of types of frequency X		
	$\%FX$	The ratio of each FX figure over the type total (20,-892) as a percenatge	$SUM\ FX.X = \Sigma fxX$	Sum of tokens due to frequency X and preceding values of X
	$SUM\ FX = \Sigma fx$	Sum of types due to frequency X and preceding values of X	$\%FX.X$	The relative per cent frequency of tokens
	$CUM\ \%FX = \%\Sigma fx$	Per cent of types due to frequency X and preceding value of X	$CUM\ \%FX.X = \%\Sigma fxX$	Per cent of tokens (total 428,647) due to frequency X and preceding values of X

X	FX	%FX	SUM FX	CUM %FX	FX.X	SUM FX.X	%FX.X	CUM %FX.X
28754	1	0.004786	1	0.004786	28754	28754	6.708083	6.708083
16510	1	0.004786	2	0.009572	16510	45264	3.851654	10.559737
9900	1	0.004786	3	0.014358	9900	55164	2.309592	12.869329
8073	1	0.004786	4	0.019144	8073	63237	1.883367	14.752696
6650	1	0.004786	5	0.023930	6650	69887	1.551393	16.304089
6383	1	0.004786	6	0.028716	6383	76270	1.489104	17.793193
5627	1	0.004786	7	0.033502	5627	81897	1.312735	19.105928
4917	1	0.004786	8	0.038288	4917	86814	1.147097	20.253025
3381	1	0.004786	9	0.043074	3381	90195	0.788760	21.041785
2975	1	0.004786	10	0.047860	2975	93170	0.694044	21.735829

Example 5.9   Word-frequency distribution in Pope's poetry.

Using Alternatives to the Printed Concordance

Some users of concordances argue that the printed context is not necessary, especially in this day of electronic access to texts. One means of publishing a concise concordance is the key word-out-of-context (KWOC) format, which includes an alphabetical listing of all the words and their location but requires the user to consult a copy of the work for the context. Such a concordance would look much like the sections of the Racine and Fitzgerald concordances (see Examples 5.3 and 5.6) that list only locations for the most

A
DÂ
ALDÂ
CHANANEA
ARCHA
ARABIA
TOBIA
CANDACIA
ACCIA
INDIA
CHORINTHIA
ARMENIA
OMNIA
MACEDONIA
BABILONIA
ANTONIA
AMAZONIA
ANDRIA
ALEXANDRIA
PERSIA
GAPADOTIA

Example 5.10   List of the words in *Alexander* in reverse alphabetical order.

DÂ   V719 nâch   V1278 nâ   2613 Armenia   2806 Batra   4716 India   5057 Accia   5540 Jâ
    6451 Alexandria   6555 Cassandra

ARABIA   2132 Amenta

CANDACIA   5521 undertân

ACCIA   5058 dâ

INDIA   4717 dâ

ARMENIA   2614 dâ

MACEDONIA   2198 Persia

ANTONIA   V446 gâch

ANDRIA   2621 nâ

ALEXANDRIA   6452 dâ

PERSIA   2197 Macedonia

Example 5.11   List of rhyming words in *Alexander*.

common words.[4] The KWOC format can be quite awkward if you are using a printed copy of the work or a microfiche. However, if you have the work in machine-readable form, all you have to do is type the line number in which the word occurs, and the computer responds immediately with as much context as you desire (within the limitations of the size of the screen, normally about 25 lines).

Recent developments in microcomputers have made it possible to obtain the same kind of information about a text without any kind of printed material. A program such as the Brigham Young Concordance System, which costs only $99,[5] provides instant retrieval of all occurrences of a word or group of words, with whatever context you desire (line, sentence, paragraph, etc.). The key word is highlighted (or in a different color with a color monitor). This program can do almost anything a mainframe concordance program can, such as find occurrences of words within a certain distance of other words, though it cannot print a complete concordance. It can print information about specific words, however.

Thus, if you are willing to work with a screen instead of with a book, there may be no real need for a printed concordance. However, there are still some important limitations. First, you must have a computer handy; even if you have easy access to one with enough memory to store a long text, you do not always want to be tied to one work station; even the most portable computer is less portable than a book (though perhaps not *much* less than a multivolume concordance). Second, you must have a copy of the necessary texts in a form that the concordance program can read, and this is not always possible. If not, you can link your local computer to a data base that contains the texts and retrieve the necessary information in much the same way you would on your own computer. This procedure is especially desirable when the text in question is of great length and you need information about only a few words.

One of the best means of retrieving information from a distant data base is through a program called ARRAS (ARchive Retrieval and Analysis System); it allows you to get beneath the surface and to the heart of the matter quickly, though it does cost more than a ducat. You can use ARRAS on a terminal connected to a mainframe or on a microcomputer connected to a data base telecommunication link.[6] Even when you are working with huge texts, it can provide concordance-type information instantaneously: word lists, frequency counts, indexes, and the like. It allows the creation of categories (and of subcategories within categories) of related words, such as *heat, hot, warmth,* and *burn* in a category called "fire." ARRAS can find all occurrences of these words—separately or in any combination—and list them or create a graphic representation of where they occur in the text (Example 5.12).

Creating a Printed Concordance

If you need a printed concordance for the sake of portability or convenience, and it doesn't already exist,[7] it is quite simple to produce one if you have the text in a machine-readable form. For example, you can use the Oxford Concordance Program (OCP) to create "a concordance of a simple piece of text in the English alphabet" by entering only the following commands:

```
*ACTION
DO CONCORDANCE
*GO
```

The result will be a list of words in alphabetical order, including the frequency of occurrence of each word and the context of each occurrence.

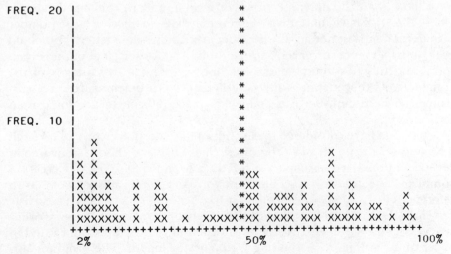

DISTRIBUTION: FIRECAT

Example 5.12   Graph generated by ARRAS.

You must of course choose an edition of the text that is as definitive as possible and to which other scholars have easy access. You must also decide what to do about variants and about quotations from other authors and passages in foreign languages. There is often some editing to do on a text, because it must meet the specifications of the concordance program. It must, for example, contain clear demarcations of any divisions of the text that are to be used to establish locations (paragraph, page, chapter of a prose text, for example, or character, scene, and act of a play; the computer can keep up with the line numbers). Often you must add special characters to distinguish among homographs, to distinguish between words in two languages that are spelled the same, or to identify proper nouns. You will need to identify any characters that are not part of the normal English alphabet or punctuation, and you must tell the computer how to treat these special characters in alphabetizing the list of words. (In French, where do *é* and *è* come in relation to *e*, or *ch* in relation to *c* in Spanish? Should apostrophes and hyphens be ignored in alphabetizing?)

A particularly sticky problem is lemmatization (see pp. 112–113), because at this time there is no satisfactory computer program to group all forms of a noun or adjective under the masculine singular form or all forms of a verb under the infinitive. Even a relatively uninflected language (such as English) contains more rules and exceptions than current programs can keep up with, and languages that contain separable prefixes (such as German) present a special problem. Some editors have pre-edited their texts or typed in long lists to tell the computer which forms go with which stem, but this is an extremely laborious process. Others, such as Wisbey and Freeman, have at least partially lemmatized the frequency lists but not the concordance itself. The lack of lemmatization is not a major problem if you are studying only uninflected forms such as prepositions and adverbs, or a few English nouns. However, when you are working with Latin where verbs can have more than 120 different forms, or even a modern romance language where they can have more than 40, you may have to check a large number of different entries, not all of which begin with the same letter. You could easily miss some occurrences because of having forgotten about a certain form, and this possibility neutralizes one of the main advantages of the computer, its thoroughness and completeness. An unlemmatized concordance can be useful, but it is somewhat more difficult to use for certain projects.

Once you have considered these and similar questions, you can take full advantage of the power of a program such as OCP and choose from among several options (see Examples 5.1–5.5, 5.7, and 5.8). You can create a complete concordance with context, or you can compile a list of words with references (locations) or just with their frequency of occurrence. These lists can show the words in forward or reverse alphabetical order (reverse order is very useful for studying rhyme or morphology and syntax) and listed in order of ascending or descending frequency or length. The program also calculates statistics about cumulative vocabulary frequencies (the X most frequently used words make up *Y* percent of the text; see Example 5.9) and about type/token ratios (individual words compared to all the occurrences of these words, so you can tell how often an author reuses a word and thus how rich her vocabulary is; see Chapter 6 for more details).

Another useful feature of a concordance program such as OCP is that it enables you to look at combinations of words. If you were puzzled by exactly what Keats meant by "Beauty is truth, truth beauty," you could ask for all combinations of *beauty* and *truth* in Keats's works. You can include or exclude any combination of words by indicating specific words, by placing a limit on the alphabetical or frequency range or on word length, or by specifying how close to other words a word must occur. If you wanted to know which adjectives are used often to describe Captain Ahab, you could ask for a list of all words longer than two or three letters that occur more than five times in the text and that are located within five words of *Ahab*.

HOW IS THE CONCORDANCE USED IN LITERARY RESEARCH?

Finding Specific Passages

Once you have a concordance, or the results from some concordance-type program, how can you use these lists of words in literary research? The most obvious way is as an aid in finding specific passages in a text. It can be rather frustrating to look through *Paradise Lost* or *Faust,* much less *A la recherche du temps perdu,* for a specific quotation, especially if your memory is less than photographic. With a concordance, however, all you have to remember is one word. Unless it is an extremely common word, a concordance can immediately provide the location of the passage—and perhaps enough context to help you remember the specific quotation without even looking it up in the complete text. If you have a concordance in which the occurrences are listed alphabetically by the preceding or following word (see Example 5.4), it is even easier to find passages.

Analyzing the Use of Particular Words

Concordances are probably employed most often to study how certain words are used. This is obviously important in literary research, and it can be a useful teaching tool in that it helps students to see how an author uses vocabulary and imagery. You may be interested in how Flaubert uses water or the color blue in *Madame Bovary,* for example. Rather than make generalizations about Flaubert's use of nature and color, you can look at the occurrences of the words that are used to make up these images and then document your interpretation with complete information. (Unfortunately, the computer cannot keep you from drawing bad conclusions from the information it provides.) Are you often struck with how an author uses a certain word, and do you find yourself wondering whether it is used in a similar way in other parts of the text? If the work is too long for a manual investigation, a concordance might be your solution. Besides, human readers sometimes miss things. The computer doesn't, and it doesn't mind how long the work is. Your only limitation may be your computer budget.

To take an interesting example, Robert F. Allen, in a paper presented at the 1984 MLA convention, studied the word *jeune* ("young") in Stendhal's *The Red and the Black.* He chose the word because it was one of the most common adjectives in the novel, and he expected it to be used in reference to Julien's (the hero's) age. It turned out, however, that it is used extremely often in a figurative sense, with little reference to the age of Julien. A character's reference to Julien as "young man" usually says more about the character's attitude (condescending, jealous, paternalistic, for example) than it does about Julien's age.

Even the oft-maligned (and omitted from concordances) function words can be well worth studying, especially when the computer can provide a list of all occurrences of them in several different orders. Conjunctions such as *and* are often neglected (Freeman provides only the locations in his Racine concordance, and Hockey suggests that *et* could have been left out of the concordance of Ammianus Marcellinus; *Guide,* p. 49), but they can often provide crucial information about how an author constructs sentences, especially when the author chooses a fairly "innocent" conjunction such as *and* instead of a stronger, more logical one or in place of *but.* Even simple prepositions can be an important indication of an author's style, as can the almost trite interjections (*oh* and *alas,* for example) with which a dramatic poet fills lines.

A list of all the words in a large body of texts can be extremely useful in devising materials for teaching foreign languages or English as a second language. You can find out which words are the most frequently used and base your vocabulary lists on this information. You can also see which forms of verbs are most frequently used and concentrate on them. Writers of books to teach technical German, for example, found that they could omit the first-person and second-person forms of verbs because these words are used so rarely in technical literature. (For this application, an unlemmatized list is what you need.)

Identifying Frequently Used Words

One of the first (and most controversial) uses for concordances was in the study of a text in terms of its most frequently used words. Baudelaire, echoing Sainte-Beuve, thought it would be possible to get to the "obsession"—the nature of the talent—of a writer if you knew what the most frequently words in his writings were, and many critics have tried to make generalizations about the relative frequency with which writers use certain words. It is not surprising that *Dieu* ("God") is the most frequently used word in Pascal's *Pensées,* a book that deals with ways of defending Christianity, but it is perhaps comforting to know that *homme* ("man") comes in second. You have to be careful in interpreting frequency lists (see Chapter 7), but they can suggest fruitful avenues of research. For example, if you perceive similarities among several frequently used words, you might pinpoint a thematic group that could otherwise have gone unnoticed. More frequently, though, you can use a concordance to check out a hunch, such as when you begin to suspect that a certain word is used more often than one would expect, and in crucial places in the text. For example, many readers notice the frequent use of the word *monster* in Racine's *Phèdre.* Sure enough, a quick look at a concordance reveals that it is used there more than six times more frequently than in his other tragedies.

These last two characteristics of word use can provide good examples of the care you must exercise when using concordances and frequency lists. Often you must be aware of how frequently other authors use the same words or of where these words occur in the work you are analyzing. (Are they spread evenly throughout the text or grouped? Do they occur at crucial points in the text?) In the first instance, you can usually obtain frequency lists for other texts written in the same language at about the same time, though you must be careful to make appropriate comparisons.[8]

The calculating and graphics functions of a computer can provide easy means of displaying word distributions and frequencies. Some concordance or retrieval programs (ARRAS, for example; see Example 5.12) have this capability, but if yours doesn't, you can use one of the numerous simple programs that can take word counts generated by the computer (already in machine-readable form) and present them graphically. SAS, for instance, a statistical analysis program now available in several versions for microcomputers as well as for mainframes, can produce anything from graphs like the one shown in Example 5.12 to much more complex representations. For example, you can see how often the verb *être* ("to be") occurs in each of ten sections of Pascal's *Pensées,* compared to a norm based on the occurrence of the verb throughout the work (Example 5.13). The rectangles represent the range of occurrences near the norm; the + signs represent the mean, and the hyphen the median. The zeroes outside the rectangles represent occurrences far from the norm.

Investigating the Use of Combinations of Words

A concordance program can be a useful tool in the study of special combinations of words that are peculiar to a specific text. Once you have noticed which individual words seem important, you can use a concordance to investigate related word usage. A quick look at a frequency list will reveal whether the word is used an unusual number of times, and the concordance itself will show quickly how the word is used, which should give a good indication of whether it is significant. Of course, the word may be significant even if it is not used frequently, and a concordance makes this

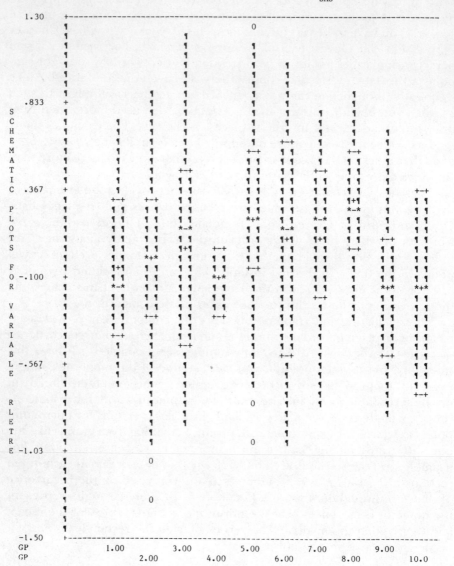

Example 5.13   Occurrences of *être* in Pascal's *Pensées* compared to the norm.

easy to investigate also—a glance at contexts and locations usually does the trick.

Often the computer simply confirms or follows up what you noticed in an impressionistic study. Sometimes, though, the concordance suggests routes for investigation. Say you have noticed an important word. Most concordance programs can generate lists of all words used more than a certain number of times within a certain distance of that important word. You can use such a list in much the same way you would have used a list you drew up by thinking about related words, but a computerized list has the advantage of being complete, within the limits of the instructions given to the computer. It may, of course, come up with frequently used words that are not significant at all, and, as in all cases of literary research with a computer, it is up to the human user to make the important interpretative decisions.

Examining Formal Structure

A concordance can be of special value when you are studying texts by authors who are particularly conscious of formal structure and word play. You can determine the length of individual sections of the work to look for formal balance, and you can find out whether certain words occur at specific intervals. You can also search for word combinations that reappear, though you can do this more easily with your own program designed to find any combinations you might be interested in. A concordance program can normally find combinations only after you have given it at least one word (*something*, for example, if you're studying Mr. Micawber) and asked it for other specific words that occur with that word (*turn, up*), but you can design your own program to find any words that appear together more than a certain number of times.[9] In writers such as Joyce and Nabokov, who are fond of puns, or such as Mallarmé, who uses words associated with the sound and spelling of other words, a concordance can help you find occurrences of words with similar spellings.

A concordance can even help you decide whether it would be fruitful to study an author from the point of view of formal structure: the careful arrangement of words or syntactic groups. For example, Bernet's study of Racine's vocabulary reveals that Racine uses only 3,263 words in his 11 tragedies, though he uses these words approximately 162,000 times. This is an inordinately small vocabulary and an equally high number of occurrences for each word; it is immediately clear that Racine must use these few words in a variety of sophisticated ways to obtain all the different effects achieved in these tragedies. A concordance is an ideal tool for investigating such matters, for categorizing the different meanings and implications of a word, and for determining in which parts of the text and in what context the word is used. With concordances, you can carry out this process for each play, find out which words dominate a particular play, and then study how certain words occur at key places in the text and which characters use them.

The preceding example makes it clear how well suited a concordance is to the study of plays written in end-stopped verse. You almost always have a complete context; the references to play, act, scene, and line show exactly where words occur; and the references to characters make it easy to study the specific vocabulary of each one. If the verse is rhymed, you can list words in reverse alphabetical order so that most rhyme words are listed together (see Example 5.10).

Comparing Different Authors' Works

Concordances can also be very useful when you are comparing works by different authors. Any information that proves significant in one author can be obtained for others so that you can tell whether a usage is unusual or search for instances of imitation. In particular cases where an author is known to be influenced by another, a concordance can help show the specifics of the influence, such as word choice, rhyming words, and imagery.[10] Words written in homage to another writer present a particularly interesting case: it is not always clear at a first reading just why one work might be "in the spirit of" another. In the case of Mallarmé's notoriously difficult *"Tombeau de Charles Baudelaire,"* one helpful approach is to use a concordance to see how Baudelaire used the words that Mallarmé uses in his poem of homage. Much of the vocabulary and imagery makes more sense in the light of Baudelaire's poetry than it does when you try to understand the Mallarmé poem in a vacuum.

A concordance sometimes reveals totally unsuspected characteristics of a text, but more often it allows the literary scholar to analyze rapidly and completely what she has already sensed. The following chapters discuss other ways of using a computer in literary analysis.

NOTES

1. The text for which a concordance is generated does not have to be made up of words. One can generate a concordance of phonemes, of stresses, or of anything else that can be represented by characters that the computer can read. Some examples will be given when projects involving morphology, sound patterns, and metrics are discussed in Chapter 7.
2. Such an appendix can be printed in a less expensive fashion. Another way to save space and money is to print the context and/or locations of these extremely frequent words on microfiche, which can be included with the published concordance, or to make them available on magnetic tape for interested scholars.
3. To be really useful, a frequency list should be lemmatized so that, for example, you can see at a glance how often a particular verb is used without having to look up each form of the verb. We will discuss lemmatization further in Chapter 7.
4. A justification for the KWOC format appears in Jacobson, Parins, Dilligan, and Bender, "Report on the Project in Literary Applications of Computer Technology at the University of Wisconsin-Madison," SIGLASH Newsletter 7.3 (1974): 12–14. Jacobson, Dilligan, and Bender are the editors of a concordance to Conrad's "Heart of Darkness," published in 1973 on two microfiches.
5. For more information, contact the Humanities Research Center, 3060 JKHB, Brigham Young University, Provo, Utah, 84602.
6. ARRAS was developed by John Smith at the University of North Carolina and will run on an IBM mainframe computer operating under CMS or TSO. See John Smith, "A New Environment for Literary Analysis," *Perspectives in Computing* 4.2–3 (1984):20–31. MICROARRAS, a version for microcomputers, will be

available soon. It will incorporate the features of the mainframe version and will also allow syntactic analysis (parsing) and simultaneous inquiries into more than one text.

7. It is often possible to obtain a printout of a concordance from the maintainers of a data base, even if it has not been published.

8. Differences in genre, length, and subject matter can cause certain words to occur in atypical ways, and it is usually best to work with a fairly large sample. If this is possible, there are methods for making statistical comparisons (most are related to the central limit theorem). Almost all the statistical packages available for microcomputers and for mainframe computers can analyze data derived from word counts, predict a normal frequency of occurrence, compare the data to this norm or to a norm based on a larger body of texts, and calculate whether the usage in the text deviates significantly from the norm. See Chapter 7 for more details.

9. See Chapter 7, especially the discussion of collocation, for more information.

10. See the discussion of the influence of Milton on Shelley (pp. 117–118).

CHAPTER 6

Interpreting Computer-Generated Data about Literary Texts

Because it can provide important information about a text and supply it in a convenient format, a concordance is an excellent starting point for many literary research projects. If, however, you need to find elements of a text other than words (or whatever else you have generated a concordance of) with their contexts and frequencies, then, unless a suitable program has been developed by someone else, you need to design (or have a programmer design) a program that meets your needs. There is a wide variety of such programs available today, designed for many different types of research. For example, you can find out how many times in a work the average word is used, how long the average word or sentence is, how often different parts of speech are used, which sounds are most common, and where the major themes occur in the text.

To use the information you have gleaned from a concordance or some other program, you have to know what to do with it and how. Suppose you know how often Shakespeare uses the word *ghost* in *Hamlet* or how long Hemingway's sentences are. To use this information, you have to know what word frequency or sentence length can tell you, as well as how often *ghost* and other words are used in other plays by Shakespeare and in plays by other writers. You also need to know how long a typical sentence in a novel is. To answer such questions you obviously need more data, but you also need statistical means of comparing and interpreting the data you have. And, most important, you need to decide what to look for.

AUTHORSHIP STUDIES

Some of the best examples of how to use computer-generated data about literary texts are in authorship studies, which establish criteria for comparing similar stylistic features in different texts. You decide what features might be unique to an author's works (or at least significantly different from those of other authors) and determine what is called a "wordprint." A wordprint can be one of several different types and is based on how frequently an author uses a variety of stylistic features, such as word and sentence length, how often words are repeated (type/token ratio), and the frequency of occurrence of certain parts of speech (especially conjunctions).

In the words of A. Q. Morton, the best-known if not the leading practitioner in the field, there is a science of stylometry "which describes and measures the personal elements in literary or extempore utterances, so that it can be said that one particular person is responsible for the composition rather than any other person who might have been speaking or writing at that time on the same subject for similar reasons."[1]

Once you have determined these "personal elements," or wordprints, you can use the computer to compare texts or samples of texts. The difficult part is choosing the criteria: They have to be meaningful, and they have to be made up of elements a computer can count. Much of Morton's work with Biblical Greek texts deals with the occurrence of *and (kai),* and he has had to refine his criteria as he went along, because his criteria and his methods have often been criticized. (He once helped an accused prisoner convince the court that statements attributed to him by the police could not have been written by him.) For example, rather than just comparing numbers of occurrences of *kai,* he has looked at intervals between its occurrences, words it frequently occurs with (collocations), and the part of the sentence in which it occurs. Such methods are especially important when one is dealing with language rather than with numbers or other randomly arranged data, because words are not chosen—nor do they occur—with perfect randomness. The choice is often determined by the subject matter, of course, as well as by preceding and following words. There are only so many words that can fill in the blank in a sentence such as "I ate ____ apple," and careful authorship studies, like any stylistic analysis, need to take this limited choice into account by looking at combinations (collocations, clusters) of words as well as at individual occurrences.

Use of Function Words as a Criterion

One of the earliest and most successful authorship studies, that of Mosteller and Wallace on the *Federalist Papers,*[2] is an excellent example of how the computer can help investigators come up with evidence that almost everyone finds conclusive. First of all, it was a perfect case to study because there were only two possible authors for the disputed texts—Hamilton and Madison—and both had written enough other works on similar subjects to provide a suitable basis for comparison. Furthermore, the disputed texts (25,000 words) and the known texts by Hamilton and Madison (70,000) were short enough to be analyzed in full.

Mosteller and Wallace first tried comparing sentence length and word length. In the former case, results from Madison and Hamilton were too similar to offer any means of associating the disputed text with either author; in the latter case, there was too much variation within each author. Later they tried a more systematic approach, using a concordance to identify words that occurred frequently in the work of one author but not in that of the other, and identified several function words (*enough* and *while,* for example) that occurred frequently but independently of subject mat-ter. They used the computer to count occurrences of these words and applied various statistical tests to interpret the results. (Most important, they devised a way to predict how frequently these function words would occur in the disputed texts, so there would be something to which to com-pare the actual findings.) In almost every case, the characteristics of the disputed texts resembled Madison's texts significantly more than they did those of Hamilton's. As a consequence, it is highly improbable that Madi-son is not the author.[3]

Other Criteria

Unfortunately, Mosteller and Wallace's method yields much less conclusive results with other texts. Each case must be approached on an individual basis, and, as in almost any kind of computer-assisted analysis, the hardest job is usually to determine what criteria to use; once you have satisfactory criteria, you can instruct the computer to search for the appropriate data and to perform statistical texts on the results.

More recent authorship studies have used new tools to develop crite-ria, some of which are treated in more detail in following chapters. Most start with a concordance, but several other available programs can help analyze a text and determine which features will be the best indicators of authorship. Ranson and Knepley, for example, in their investigation of the possibility that *Edmund Ironside* was written by Shakespeare,[4] have used modified versions of EYEBALL, THEME, and KYST, as well as the Ox-ford Concordance Program. EYEBALL is a program that searches texts for "such well-defined features as word lengths and syntactic categories" (see p. 115) and that can provide statistics such as type/token ratios. THEME finds and counts occurrences of words related to specific themes, and KYST produces a graphic representation of how the themes are related (see pp. 120–121 for an example). Armed with the data produced by these programs, Ranson and Kepley have been able to study colloca-tions of function words as well as stocks of images (themes), and their preliminary findings are "not incompatible with the thesis that the same author was responsible for both texts" (abstract).

Another well-known authorship study involves accusations that Mikhail Sholokhov plagiarized *The Quiet Don* from Fyodor Kryukov. A research team led by Geir Kjetsaa has carried out detailed stylistic analysis of large seg-ments of text from the novel and of texts known to have been written by Sholokhov and by Kryukov.[5] Kjetsaa employed sentence length, distribution and position of parts of speech, and how often certain forms of words were used in comparison to the rest of the text. These criteria were well adapted to Russian, which is highly inflected and free in word order. Although Kjetsaa was unwilling to make a definitive pronouncement, all of his tests excluded Kryukov as author but not Sholokhov.

MORE HELP FROM THE COMPUTER

In all of these authorship studies, the scholars had to get the computer to produce data about stylistic features and then to perform some sort of statistical analysis on the results. The first step is usually to generate a concordance, because it both tells you a lot about a text and provides a list of words that the computer can use easily to get more information. An extremely elementary program can count the letters in words to arrive at word length; to get sentence length, you just count the words or characters between periods. (You do have to tell the computer about abbreviations, ellipses, and decimal points, though, teaching it to recognize and *overlook* them when looking for a period that ends a sentence.) The computer can also use the frequency list generated by a concordance to calculate a type/token ratio by comparing the number of individual words (types) to the number of occurrences of all these words (tokens); this will show whether the writer has a varied vocabulary or uses the same words over and over.

Programs such as CLAS (Computerized Language Analysis System) and PROVIDE perform such operations as well as generating a concordance (though without context, in the case of PROVIDE).[6] They can even tell you the number of syllables per word or sentence or how often each punctuation mark is used, and give you a lot of statistics about what they have found.

It is slightly more complicated to pick certain categories of words out of a text. The process is basically the same for all categories, such as parts of speech (see the discussion of lemmatization, pp. 112–113), verb tenses, themes, direct discourse, or text in a foreign language. If you need a list of proper nouns, for example, the computer has to know what a proper noun is. (You have to be sure you do, too; computers don't work well with fuzzy definitions.) One way is to give the computer a list of all the proper nouns in the text, so it can match each word of the text against the words in the list. Another way is to identify (tag) each proper noun, either as you type it in or as you edit it.

A third way to get a list of proper nouns, which involves more programming but saves a lot of work in the long run, is to have the computer find all words beginning with capital letters. (This wouldn't work too well with a language such as German, which capitalizes all nouns, but on the other hand, this characteristic of German makes it easier to identify nouns.) You could print these words in two lists, the first of which would include only words that don't begin a sentence, because they are almost sure to be proper nouns. The second list would consist of the first word in each sentence, after function words had been eliminated. (Function words are words such as articles and conjunctions, which don't express content; 250 of these function words make up roughly half of a normal English text and an even greater percentage of sentence-beginning words.) All you would have to do is to check this second list for words that aren't proper nouns, eliminate them, and then merge it with the first list. This would be much easier and quicker than either identifying all of them in the text or drawing up a complete list.

Statistical Analysis

The information you get from a concordance program or from programs such as CLAS and PROVIDE is usually numerical (how many times certain stylistic features occur in a text), and you will generally have to apply some type of statistical analysis in order to interpret it. (Many of these programs can take care of the simple operations themselves, such as computing means.) You will almost always need to know some averages, or how much a feature deviates from the average, and whether this deviation is significant; otherwise, the fact that a word occurs a certain number of times in a text may be of very little use. For example, the type/token ratio for the complete text is an indication of how many times the average word is used. Because the computer knows (after a concordance program has been run) how many individual words (types) are in the text and how many occurrences (tokens) of these words there are, it can provide this ratio instantly, whereas it would take days to do this if one were counting "by hand." A quick comparison of the ratio for any word to that for the complete text will show whether the number of times the word occurs is below or above average for that text, or for any other text for which similar information is available.

Averages (means) and ratios may be all you need. If you have an idea, for example, that a certain word is used especially often in a text, a quick look at type/token ratios will provide quantitative verification. If, like all students of French literature, you have to compare the tragedies of Corneille and Racine, you might know that duty is an especially important concept in Corneille, and that the noun *devoir* is one of his most frequently used words. So you look up *devoir* in the Racine concordance and find that it occurs 46 times. That might look like a lot—until you check the type/token ratio for Racine's tragedies and find that the average word occurs 49 times. Your idea that the word is important is not necessarily invalidated by such knowledge. All the computer has done is suggest a new way of looking at the text (and at the way you read) that might not have been apparent without its aid. Indeed, a closer look reveals that a third of the occurrences of *devoir* are in one play, *Mithridate,* and that another 20% are in *Bérénice,* suggesting that those plays are much more Cornelian than the others.

More often, though, you will need to know more than just an average, especially when working with more than one word at a time. You will want to know just *how many times more or less often* than the average word a word has to occur for the difference to be statistically significant—that is, to know whether the difference can be attributed to the random distribution of words in the text. You will also want to know whether there are many words whose frequency is far from the average, so you can tell whether a word that occurs much more than the average is really unique. Tests that provide an excellent means of measuring these differences can be run on any computer (and even on some calculators). The standard deviation, for example, measures how close the actual frequencies of occurrence for a group of words are to the average, and the chi-square test helps determine whether (1) the differences between the actual frequencies of occurrence and the average can be attributed to a random distribution of the words or (2) the differences are truly significant.

One way to use the standard deviation is to look at the distribution of features throughout a work or corpus, rather than at the significance of individual words. If you are interested in looking at highly descriptive passages, the standard deviation can show that in, say, two texts with the same average number of adjectives per hundred words, in one text the number of adjectives varies greatly from one part of the text to the next, whereas in the other it is quite consistent. You might have a text with adjectives distributed something like this:

NUMBER OF ADJECTIVES

		TEXT ONE	TEXT TWO
Segment	1	8	8
	2	6	11
	3	7	4
	4	10	7
	5	9	9
	6	7	14
	7	8	6
	8	7	5
	9	10	8
	10	8	8
Average (mean):		8.0	8.0
Standard deviation:		4.0	8.7

If you looked only at the averages, you would think that both texts had a similar distribution of adjectives per segment. But if you compared the standard deviations, you would see that there is something unusual in text two and that you should look at the individual segments. You would soon see that segment 6 contains considerably more adjectives than segments 3 and 8 and that it would be a good candidate for a highly descriptive passage.

You could then use the chi-square test to determine whether the differences could be expected to occur by chance or can be considered significant. Statisticians assume that if a feature (such as the number of times a word occurs in a work) can be expected to occur by random happenstance no more than 5 times in 100, it is significant—that is, not attributable to chance. (You can choose another "degree of significance" if you like.) The chi-square test gives you a number that reflects the probability of the feature's occurring, and you compare it to numbers in a table. You get from the table the number for a probability of 5/100 (or .05), and compare to see whether the number you got from your chi-square test is larger than that number. If so, you can assume you are dealing with a significant feature.

Take the example of two important words in Racine's *Phèdre:* the words *innocent* and *aveu* (avowal). The former occurs 19 times in *Phèdre* and 81 times in Racine's 11 tragedies, whereas the latter occurs 4 times in *Phèdre* and 17 times in the tragedies. Thus they both occur approximately 2.6 times more often than one would expect: 19/(81/11) and 4/(17/11). However, the probability of a word's occurring 19 times in one play and 81 times in all 11 plays is well less than 1 in 1,000 (chi-square of 18.81), whereas that of a word's occurring 4 times in one play and 17 times in all 11 is slightly more than 5 in 100 (chi-square of 3.99). The numerical "weighting" in favor of both *innocent* and *aveu* can be considered significant, but that of the former is much more so.

More powerful statistical procedures can look at a text, search for combinations of features, reveal patterns of distribution (individually and in combination), and determine their significance. A "clustering" procedure, for example, can take a list of words that make up a theme (such as *light, sun, bright, clear, shine, radiant,* and *glow*) and show graphically any parts of the text where combinations (clusters) of these words are found to a significant degree. The graph from Bratley and Fortier's study of Gide's *L'Immoraliste* (see Example 7.4) is an example of the use of a clustering program.

You could also use clustering in linguistic research to find out whether certain combinations of phonemes occur consistently among groups of speakers of a language or dialect or to study groupings of parts of speech, as Brainerd did with pronouns and articles as indicators of genre. He found 6 distinct groupings among his 50 samples of plays, literary works ("belles lettres") and expository writing ("exposition"), ranging from expository works high in articles (vertical axis in Example 6.1) and low in pronouns (horizontal axis) to plays at the opposite extreme. The circular lines indicate clusters of texts that are more similar to each other (in terms of the number of pronouns and articles) than to the other texts.[7]

In the examples we have examined dealing with adjectives in segments of a text and with the vocabulary in Racine's tragedies, comparisons are fairly easy to make because the segments and plays are of similar length. However, if you are working with sentences or paragraphs that differ greatly in length, you need to use a somewhat more complex statistical procedure. A long sentence tends to have more conjunctions than a short sentence, and a long paragraph gives the writer more room than a short one to repeat words and develop a network of related words. Therefore, if you are interested in how many conjunctions a writer uses in a typical sentence, you need a program that looks at each sentence, compares the number of conjunctions to the total number of words in the sentence, determines a typical (average) number of occurrences for sentences of a certain length, and then determines how each sentence compares to the norm for sentences of that length. A microcomputer can perform this procedure for 1,000 sentences in less than a minute.

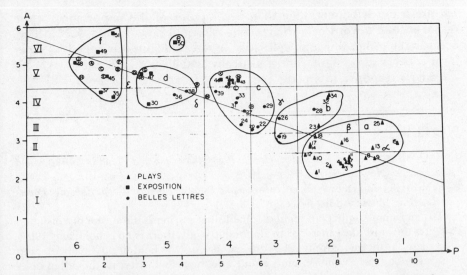

Example 6.1 Clusters of texts that are similar in terms of the number of pronouns and articles.

A Note of Caution

Statistical methods are available for handling almost any quantitative information you can derive from a literary test—sounds, rhythms, vocabulary, parts of speech, themes—and we will look at many of them in Chapter 7. The distribution of features in literary texts does not always follow the patterns with which statisticians are most familiar (a statistician would prefer a situation in which each letter of the alphabet occurred an equal number of times, for example), but it is by no means impossible to find patterns that statistical methods can help you analyze. If you aren't familiar with statistical methods, you can consult one of the books or articles dealing with the subject from a literary point of view (see Appendix III). Most major universities have statistical laboratories that offer free consulting. Don't be afraid to ask for help; statisticians are often fascinated by the new kind of data a literary text can generate and are more than willing to help.

Just as important as knowing when to use statistics is knowing when to ignore statistics. As Paul Bratley and Paul Fortier point out in "Themes, Statistics and the French Novel," there is a distinction between literary analysis and statistical analysis. The latter can confirm the former or suggest new possibilities, but it is useless without your firm control of the process. Literature is art. It uses carefully controlled structures (authorship studies have been much more successful with prose than with verse), not the random distribution of items (words) with which statisticians are familiar and on which their methods are based. Even the standards for determining significance (5 chances or 1 chance in 100, for example) are subjective, and *you* are a much better judge than a computer of the importance of the occurrence of a word or a theme. You can't tell how often a word occurs compared to other words as well as a computer can, but you can tell whether what appears to be significant statistically actually *is* significant in terms of a reader's response to a text.

NOTES

1. A. Q. Morton, *Literary Detection: How to Prove Authorship and Fraud in Literature and Documents* (New York: Scribner's, 1978).
2. F. Mosteller and D. L. Wallace, *Inference and Disputed Authorship: The Federalist Papers* (Reading, Mass.: Addison-Wesley, 1964).
3. To determine whether it is highly probable that a writer is the author of a disputed text is the most one can ask of an authorship study; there is no proof that is 100% certain. Furthermore, only when one can narrow the field of possible writers to two can one have some certainty about who the actual writer is (though in cases where there are several possibilities one can at least determine that it is highly *improbable* that a particular writer is the author).
4. Nicholas Ranson and Jean Knepley, "Edmund Ironside: A Reappraisal Appraised," paper at 7th International Conference on Computers in the Humanities.
5. Geir Kjetsaa, "Storms on the Quiet Don: A Pilot Study," *Scando-Sclavica* 22 (1967):5–24.
6. George A. Borden and James J. Watts, "A Computerized Language Analysis System," *Chum* 5 (1971):129–141. Boyd K. Swigger, "PROVIDE—A Preliminary Program for Text Analyses," *SIGLASH Newsletter* 6, No. 5 (1973):3.
7. Barron Brainerd, "An Exploratory Study of Pronouns and Articles as Indices of Genre in English," *Language and Style* 5 (1972):239–259.

CHAPTER 7

Stylistic Analysis

Many people talk about style, but not always in a meaningful way. There is confusion about whether style is found in the author, the reader, or the text, and especially about how to describe it. As Donald Ross points out in the introduction to his description of his parsing program EYEBALL, "Most comments about style are quite general, and they often tend toward the metaphorical: Keats is 'florid,' Beethoven is 'heroic,' Cézanne is 'rustic' " (85). Literary critics are in a better position than critics of art and music, because most readers know more about putting words together than they do about composing or painting, but it is still difficult to say something meaningful about style without using impressionistic labels that convey very little information. A computer can provide you with more than enough precise information to keep you from having to make vague generalizations, but you still have to be careful to avoid the other extreme—publishing too much detailed information.

The most commonly accepted definition of style is "the use of language to express thought and emotion." Style is a particular means of handling language so that its form and structure convey messages that supplement the meaning of the words. Cardinal Newman put it more succinctly. Style, he said, is a "thinking out into language."[1] We can argue about whether stylistic effects are consciously intended by the author, a reflection of the subconscious operation of the brain, or are just chance combinations of words, "mere variants of typical expenditure of linguistic material,"[2] but it is hard to deny that these effects are there. They are present as structures, as patterns that affect the reader and that can be detected by the trained eye.

The eye can use help, though, either in checking out an intuition or in looking for patterns that even the best-trained eye might miss. It can also use the help of a more patient, objective eye that can look for any possible pattern without necessarily being influenced by what it already knows (or thinks it knows), and it can *certainly* use the help of a fast, tireless eye that doesn't mind going through a text over and over again. Don't worry, though, that the computer might replace you. You are still indispensable. You tell it what to look for, inform it what constitutes a pattern, and evaluate its findings. But give it this help, and the computer can do in a few minutes what would take you weeks, even years. It can undertake projects that you probably wouldn't dream of doing by hand and come up with fascinating results.

A computer can help you study style at any level, from individual sounds to the largest macrostructures. Let's look at some possibilities and at some examples of what has already been done with such aspects of style as sound, meter, morphology, vocabulary, syntax, and theme, working up from the basic elements of literary style to its most complex features.

SOUND PATTERNS

Literary scholars have always studied sound patterns, looking at alliteration, for example, from *Beowulf* to Hopkins. Dell Hymes looked for "summative words" in which the dominant sounds of a poem appear and that express the theme of the poem (for example, *sea* in William Carlos Williams's "Flowers by the Sea").[3] He used quantitative analysis of phonemes and statistical measures of their significance, but he makes no mention of having used a computer. You can certainly count phonemes by hand and come up with a good idea of which sounds are significant, especially if you're looking only at 20 sonnets, but it makes your job much easier when all you have to do is supply a computer with a machine-readable version of your text. A simple program can then isolate all the phonemes and count them, calculate chi-squares to see which ones are significantly frequent, and produce a list of words that contain the most important phonemes.

You can take a similar approach to any project that deals with sounds. You can look for rhyme, alliteration, or assonance; determine which sounds are the most frequently used; and find out which sounds are associated with each other. Much of this is easy enough to do by hand with a sonnet, but if you are curious about whether Milton associates certain sounds with Satan throughout *Paradise Lost,* or whether certain passages have a higher-than-normal density of alliteration, it is much easier to ask a computer. You could quickly have a list of the most frequent sounds that occur within, say, ten words of "Satan" and other words associated with him. You could also learn how much alliteration occurs in each section of the poem. And you could define your sections as you like and take their length into account.

Even within a poem as short as a sonnet, or within a stanza, there might be repeated sound patterns you do not notice (you can be aware of only so much as you read). You might be struck by the sensuous beauty of Keats's "jellies soother than the creamy curd" in stanza 30 of "The Eve of Saint Agnes," but would you always take the time to figure out why and then look at other lines in the stanza containing similar sounds? If so, you would find the combination of *s, l* and *u* in "azure lidded sleep," "blanchèd linen smooth," and "lucent syrups." But what about similar combinations throughout the poem, or even one in the same stanza that you might have missed? Let the computer print out every occurrence of such a repeated combination within a line or a certain number of words, and then use your literary judgment to decide which combinations are important enough to mention in class or to include in your article.

The computer's speed and accuracy can be helpful when you want to search for features within a large number of works. If a rhyme or sound pattern strikes you in one poem, it would be interesting to know whether it occurs in others, but you probably wouldn't take the time to read through hundreds of poems to find out; the computer wouldn't mind at all. The computer could produce a concordance-like list of where the feature occurs and in what context, or you could ask it for some sort of graphic representation of what it found. This could show you at a glance where the feature occurs in a work or, in the case of rhyme, the relationships between rhyming words. The simple graph produced by ARRAS (see Example 5.12) can serve as an example of the first possibility, and J. Joyce's work with mathematical graph theory exemplifies the second (see Example 7.1 here).[4]

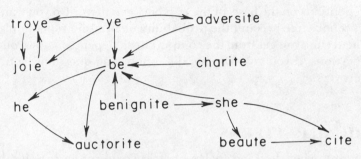

Example 7.1 Words rhyming with *be* **in** *Troilus and Criseyde.*

The computer can also help us correct false impressions based on subjective judgments. David Packard's study of sound patterns in Homer mentions cases where earlier scholars had cited lines containing an unusual number of occurrences of certain sounds the incidence of which really was not unusual at all.[5] For example, a line in the *Odyssey* that had been cited as unusual because of its three gutterals turned out to be only one of 2,414 lines with that many gutterals. This doesn't mean that the sounds are not important or that the line is not effective, but you wouldn't want to go out on a limb and say it represents an exceptional case.

The only limitations on a computer's ability to help you study sound patterns involve difficulties that arise in determining which phonemes the spelling of a word represents. You can't just look for every occurrence of the letter *a* if you are interested in the sound *ah.* You have to define the sound *ah,* giving the computer rules for distinguishing between the sound of *a* in *father* and in *fat,* for example. Most languages have firm enough rules and few enough exceptions to enable a fairly simple program to read a work and break each word into phonemes, though a language such as English (with its various pronunciations for combinations such as *ow* and *ough*) can make life difficult. If there are too many problems of this kind, you can enter all or part of your text in some sort of phonetic transcription, though such a procedure will slow you down.

Let's consider alliteration as a good example of what you have to keep in mind in defining features for a computer search. It would be simple enough to define combinations of consonants that have the same sound (*k* and *c* + *a* but not *c* + *e,* for example). Then you would have to decide whether you were interested only in sounds at the beginnings of words or in sounds anywhere in a word. Next would come questions such as whether alliteration among stressed syllables is more important than that among unstressed syllables. In a language such as German, do the numerous function words beginning with *d* and *w* deserve less weight than content words, especially when the latter come at a stressed point in a line? How many repetitions of a sound are necessary before it counts as alliteration? Just two, or more? How close do the repetitions have to be to each other? Do you want to use various statistical procedures to calculate the relationship between repetitions on the basis of the gap between them? Do you want to use statistics to take into account the probability of a certain repetition's occurring? The results you get from the computer will depend on how you answer these questions. If you give it vague definitions and questions, you will get vague answers.

METRICAL PATTERNS

A computer can help find and analyze metrical patterns much as it can sound patterns. It is usually possible to teach the computer to perform metrical analysis with 95–98% accuracy, scanning a line of verse and finding the length or stress on a syllable. The computer usually knows when it is having trouble scanning a line and can mark such lines for your attention; in most cases, it has trouble with a line because of an exception to the rules that would bother a human as much as it does the machine.

There have been several successful projects dealing with the analysis of verse in Latin, Greek, Sanskrit, English, German, and French, though in some cases it has been necessary to include a list of words that the computer consults to find out about stresses, or to mark the stresses as the text is prepared for the computer. Such a list, or dictionary, is usually prepared starting from a concordance, which provides a handy list of all the words in the text, in forward or reverse alphabetical order. This dictionary can then be used as a basis for a study of other texts, especially if they are by the same author.

It is not always necessary to write a special program to give you the information you need. If your text already contains special characters that carry the necessary information about syllable length and stress, a concordance package can probably tell you all you need to know, including the listing of lines by metrical pattern and the number of occurrences of each pattern. For example, Wendy Rosslyn coded the lines of Pasternak's *Volny* according to stress and rhyme.[6] She used 0, 1, -, and * to indicate unstressed and stressed syllables in weak and strong positions, respectively; to separate metrical words; and letters to indicate types of rhyme:

Здесь будет спор живых достоинств	)*)10)1)01)010,)ADE
И их борьба, и их закат,	)01)01,)01)01,)BDF
И то, чем дарит жаркий пояс,	)01,)010)10)10)ADE
И чем умеренный богат.	)01)010-)01.)BDF

She used COCOA to analyze these codes and was able to produce lists and concordances of metrical words, rhymes, punctuation, and line types.

There are many ways of using such results. Authorship studies, for example, have looked at how much the metrical stress in disputed texts differs from the norm and from the metrical stress in other texts by authors who might have written the disputed texts. Daniel L. Greenblatt found that metrical patterns are a much more reliable criterion for distinguishing between the styles of Donne and Jonson than are the vocabularies of the two writers,[7] because the samples of their lyric poetry are too small. He was able to reject Donne as author of "The Expostulation" and to determine that Jonson could have written it, but he was not willing to state that no one other than Jonson could have been the author.

The computer's ability to scan poetry also has great potential in computer-assisted learning. A student can make an attempt at scanning a line, and the computer can check the results without relying on the instructor's having told it the correct scansion for each line. Thus there can be a tremendous pool of lines to scan, and the computer can choose lines at random for practice in scansion. The instructor can also have the computer analyze the students' errors and record the errors and error types for her to examine later (see Chapter 1).

Scholars have used the results of computer-assisted analysis of metrics, and also of sound patterns, to study the structure of languages, especially ones that are no longer spoken. Stephen V. F. Waite studied the "interplay of verse ictus and word stress" to determine to what extent word stress (in addition to syllable length) influenced poetic composition in Latin poetry, and especially in Plautus.[8] Yuri A. Tambovtsev has used the computer to study the metrical characteristics in several Siberian languages in his efforts to classify members of a language "family."[9] The computer can produce lists of rhyming words to help determine how words were pronounced at some time in the past or to help isolate certain phonemes for study.

In literary research, all the information the computer can produce about metrics and rhythm can be used in analyzing the structure of a text. Scholars such as Wilhelm Ott have published several volumes of data on Latin hexameters—including accent, elision, hiatus, an index with a frequency distribution of all metrical forms, and listings of all verse types according to their meter, rhyme, or other ending. It is generally possible to gain access to similar data for other texts even if their compilers have not published them.[10] Farber and Zhu have related anomalies within metrical regularity to syntactical structures and formulaic patterns,[11] and many scholars have been able to isolate unusual and significant lines of verse by having the computer look at the overall metrical structure of a work. The computer can find other examples of patterns you have already noticed or point out unusual patterns for you to look at more carefully. In texts that exhibit a very regular pattern/such as iambic pentameter, you can get a list of lines containing irregular feet and can examine them on the assumption that they would be there for a special effect. In a form characterized by more metrical freedom, such as the French Alexandrine (wherein any grouping of the six syllables of each hemistich is permitted), it is often worthwhile to look for excessive *regularity,* because several lines in a row divided 3-3/3-3 reveal either a monotonous poet or, more fruitfully, a special reason for regularity, such as the climax of an important passage or the evocation of calm.

PREPARING TO STUDY WORDS AND LARGER STRUCTURES

Most studies of style have dealt with complete words rather than with sound and meter, to a large extent because it is easier to isolate words from a text than phonemes and syllables—all the computer has to do is look for spaces and punctuation. If you want to work with the words in exactly the form in which they appear in the text, you're ready to go. But suppose you want to know how often a certain verb occurs, and you're dealing with a Romance language in which there can be well over 40 forms of a verb, some of which have the same spellings as a noun or an adjective? (And Latin verbs can have three times as many forms!) You could find all the different spellings of most regular verbs grouped together in an alphabetical list generated by a concordance program, but what about irregular verbs (remember French with *est, fut,* and *soit* as three of the forty forms of the same verb)? And do you relish the prospect of counting all 40 forms and adding them up every time you want to know how often a verb is used? If not, you need to lemmatize your text—that is, to group all forms of a word under its stem (infinitive, masculine, singular, etc.)—and this can take forever without the help of a computer.

Lemmatization

Lemmatization is useful for many other applications than the study of literary style. In fact, lemmatization is more of a prologue to literary study than an aspect of it, because it is normally used in preparing to study vocabulary and syntax. It is a wonderful tool for linguists in the study of morphology and for lexicographers in the compilation of dictionaries. It has been used in the preparation of foreign-language textbooks to help determine the most frequently used words and also the most frequently used forms, so teachers can tell what words and which tenses, for example, to emphasize. You can even use it "backwards," so the computer can help students learn verb and case endings. Students type in an infinitive and specify a tense, and the computer checks to determine whether they can give all the correct forms. As in the use of computer-assisted learning in metrical analysis, the computer can "know" these forms without your having to give it every correct answer.

For such a program to work, and for a computer to be able to help with lemmatization, the computer must have a list of rules or a dictionary to consult. The rules tell it what is a stem and what is an ending, and the dictionary contains the lemma (the basic form, or dictionary heading) for each word in the text. Most concordance programs allow you to include a brief dictionary (a few hundred words at most), but this is useful only when you are interested in a small number of words. If you need to lemmatize an entire text, you need a complete dictionary.

Such dictionaries in machine-readable form exist in several languages, and you can often adapt a dictionary established for one project to another project dealing with a text in the same language. In Italian, for example, the Institute for Computational Linguistics (ILC) at Pisa has developed a program to work with their dictionary and can lemmatize all words except for the rather large number of homographs in Italian. A second program (see page 114 for an example) can take care of 85% of these homographs, and though this still leaves work for the scholar, it is much less than if she or he had to do it all by hand.[12]

A project in French has enjoyed a 95% success rate without the need of a large dictionary because of the "highly rigorous system of flexional regularities" in French.[13] A dictionary of function words takes care of words that are not inflected, and a program then works on the remaining words and separates stems from endings. It builds a list of possible endings as it goes along, so this process can be completely automatic. The scholar has to deal with only the 5% of words that remain.

Even working without a full dictionary, you can expect a similar success rate with other highly inflected languages, but not with all languages. English, for example, wherein words are sometimes inflected and sometimes not, and where suffixes are hard to distinguish from the rest of the word, is harder to lemmatize automatically than languages that are highly inflected. Still, a computer can make any lemmatization project easier. If nothing else, a concordance package like WATCON enables you to go through the list of words in a text, in alphabetical order, and type in at the terminal the form under which each word should be lemmatized. For example, in a German text you might have *Aug, Auge, Augen, Auges,* and *Augs* near each other in a word list, and you would type in *Auge* as the lemma for each one. This can be slow, but it is much easier than sorting and counting everything by hand. Once you have entered all the lemmas, the computer does the work of rearranging your list and counting the number of occurrences of each lemma, and it gives you all the options contained in the concordance package by lemma rather than occurrence (by type rather than token).

Conflation

Similar to lemmatization is what can be called conflation: the grouping together of all words with the same stem or root, whether or not they are forms of one lexeme. *Love, loves, loved,* and *loving* make up the lexeme *love,* but you might want to look at *lovable, lovelike,* or *lovely.* A computer can help you do this in much the same way in which it performs lemmatization, but it can never be completely successful in a language such as English, where *hunting* is related to *hunt* but *bunting* is not always related to *bunt,* or where a mixture of Latin and Germanic origins can result in the computer thinking that *manlike* and *manual* go together as *habitlike* and *habitual* do. You will have to do some editing when the computer has finished conflating, but you will have a very good starting point for finding related words in a text.

Parsing

Parsing is to syntax what lemmatization is to vocabulary. You can't achieve complete understanding of an author's vocabulary without some information about the syntactical context of some words, because you can't place a word such as *bear* in a category without knowing whether it is a noun or a verb, especially in view of the fact that its meaning would be completely different depending on its grammatical use in the sentence. Even in a case such as *after,* where you can tell what the word means without knowing whether it is a preposition or a conjunction, you can't really be sure how an author is using it without looking at the context. The work of the Italian Institute for Computational Linguistics furnishes a good example:

LO MENO

lo	= a) pronoun	(it, him)
	b) article	(the)
meno	= a) masculine noun	(least)
	b) adverb	(less)
	c) preposition	(except)
	d) verb	(lead)
	e) adjective	(less)

Lo and *meno* can theoretically combine in ten different ways, but the rules eliminate all possible combinations except article + noun and pronoun + verb, and the context permits a correct choice between the two possibilities, so the computer can tell you that in this case *meno* is a verb. The ILC has achieved an 80% success rate in this kind of parsing, even when working with the extremely high number of homographs and ambiguous forms in Italian (Picchi, Ratti, Saba, and Catarsi).

This is a fairly simple type of parsing, which aims not at the syntactical structures of the sentence but at distinguishing homographs that a dictionary-based lemmatization program has not been able to distinguish. No programs exist that can parse a text with complete success, but programs are getting better and are requiring less and less human intervention.

A good example is EYEBALL, developed at the University of Minnesota by Donald Ross.[14] It uses a dictionary of function words to determine the syntactical category (part of speech) of as many words as possible (about half) and to determine where clauses and prepositional phrases start. The computer carries out this stage automatically, but in the next stage the user must help by identifying the category of main words in the clauses and phrases and must check for errors. Once this process is complete (Ross reports that it takes less than an hour for 500 words, including typing in the text), an "augmented text" is produced, such as the one shown in Example 7.2 for the third sentence of Crane's *The Red Badge of Courage*.[15] You now have a complete parse of the sentence in a form the computer can read and analyze statistically. You have to help more than you would in many computer-assisted projects, but parsing programs are improving, and they even run on fairly small personal computers with as little as 64K of memory, using BASIC.[16]

Ross and other authors of parsing systems do not claim that they have given you a "comprehensive description" of a sentence (p. 95), but they do give you enough for you to carry out most stylistic studies. You can identify the function of every word as you prepare to analyze an author's characteristic vocabulary, you can search for unique combinations that characterize style and create themes and images, and you can identify phrases, clauses, and other constituent elements of the sentence with an eye toward larger formal elements of the text. Basically, you can see how a writer's language works, either within a particular text or in comparison to others by that writer or by others.

Vocabulary location of first instance	Location			Syntactic class		Phrase-clause location	Word	Punctuation
	Para.	Sent.	Word	Category	Function			
43	1	3	1	PRON	SUBJ	1 0 0	It	
44	1	3	2	VERB	PRED	0	cast	
45	1	3	3	DET	COMP	0	its	
46	1	3	4	NOUN	COMP	0	eyes	
47	1	3	5	PREP	APRP	0	upon	
1	1	3	6	DET	APRP	0	the	
49	1	3	7	NOUN	APRP	1	roads	
50	1	3	8	SUBD	SUBJ	1 0	which	
51	1	3	9	AUXV	PRED	1 0	were	
52	1	3	10	VERB	PRED	1 0	growing	
5	1	3	11	PREP	APRP	1 0	from	
54	1	3	12	ADJ	APRP	1 0	long	
55	1	3	13	NOUN	APRP	1 1	troughs	
41	1	3	14	PREP	APRP	1 0	of	
57	1	3	15	ADJ	APPP	1 0	liquid	
58	1	3	16	NOUN	APRP	1 1	mud	
27	1	3	17	PREP	APRP	1 0	to	
60	1	3	18	ADJ	APPP	1 0	proper	
61	1	3	19	NOUN	APRP	6 1 6	thoroughfares	.

Example 7.2   EYEBALL "Augmented text" for a sentence in *The Red Badge of Courage*.

VOCABULARY AND CONTENT STUDIES

Choice of Words

Any writer has a characteristic vocabulary made up of words the frequency of which in a text or part of a text differs notably from the normal frequency.[17] The simple statistical procedures mentioned in Chapter 6 will give you this information, as will a program like EYEBALL. You can break this characteristic vocabulary down into parts of speech, function words, content words, proper nouns, or whatever, depending on what you find significant about an author's style. It is important that you make the choice, because what is a useful way to characterize the style of one author is not necessarily useful in characterizing the style of others. For example, Louis Milic found that verbal forms make reliable discriminators when one is studying the styles of Swift, Addison, Johnson, Gibbon, and Macaulay,[18] but Bernet found verbs to be the least useful part of speech when one is studying Racine's tragedies, because their usage changes very little from play to play. Look at the text and follow your instincts. When you suspect that a text is extremely forceful and active, comparing the number of verbs to the number of nouns could confirm that suspicion, even if the author's use of verbs is not especially unusual.

Let's take another example of a process you might go through. If you were looking at polemic prose, a study of connectives such as subordinate conjunctions could suggest that the reader is being led along the logical path step by step *or,* if it turns out that there are *few* strong connectives, that he is being persuaded in some less rational way. And if you're stumped, for the moment, about just what this less rational way might be, you could look at the frequencies of other types of words and perhaps discover an unusual number of adjectives. You could look at them in context and see what kinds of adjectives most of them were, or you could have the computer tell you which nouns were used right after adjectives. If you had (or wanted to prepare) a list of common concrete and abstract nouns for the computer to read, you might find out that there are many concrete nouns and that descriptive imagery is more important than logic in your text. Of course, you may have noticed this by yourself (perhaps not, if you were working with a long, complex text), but it is nice to have your hunch confirmed. Even if you had noticed a preference for a descriptive style over a logical one, you almost certainly wouldn't have been able to say whether that preference held for the whole text or just for certain parts. The computer can tell you exactly to what extent each style is used in each part of the text; then you can figure out why.

To identify an author's characteristic vocabulary, you can use several different criteria, all of which can help you understand the style and content of a text. These criteria have also been used, with varying degrees of success, in authorship studies to compare texts, because an author's "plus" words (as Warren B. Austin calls words that occur with an unusually high frequency in one writer's works but not in another's[19]) can be an excellent discriminator in comparing texts. Even criteria that don't tell you much about one text can be useful in authorship studies, if you can determine their absence or presence in other texts.

Infrequently used words can be equally useful in identifying an author's characteristic vocabulary. This is especially true in the case of a writer such as Racine, who doesn't use a large variety of words in the first place. You would expect him to use all of his 3,263 words (in the 11 tragedies) often, but in fact 680 of them are used only once. Bernet has shown that these words that are used only once (hapax logomenon) are particularly useful keys to the main subjects of the plays, as well as to the general nature of the vocabulary of each play. For example, *Athalie* has the most original vocabulary of all Racine's tragedies if we judge by the number of words that occur in it and in no other play. This vocabulary includes not only the expected religious words but also a group of extremely concrete, "unracinian" terms that suggest a special approach to the play.

Word and sentence length are also useful indicators of the characteristics of a writer's vocabulary and style, and they have been among the most commonly used tests in authorship studies. Word length has been shown to be related to frequency of occurrence, and a high number of unusually frequently used long words can be an indication that they have been very carefully chosen and are thus especially important to an interpretation of a text.

You might want to compare one writer's vocabulary to another's—either in terms of general characteristics that would provide useful points of comparison (this is often the approach taken in authorship studies) or in terms of specific words that one seems to "borrow" from the other, consciously or unconsciously. One of the earliest examples of this second type of study was Joseph Raben's comparison of the vocabularies of Milton's *Paradise Lost* and Shelley's *Prometheus Unbound.*[20] Aware that Shelley was reading Milton as he wrote his drama, Raben wanted to find out how much of Milton's vocabulary was "assimilated" by Shelley. He decided to take the sentence as his basic unit and, with the help of a programmer, devised an efficient means of finding and cataloguing each sentence in the texts that contained at least two content words in common. (The scholar then looks at each pair of sentences and decides just how similar the two sentences are.) Raben's program unearthed thousands of such sentence pairs, including one with seventeen words in common. His project offers an excellent example of how a computer can help you carry out a thorough investigation of something you have noticed in a work. You could certainly notice many of the pairs yourself, but by no means all, especially in cases where passages in Shelley seem influenced by two different passages in Milton:

> I curse thee! let a sufferer's curse
> Clasp thee, his torturer, like remorse;
> Till thine *Infinity* shall be
> A **robe** of **envenomed** agony;
> And thine Omnipotence a **crown** of **pain**,
> To cling like burning gold round thy dissolving brain.
> *Heap* on thy soul, by virtue of this Curse,
> Ill deed, then be thou *damned,* beholding *good*;
> Both *infinite* as is the universe
> And thou, and thy self-torturing solitude.

> *Prometheus Unbound,* I, 286–295

> That with reiterated crimes he might
> *Heap* on himself *damnation,* while he sought
> Evil to others, and enrag'd might see
> How all his malice serv'd but to bring forth
> *Infinite goodness,* grace and mercy . . .

> *Paradise Lost,* I, 214–218

> Others with vast Typhoean rage more fell
> Rend up both Roces and Hills, and ride the Aior
> In whirlwind; Hell scarce holds the wild uproar.
> As when Alcides from Oechalia **Crowned**
> With conquest, felt th'**envenom'd robe**, and tore
> Through **pain** up by the roots Thessalian Pines . . .

> *Paradise Lost,* II, 539–544

Raben noticed metrical resemblances in many of the comparable passages, such as "Heap on himself damnation" (Milton) and "Heap on thy soul by virtue" (Shelley). He could have had the computer help find these matching metrical patterns, but it is probably easier to do it by hand when working with a limited number of examples (in this case, the ones you have decided are interesting and have selected from the complete list the computer generated).

Combination of Words

What we are after in any vocabulary study—indeed, in any literary study—is why an author has (1) chosen certain words and (2) put them where she did—what Jakobson calls selection and combination.[21] Looking at vocabulary from the point of view of richness, originality, and other aspects of frequency helps us understand selection, but this is only part of the process. We also need to look at where the words go and with which other words they are used.

In addition to looking at individual words, more and more computer-assisted studies of style have used what is called collocation. The term, introduced by J. R. Firth in 1951 in "Modes of Meaning," means not only the co-occurrence of certain words but also a comparison of all co-occurrences so that we can establish a norm and compare each individual case of co-occurrence to it, taking into account how many times the co-occurring words appear in the text separately.[22] By comparing the occurrence of a combination of words to the probability of that occurrence, we can tell how significant the combination is, just as we can tell how significant the occurrence of an individual word is by comparing it to the average frequency of occurrence for the text.

Scholars such as Godelieve L. M. Berry-Rogghe have devised a measure called the "z-score" that makes it possible to tell at a glance which combinations are significant.[23] She worked with texts by Charles Dickens, Doris Lessing, and Giles Cooper and gives the example of words that occurred within a span of three words on each side of the words *house*. Function words (words that were grammatically linked to *house*) generally had extremely low z-scores, but certain more interesting combinations had very high scores (Example 7.3). You can choose whatever span of words suits your text best and reveals interesting combinations without too many of what Berry-Rogghe calls "intruders"—words that your literary intuition tells you do not make significant combinations. One thing to keep in mind in choosing your span is the average sentence length of your text, because most collocations occur within a sentence. A wide span for a text with short sentences would

SOLD	24·0500	ONLY	2·0441	DID	0·6462
COMMONS	21·2416	COULD	1·9887	ABOUT	0·5363
DECORATE	19·9000	SOMETHING	1·9026	BUT	0·3641
THIS	13·3937	UP	1·8829	NOT	0·3221
EMPTY	11·9090	HAVE	1·8682	LIKE	0·2833
BUYING	10·5970	IN	1·7299	HIS	−0·0385
PAINTING	10·5970	MYRA	1·7232	WAS	−0·0890
OPPOSITE	8·5192	OTHER	1·6889	KNOW	−0·1038
LOVES	6·4811	BEFORE	1·6451	ALL	−0·1060
OUTSIDE	5·8626	TONY	1·4459	WELL	−0·1209
LIVED	5·6067	GHOST	1·3916	FOR	−0·1794
FAMILY	4·3744	MORE	1·3740	IF	−0·2197
REMEMBER	3·9425	MUCH	1·3227	IT	−0·4368
FULL	3·8209	WHERE	1·2896	THEY	−0·5175
MY	3·6780	ONE	1·2879	YES	−0·5818
INTO	3·5792	GET	1·1949	BE	−0·6557
THE	3·2978	OUT	1·1348	I	−0·6865
HAS	2·9359	OR	0·9316	DO	−0·6993
'RE	2·5999	PEOPLE	0·9220	WITH	−0·9090
NICE	2·3908	OF	0·9096	TO	−1·6660
YEARS	2·3712	MOTHER	0·8558	THAT	−1·8030
IS	2·1721	SEE	0·8503	YOU	−2·6034
EVERY	2·0736	BEEN	0·7713	AND	−2·6488

Example 7.3 Collocates of *house* in decreasing order of significance.

allow all sorts of intruders; you would be including almost the entire sentence every time.

Theme

Collocations are very useful in authorship studies, as are frequently occurring groups of three of more words. You and the computer can put collocations to even better use, however, by searching for collocations that are related to the ones you have already found in order to build up groupings of related words or groups of words. The computer can easily find all the collocations of each word related to *house* and plot the results so that you can see what combinations (often called clusters) exist and which ones are worth investigating. You could get a graph something like that of rhyming words in *Troilus and Criseyde* (see Example 7.1), which would show you groups of related words that constitute the themes of a work.

Paul Bratley and P. A. Fortier have taken this process of collocating the results of a collocation a step further in developing their series of programs called THEME.[24] Rather than going through lists the computer had come up with, they developed by hand (that is, by intuitive reading) lists of words making up themes that could occur in any work. They then had the computer search for correlations among themes. In the case of their work with André Gide's short novel *L'Immoraliste,* they divided the text into 3-page sections and searched for words that evoked any of their 22 themes. A high correlation value indicates that when words that evoke one theme occur more or less frequently than usual, then so do words evoking the other theme; a low correlation indicates that when one theme is frequently evoked, the other is not. The result was a list of which themes occur in correlation with each other and to what extent they are correlated.

Bratley and Fortier also had the computer produce a graphic representation of their findings, using a program called KYST that performs "multidimensional scaling." This program groups similar themes (those with high correlations) together and dissimilar ones apart, yielding a picture of related groups on one side and their opposites on the other (Example 7.4). You can see that themes related to well-being *(bien)* and health *(santé)* are far to the left, whereas themes related to illness *(maladie)* and weakness *(faiblesse)* are far to the right. A separate group related to beauty *(beauté),* light *(lumière),* and warmth *(chaleur)* appears at the lower left.

One interesting feature about Bratley and Fortier's work—a feature that makes theirs one of the most useful brief computer-assisted studies of style —is their constant awareness of just what the computer can do for them and of how literary analysis is different from and complemented by statistical analysis. They had already used literary analysis to posit which themes would be related, and they found that "a slight clockwise rotation of the axes [of the graph shown in Example 7.4] would divide the themes clearly into the groups that we postulated as a result of literary study," sickness and health (23). They were surprised, however, by how the computer arranged

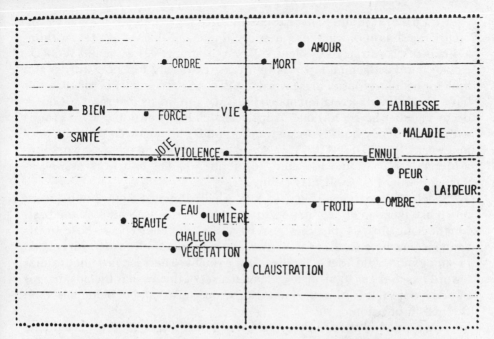

Example 7.4   Graphic representation of themes in Gide's *L'Immoraliste*.

the three themes *ordre, amour,* and *ombre* and were able to refine their original analyses.

Bratley and Fortier's method of creating their own lists of words that constitute themes gives a more general set of themes that could be used for any work, but the ideal solution would be to let the computer search for significant combinations of collocations in a large number of texts and to use the results to draw up the lists of words that constitute each theme. Bratley and Fortier say they were not able to detect important themes automatically, but they don't give any details. Such a text-based list would take care of the problem that they mention, that "a number of words important to a given theme in *L'Immoraliste* have not been counted" (24).

Scholars have had similar problems when doing thematic research with the General Inquirer (GI) system, a set of programs developed by the Harvard Laboratory of Social Relations in the early 1960s. This system uses a dictionary of words classified into semantic groups (based on categories such as sex, cultural setting, and attitude toward others), counts "occurrences and specified co-occurrences" of members of these groups, and performs various statistical tests.[25] The GI was designed to help analyze a patient's attitudes, but it has been used with modified dictionaries to study political, anthropological, and literary texts. It can be helpful in analyzing content, but much depends on how the dictionary has been established. Setting up such a dictionary involves a certain amount of subjective judgment and is a tedious task.

Howard P. Iker and Sally T. Sedelow are two scholars who have developed programs in which a computer can find major themes of a text without a dictionary constructed by hand.[26] Iker's programs SELECT and WORDS isolate the most common words in a text (excluding function words) and look for combinations of these words. Words that frequently occur together have a high "intercorrelation matrix" (ICM), and words that rarely or never occur together have a low one. Iker's research has shown that word groups with a high ICM "both represent and identify the major content themes" in a work ("WORDS," 430). He uses his programs in psychiatric work, but a literary scholar could use them to identify themes in a work as well as passages where these themes occur.

Sedelow's programs, called VIA (Verbally-Indexed Association), work much like Iker's in finding important content words that could be the basis for thematic analysis, but they also have the computer check these words against a machine-readable thesaurus so that it can find words with related meanings and build a set of themes. Once you have decided how many times a word has to occur to be included, such a set of themes has the advantages of being objective (within the limits of the thesaurus) and of being based on the text in question.

You would still need to check the list of words that constitute each theme and bring your literary judgment to bear to see how usable it is. The computer is doing nothing but counting and comparing, which must remain a preliminary step. But just think how much easier it is to check a list for errors or omissions than to build such a list from scratch. When it comes to finding out where, how often, and in what context certain words are used, you are no match for a computer. Your advantage is that you are like Pascal's thinking reed, who even though it is weaker than the forces around it, can understand what is going on.

STUDIES OF SYNTAX

Bratley and Fortier preface their discussion of their work on *L'Immoraliste* with Baudelaire's idea that "a successful work of literature is an organic whole in which every aspect, even every word, contributes to the overall aesthetic effect" (18). We have seen how the computer can help you understand how each phoneme, word, and word group is used, but there are even larger structures with which the computer can help. In particular, once a text has been parsed (ideally with the help of a computer), you can look at an author's syntactical patterns and examine how they constitute individual style.

Studies such as those of Louis Milic and Robert Cluett take the approach of having computers go through large quantities of data to find patterns they might not have thought of themselves. You might suspect, for example, that a writer uses conjunctions or some other part of speech a great deal, but you might not be sure in what way. Rather than make a guess and see whether the computer can confirm it, you could have the computer search for all sorts of combinations involving conjunctions and then review the material yourself to discover which combinations are significant. You could also have the computer produce some statistical data for ranking the patterns in some order, such as how unusual they are compared to the rest of the text or to other texts. By working in this way, you take advantage of one of the computer's most valuable capabilities, that of checking out all the possibilities. You would probably not have time to be that thorough yourself, yet it is useful to know that you haven't missed something important. The computer makes this thoroughness possible, but it still needs you to tell it what to look for and then to evaluate its findings.

Milic's work with Jonathan Swift is one of the first major contributions in this area, and it has been adapted to other texts numerous times. Milic looked at combinations of 24 word classes (parts of speech and function words, using Fries's *The Structure of English*)[27] in Swift and in four comparable control writers. The computer produced a huge quantity of evidence, much of which was not useful, but it also discovered patterns that no one is likely to have noticed using traditional methods of literary research. Milic found that Swift had a marked preference for certain word classes in certain parts of the sentence, such as connectives at the beginning, and that his writing exhibits a distinctive use of series. Milic also calculated a *"D* value" that "represents the number of different arrangements of the twenty-four word-classes" in a text and reveals "a varied repertory of possible syntactical constructions" (208). Milic used the D value to compare the variety and density of Swift's style to those of his contemporaries.

The scholars who have followed Milic's example include Cluett, who used the D value and everything from sentence length to word clusters and parallelisms to determine the characteristics of different types of style.[28] For example, he worked with Hemingway's "simple," "plain" style and found it to be surprisingly complex. Compared to those of 16 of his contemporaries, his sentences are not particularly short, unsubordinated, syntactically repetitive, or high in the use of *and.* The staccato, telegraphic sentences are there, but they are hardly dominant. Cluett was able to make many useful generalizations about the historical development of English prose style, noting a decline in period length and subordination and an increase in participial and progressive constructions as well as in the overall use of nouns (258).

Mary Lynn Flowers used sentence structure to study characterization in Racine's theater.[29] She had the computer calculate sentence length, compare sentence length to that of the alexandrine line, and determine the distribution of terminal punctuation, and she discovered that certain characters consistently used specific types of sentences. Flowers found, for example, that emotional characters use shorter, more irregular sentences and that sentences in highly charged scenes are generally shorter than those in other scenes. She was also able to show that Racine uses more consistent sentence structure as his career develops and to show how he differs from other playwrights of the time—especially from Pradon, the author of a rival *Phèdre.*

STUDIES OF OTHER STRUCTURAL PATTERNS

There are all sorts of other structural patterns in literary works that the computer can help you find. A simple example is the counting of the lengths of chapters or other divisions of a longer text to determine whether the author has set up some kind of symmetry that could suggest how these divisions are related. You wouldn't always need a computer to do this, but in some books it isn't easy to tell exactly how long chapters (or parts, acts, scenes, or cantos) are, especially if there are many of them. In texts made up of dated sections, you could find clusters of letters written within a brief period of time and see whether other structures in the work fit this temporal pattern. Christiane and Claude Allais did this with Laclos's *Les Liaisons dangereuses*[30] and found a five-part structure within the ten temporal divisions of the novel. You could do similar analyses of how characters in a play interact or of where geographic locations are mentioned.

In the future, we should have enough information about literary texts to enable the computer to probe such hard-to-identify features as irony and metaphor. This sort of investigation is difficult to carry out (with or without a computer), but it is basically a matter of knowing what standard usage would be and of noticing when something different occurs. It shouldn't be long before a computer can learn to realize that using the word *rose* to refer to a young woman is not "normal" usage and that it is highly unlikely that Swift, in *A Modest Proposal,* is advocating the selling of young children as food as a way to alleviate some of Ireland's problems.

Current methods of processing natural language by computer are not far from the capacity to recognize metaphorical language. It is already possible to store enough information and sort through it quickly enough to know to which category (in the case of the rose, plant instead of human) a word normally belongs.[31] The computer could then look at the context, determine whether words linked (by syntax or content) to that word can fit into the same category, and determine to what extent, if any, the combination differs from the norm. It could then suggest that any combination differing from the norm by more than a certain amount contains a figure such as metaphor. Similarly, it could look at syntax, recognize deviations from normal usage, and decide whether the deviation constitutes an error or a figure such as inversion or ellipsis.

When we speculate about the computer's performing such complex processing of natural language, we are getting into what is called artificial intelligence (AI). The computer has to exhibit intelligent behavior, make all sorts of decisions, and learn from its mistakes and successes, rather than simply follow explicit instructions. Rather than matching *rose* against a list of possible metaphors, it has to understand what a metaphor is and how to recognize one. In particular, it has to have the ability to parse and to analyze syntax completely, and it needs enough information so that it can categorize any word it meets. (This is not so awesome as it sounds; about 50% of the words in a text come from about 250 function words, the majority of the others from a few thousand very common words. And the computer can pause and ask for help, like a student who can't find a word in a dictionary.)

Recognizing irony would require even more complex AI programming, because the computer would have to know the society's values and what is considered normal or acceptable behavior. It would have to know enough about people in general and about a character in a work in particular to know what that character is likely to say and to suggest an ironic interpretation when the character's discourse exceeds a certain degree of unlikeliness. This is not science fiction. Such applications already exist in the social sciences, such as in the interpretation of what a psychoanalyst's patients say. Such interpretation currently takes resources beyond those of a typical microcomputer, but there are already several "expert systems" available for micros, with such intriguing names as *Lightyear* and *Reveal,* which can help the user make decisions, especially in business applications.

Research in AI is also being applied to the translation of foreign languages. Machine translation has long been a dream, but it is only recently that the complexity of the task has truly been understood—there is a lot more to it than just matching words with a dictionary. Fortunately, computers are becoming better and better able to cope with this complexity, especially the new "fifth-generation" systems.[32]

Two different types of translation systems for microcomputers are already available. MICROCAT (Weidner Communications Corp.) takes a text, asks for information about words it doesn't know, and then begins the slow process (several minutes per paragraph) of translation. The results are quite good, and you can let it do the bulk of the work at night or at some other time when you aren't using your computer.

The ALPS (Automated Language Processing Systems) is an "interactive" system that gives you a translation sentence by sentence (as opposed to a "batch" system such as MICROCAT, which processes a job without operator intervention). You check it for accuracy and style, make any corrections with a built-in word processor, and then go on to the next sentence. Many translators prefer to work this way, getting things just right as they go along instead of later going over a draft of the entire text.

Both systems can handle English, German, French, Spanish, and Italian, and more languages, including Japanese and Arabic, will be available soon. The secret is a good dictionary, especially if you are working with an unusual vocabulary. Your dictionary must include not only the right words but also all the morphological and syntactical information about them—part of speech, endings, plurals, verb forms, and so on. It can take a while to build up the right dictionary, but the results are well worth it if you have to do a lot of translating. And it's often possible to get a dictionary in machine-readable form from a data base (sometimes called a "term bank") or another translator.

Not much AI research is going on today in the area of literary research, but the great deal of work under way in the processing of natural language cannot help but spawn future developments for literary studies. One of the main goals of AI is to enable people to use their normal language to communicate with computers, and once a computer can understand everyday language, it will not be hard to teach it about literary language. For the time being, though, the most practical applications are in the areas of lemmatization and parsing and in computer-assisted instruction (see Chapter 1). If the computer can understand the structure of our language and understand our statements and questions as we normally express them, the future is almost unlimited.

NOTES

1. John Henry Cardinal Newman, *The Idea of a University,* ed. Martin J. Svaglic (New York: Holt, Rinehart and Winston, 1907), pp. 276–277.
2. Gustav Herdan, *Language as Choice and Chance* (Groningen: P. Noordhoff, 1956), p. 2.
3. Dell Hymes, "Phonological Aspects of Style: Some English Sonnets," *Style in Language,* ed. Thomas A. Sebeok (Cambridge: M.I.T. Press, 1960), pp. 33–53.
4. James Joyce, "Networks of Sound: Graph Theory Applied to Studying Rhymes," *Computing in the Humanities. Proceedings of the Third International Conference on Computing in the Humanities,* ed. Lusignan and North (Waterloo: University of Waterloo Press, 1977), pp. 307–316.
5. David Packard, "Metrical and Grammatical Patterns in the Greek Hexameter," *The Computer in Literary and Linguistic Studies,* ed. Jones and Churchhouse (Cardiff: University of Wales Press, 1976), pp. 85–91.
6. Wendy Rosslyn, "COCOA as a Tool for the Analysis of Poetry," *ALLC Bulletin* 3 (1975):15–18.
7. Daniel L. Greenblatt, "Generative Metrics and the Authorship of 'The Expostulation,'" *Centrum* 1 (1973):87–104.
8. Stephen V. F. Waite, "Word Position in Plautus: Interplay of Verse Ictus and Word Stress," *The Computer in Literary and Linguistic Studies,* ed. Jones and Churchhouse (Cardiff: University of Wales Press, 1976), pp. 92–105.
9. Yuri A. Tambovtsev, "The Relations of Some Siberian Languages from the Phonostatistical Viewpoint," *Sixth International Conference on Computers and the Humanities,* ed. Burton and Short (Rockville, Md.: Computer Science Press, 1983), p. 687.
10. Wilhelm Ott, *Materialen zu Metrik und Stilistik,* 15 vols. (Tuebingen: Max Niemeyer Verlag, 1970–83); Wilhelm Ott, "Computer Applications in Textual Criticism," *The Computer and Literary Studies,* ed. Aitken, Bailey, Hamilton-Smith (Edinburgh: Edinburgh University Press, 1973), pp. 199–223.
11. J. Joel Farber and David J. Zhu, *Metrical Analysis: Homer's Odyssey,* Paper at 7th International Conference on Computers and the Humanities, 1985.
12. E. D. Picchi, D. Ratti, A. Saba, and N. Catarsi, "A Morphosyntactic Analyzer for

Italian," *Sixth International Conference on Computers and the Humanities,* ed. Burton and Short (Rockville, Md.: Computer Science Press, 1983), pp. 512–520.

13. Jean G. Meunier, Serge Boivert, and François Denis, "The Lemmatisation of Contemporary French," *The Computer in Literary and Linguistic Studies,* ed. Jones and Churchhouse (Cardiff: University of Wales Press, 1976), pp. 208–214.

14. Donald Ross. *Description and User's Instructions for EYEBALL.* (Minneapolis: University of Minnesota Department of English, 1974); Donald Ross, "An EYEBALL View of Blake's Songs of Innocence and of Experience," *Computers in the Humanities,* ed. J. L. Mitchell (Edinburgh: Edinburgh University Press, 1974), pp. 94–108; Donald Ross, "Beyond the Concordance: Algorithms for Description of English Clauses and Phrases," *The Computer and Literary Studies,* ed. Aitken, Bailey, and Hamilton-Smith (Edinburgh: Edinburgh University Press, 1973), pp. 85–99; Donald Ross, "EYEBALL: A Computer Program for Description of Style," *Computers and the Humanities* 6 (1972):213–221.

15. Donald Ross, "EYEBALL and the Analysis of Literary Style," *Computing in the Humanities,* ed. Peter C. Patton and Renée A. Holoien (Lexington, Mass.: D.C. Heath, 1981), pp. 85–103.

16. Richard Earp, "Using a Microcomputer for Parsing Text," Paper at 7th International Conference on Computers in the Humanities, 1985.

17. Charles Bernet, *Le Vocabulaire des tragédies de Jean Racine* (Paris/Geneva: Champion/Slatkine, 1983), p. 177

18. Louis T. Milic, *A Quantitative Approach to the Style of Jonathan Swift* (The Hague: Mouton, 1967).

19. Warren B. Austin, "The Authorship of Certain Renaissance English Pamphlets," *Proceedings: Computer Applications to Problems in the Humanities,* ed. Frederick M. Burelbach, Jr. (Brockport, N.Y.: SUNY College at Brockport, 1970), pp. 93–99.

20. Joseph Raben, "A Computer-Aided Study of Literary Influence: Milton to Shelley," *Proceedings of a Literary Data Processing Conference, September 9–11, 1964,* ed. Jess B. Bessinger, Jr., Stephen M. Parrish, and Harry F. Arader (New York: Modern Language Association, 1964), pp. 230–274.

21. See Jakobson's definition of the poetic function: "It projects the principle of equivalence from the axis of selection into the axis of combination." (Roman Jakobson, "Linguistics and Poetics," *Style in Language,* ed. Thomas A. Sebeok, Cambridge: M.I.T. Press, 1960, pp. 350–377.) This definition furnishes a good rationale for studying collocations.
    Studying the patterns of occurrence of words is also a good way to look at how the brain stores and retrieves words. Like the literary scholar, the psychologist looks for deep motives in words the brain habitually couples together. See Morton, *Literary Detection,* pp. 15–16.

22. J. R. Firth, *Papers in Linguistics 1934–51* (Oxford: Oxford University Press, 1957). A technical definition is "the syntagmatic association of lexical items, quantifiable, textually, as the probability that there will occur at *n* removes (a distance of *n* lexical items) from an item *x,* the items *a, b, c* . . ." See M. A. K. Haliday, "Categories of the Theory of Grammar," *Word* 17 (1961):241–292.

23. G. L. M. Berry-Rogghe, "The Computation of Collocations and Their Relevance in Lexical Studies," *The Computer and Literary Study,* ed. Aitken, Bailey, and Hamilton-Smith (Edinburgh: Edinburgh University Press, 1973), pp. 103–112.

24. Paul Bratley and Paul A. Fortier, "Themes, Statistics and the French Novel,"

Sixth International Conference on Computers and the Humanities, ed. Burton and Short (Rockville, Md.: Computer Science Press, 1983), pp. 18–25.

25. Philip J. Stone, Dexter C. Dunphy, Marshall S. Smith, and Daniel M. Ogilvie, *The General Inquirer: A Computer Approach to Content Analysis* (Cambridge, Mass.: M.I.T. Press, 1966).

26. Howard P. Iker, "SELECT: A Computer Program to Identify Associationally Rich Words for Content Analysis. I. Statistical Results," *CHum* 8 (1974):313–319; Howard P. Iker, "SELECT: A Computer Program to Identify Associationally Rich Words for Content Analysis. II. Substantive Results," *CHum* 9 (1975): 3–12; Howard P. Iker and R. Klein," WORDS: A Computer System for the Analysis of Content," *Behavior Research Methods and Instrumentation* 6 (1974): 430–438; Sally Sedelow, "The Computer in the Humanities and Fine Arts," *Computer Surveys* 2 (1970):93–96; Sally Sedelow and Walter Sedelow, Jr., "Stylistic Analysis," *Automated Language Processing: The State of the Art,* ed. Harold Borko (New York: Wiley, 1976), pp. 201–203.

27. Charles C. Fries, *The Structure of English* (New York: Harcourt, Brace, 1952).

28. Robert Cluett, *Prose Style and Critical Reading* (New York: Columbia University Teachers College Press, 1976).

29. Mary Lynn Flowers, *Sentence Structure and Characterization in the Tragedies of Jean Racine: A Computer Assisted Study* (Cranbury, N.J.: Farleigh Dickinson University Press, 1979).

30. Chr. Allais, and Cl. Allais, "A Method of Structural Analysis with an Application to *Les Liaisons dangereuses,*" *R.E.L.O. Revue* No. 2 (1968):13–33.

31. You can already get dictionaries, thesauri, and encyclopedias for your microcomputer, and now complete data bases are becoming available on disks similar to audio compact disks; see page 78.

32. W. J. Hutchins, "Machine Translation and Machine-Aided Translation," *Translation: Literary, Linguistic and Philosophical Perspectives* (Newark: University of Delaware Press, 1984), pp. 93–149.

CHAPTER 8

Using a Computer in Scholarly Publishing

You can put a computer to great advantage in any kind of scholarly publishing, whether you are preparing your own article or book or editing someone else's work. More and more publishers have the capability of working with your text in some sort of machine-readable form, so you can avoid the step of having someone retype your text and, regrettably, introduce errors into what left your desk. If you are a bit more ambitious, or are looking for ways to save money and proofreading time, you can send a publisher computer-generated, camera-ready copy that looks as though it had been typeset. Or you can send a version of your text that can be fed into a compositor to produce proofs in a couple of hours! Let's look first at getting your work ready for a publisher. (Everything we talk about here can easily be done on a microcomputer.)

PREPARING YOUR WORK FOR THE PUBLISHER

Communicating Your Text Electronically

For submitting manuscripts, you will probably want to send printed copy for the sake of ease in reading. Once your manuscript is accepted, though, find out whether your publisher has a computer that can read your floppy disk and, if so, make your revisions and mail the disk instead of your typescript. Or better yet, send your text electronically through the telephone lines to the publisher's computer. You can do this via a direct phone connection between your computer and that of your publisher, using a device called a modem to link your computer to the phone. Modems usually come with the software necessary to enable you to communicate with other microcomputers, mainframes, or data bases; there are also freeware programs such as PC-TALK.

Easier still, you can communicate with a publisher as part of a network. Many institutions belong to a network such as BITNET or EDUNET, which joins their mainframe computers. (It's quite easy, even without a modem, to transfer your files from a micro to a mainframe, though some word processing programs—WordStar is a prime example—use certain formatting codes that can present problems.) If your publisher and your university belong to the same network, you can send your text and any necessary correspondence and get an answer back as soon as your publisher responds.

The Publisher's Printer—and Yours

Once a publisher has your text in machine-readable form, there are all sorts of ways of speeding up the process of going from text to print. The simplest is for the publisher to use a word processor and printer to produce the copy to be used for publication. Any final revisions, changes to make the material conform to "house style," and other formatting can easily be done before printing. The computer can check for spelling errors and can generate a table of contents and index. (A publisher can also use a computer for bookkeeping and to send out and keep up with reader reports.)

Once everything is ready, the publisher can use a printer attached to its micro to produce the final copy. The resulting pages can be photographically reduced a bit to make them darker and more like printed pages; then they are taken to an offset printer and a binder to produce the publication. The publisher can produce a quality product quickly, without having to pay typesetters or proofreaders. These reduced costs benefit you as well. It is mostly because you have supplied your text in machine-readable form that the publisher can save money, and some of the savings should be passed on to you in the form of a larger advance or a lower subvention.[1]

Although publishing in this simple way won't produce copy that looks just like professional typesetting, the copy can look remarkably good, and you will be tempted to acquire a letter-quality printer of your own. Printers for microcomputers *are* getting better and cheaper all the time; for less than $500 you can buy a daisy-wheel printer that produces copy as good as that of a typewriter. Such printers are slow (about 10–20 characters per second) and often noisy, and it may be worth your while to spend more for a printer that is faster, more reliable, and more generally supported (both for repairs and for alternative daisy wheels that print a variety of characters).

Don't fail to consider good dot-matrix printers. They are four or five times faster than most daisy-wheel printers at printing drafts, and when you slow them down so that they strike each character twice or four times, the results are almost indistinguishable from those of daisy-wheel printers. In fact, once you photocopy a page and reduce it a bit, it is really hard to tell the difference (Example 8.1). Dot-matrix printers with truly "near-letter-quality" output cost around $1,000, but you may not need something this good for your own computer. Excellent dot-matrix printers are available for less than $300, and there are several degrees of quality in between.

It doesn't take much more money to buy a printer that produces copy with the appearance of having been professionally set. Prices are falling rapidly, and you can now buy the Hewlett–Packard "Laser-Jet" printer for

```
     The output of a near-letter-quality (NLQ) dot-matrix printer
can be quite good--it's hard to tell that the letters are made
up of dots.  You  can print foreign characters such as é and à,
though it's not always easy to mix languages without inserting
commands to change character sets.  You can also do boldface, but
not always italics or proportional spacing.
```

Example 8.1   "Near-letter-quality" output from a $500 dot-matrix printer.

The output of a laser printer is of near professional quality, and is a good choice for printing final versions of documents for which appearance is especially important. In particular, it is well suited to producing camera-ready copy and documents with a variety of foreign characters such as é, à, ß, Ñ, and š. It also does *italics* and **boldface** very well, as well as proportional spacing and right justification.

Example 8.2   Output from a laser printer.

less than $3,000 and get results like those shown in Example 8.2. Most word processors can drive such a printer. If your word processor cannot, you can get a pre-printing program, such as *Polaris Printmerge* for *WordStar,* to serve as a go-between.

The Use of Codes

In order to get truly professional output, either you or your publisher must insert typesetting codes into your text. Once this is done, a compositor can read your text and produce proof almost immediately. It takes a little longer to get your text ready, but you save months of work and often a good bit of money too. If you are involved in any kind of publishing, it is well worth your while to consider learning how to insert these codes. You can then do it yourself before you send your text to the publisher and thus be in a good position to bargain for a lower subvention or a larger advance.

You start with the files produced by your word processor. If you're using a program such as WordStar that includes characters other than the standard 128 characters of the ASCII code, you need to convert these to the standard characters that any computer can read. There are all sorts of programs available to do this, and one often comes with the word processor. All you do is answer a few questions from a menu and wait a minute or so (for an article of average length).

The next step is to mark all the places in your text where the format is to change. For most texts, this involves only the title, subtitles if there are any, and text that is centered or indented. Choose any characters that are easy to remember, beginning with a character that doesn't occur anywhere

```
is decadence in its best sense without the
fanfare, without the outrage, but
satisfying and enduring.
/h3
NOTES
/
1 A selected bibliography of Barbey
d'Aurevilly would include the
following: Philippe Berthier, Barbey
d'Aurevilly et l'imagination
```

Example 8.3   Text with preliminary codes.

else (we use /H1, /H2, and so on for headings with different type styles; we use /EX1 and /EX2 for various centered or indented extracts), and insert them just before the text in question (Example 8.3). You also insert some character (we use / again, with nothing after it) when it is time to return to normal format.

Once this is done, you need a little help from a programmer—but only the first time you do it, because you can generally use the same program for all your publishing projects. (The actual codes that will be put into your file should be listed in a part of the program you can edit with any word processor so that, if you use a different publisher the next time, you can change the codes and use the same program.) The programmer can help you design a program that converts your codes (/H1, /EX1, and so on) into whatever codes the publisher's equipment uses. Such a program will also convert the various codes in your word processing file, such as those for underscoring (which will be changed to italics), boldface, and superscripts (Example 8.4). The results look a little odd, but you will get used to it. In fact, most editors soon find it easier to spot errors in coded text like this than in "straight" text.

You then send the disk with the output from this program to the publisher, and your proofs can be ready in minutes for an article, in a couple of hours for a journal or book. These proofs may be traditional galleys, or you can go straight to page proofs. If you've done everything right, there should be no reason to bother with galleys, because the computer rarely introduces errors. Still, even on a computerized system it is expensive to make extensive changes in page proofs, and we think galleys are a worthwhile intermediate step, at least until you've been through the process once or twice. You may have missed some typos, especially if there are foreign characters that your printer couldn't print, and you can't be perfectly sure about type styles and formats until you see some kind of proofs. And of course, once the galleys are ready, you can have page proofs in almost no time at all.

The advantages of using some combinations of these computerized systems are obvious. You avoid many intermediate steps that can introduce errors, and you save a great deal of time. Furthermore, you can save quite a lot of money, especially once you're an "old hand" and have the bugs out of the process.

```
is decadence in its best sense without the
fanfare, without the outrage, but
satisfying and enduring.<EP><UF24>NOTES<EP>
<UF25><EM><EM>$ssl A selected bibliography
on Barbey d'Aurevilly would include the
following: Philippe Bertheir, <CF303>Barbey
d'Aurevilly et l'imagiantion<CF301>
```

Example 8.4   Text with typesetting codes.

USING THE COMPUTER IN TEXTUAL EDITING

For the same reasons, you should consider using a computer in textual editing projects. Doing so can save large amounts of time and can often save money, but perhaps most important, it can help produce a more accurate and thorough edition. As Wilhelm Ott argued as early as 1973, ("Computer Applications"), "there is nowadays no other means than electronic data processing to guarantee the exactness, completeness and consistency legitimately required of a modern edition" (200). A further consideration is that, once you have your text and other information in machine-readable form, it will be much easier for future scholars to take advantage of your work.

The computer can help at every stage of the preparation and publication of a critical edition. Ott and others have generally broken down the process into several steps:

1. The collection of texts to be used
2. The comparison and collation of these texts
3. Determining the relationships among the texts
4. The reconstruction of as definitive a text as possible
5. The compilation of the critical apparatus (variants, notes, indexes, and so on)
6. The printing of text and apparatus

The beauty of using a computer in these various steps is that it can not only do much of the work in steps 1 through 5 but also store everything you deem important. Thus, when you're ready to publish your edition (step 6), you have your text and critical apparatus all set to print; no expensive retyping or proofreading is called for. Even if the computer didn't help make the first five steps easier, the advantages of having everything ready to print without the danger of introducing errors during typesetting makes using a computer the best method.

Collecting Texts

Using the computer to collect texts is not much different from using it in any bibliographic project. You can search library catalogues and other data bases to find manuscripts and published editions or to find works that might provide information about these manuscripts and editions. This may not be necessary if you are working with a text that has only a few well-known versions, but if you are trying to track down, say, all the letters of a busy correspondent, some computerized searches could speed things up considerably. (See Chapter 4 for more information about such searches.)

A portable computer can be a great help in annotating or entering text from manuscripts in libraries. You can take your computer into the reading room and almost silently enter text, avoiding the risk and tedium of having to recopy your handwritten copy of the manuscripts.

Collating Texts

One of the most time-consuming aspects of textual editing is collating numerous texts, checking for every difference among them. A computer is a whiz at such a chore, and it can compare the readings of each text—character by character—much more quickly and accurately than you can. If it finds differences, it can list them in a convenient format. This list can also help you spot errors in your text, because the same error is unlikely to occur in all versions of the text. In fact, there is usually no need to proofread your machine-readable text if you are collating it against several other versions. (At least one typesetting company types into the computer a copy of each work it is going to publish and runs a collation program on it to compare it to the text they are about to set. This process gives better results than using a spelling checker, but it does involve extra labor.)

The normal procedure in computerized collation is to compare a master text (base text or provisional copy text) to several others. Earlier collation programs, intended to provide a printout of all variants (which an editor could then use in the traditional way) list variants beneath the word from the base text, line by line. The computer compares the master text to each of the other texts and prints out any word that differs from the master text, along with the source of each variant. The editor is now ready for what R. L. Widmann, who collated some 60 editions of *A Midsummer Night's Dream,* calls "collation by eye."[2] Example 8.5 is a sample of her output. The *w* indicates a difference in line length.

More recent collation programs, such as those of Penny Gilbert and Peter Shillingsberg,[3] are designed to prepare machine-readable lists of variants that can later be incorporated into your edition, rather than just to print

2179	And this dittie after mee, Sing; and daunce it trippingly.			
q2		Ditty	me, Sing	dance	
f1		Ditty	me, sing	dance	trippinglie.
f2		Ditty	me, sing	dance	trippinglye.
f3		Ditty	me, sing	dance	
f4		Ditty	me, sing	dance	trippingly. w
r1		Ditty	me, Sing	Dance	
r2		Ditty	me, Sing	Dance	
r3		Ditty	me>w		
p1		ditty	me>w		
p2		ditty	me>w		
t1		ditty	me>w		
t2		ditty	me>w		
h1		ditty	me>w		
wa	Sing, and dance it trippingly.>w				
j1		ditty	me>w		
ca		ditty,	me,>w		
h3		ditty,	me,>w		
ma		ditty,	me,>w		

Example 8.5 Variants of a line from *A Midsummer Night's Dream.*

out visual aids for the traditional collation process. Gilbert's program COL-LATE prints out 15 lines of text followed by a listing of variants. The variant is printed beneath the corresponding words from the master text (Example 8.6.). You then use the computer to edit this list, discarding any variants that are clearly errors or that you don't think are significant enough to be included in your edition. The program next creates a file with the variants in traditional variant-note style, distinguishing omissions and deletions from alterations (Example 8.7). This file is then used to add the variants to the proper page of the edition. Example 8.8 shows a page of the published work.

In the process we just described, the computer compiles a list of variants automatically, continuing until it has gone through the entire text or until you tell it to stop. For the process to work correctly, the computer must always know which words in the texts being compared to the base text correspond to specific words in the base text. Unfortunately, this is often difficult, and the computer has been known to "lose its place." This can happen, for example, when blocks of text have been added to or deleted from the texts being compared, or when there are so many changes that it is hard to tell just what is a variant of what. It isn't often much of a problem in poetry (because the computer can usually find its place when it gets to a new line), but in prose the computer can come up with many spurious variants if it doesn't realize that two considerably different passages are still variants of each other.

DANUS Q*UAESTIONES SUPER M*ETAPHYSICAM   L*IBER I*V*. Q*UAEST. I*

2100	B	04	01021	QUALITATIS AUT QUANTITATIS ESSENT ADINVICEM DIVERSI, NON SOLUM
2200	B	04	01022	SPECIE VEL GENERE, IMMO GENERE GENERALISSIMO. C*ONSEQUENS EST
2300	B	04	01023	FALSUM, IGITUR ET ANTECEDENS, SCILICET CONSEQUENS APPARET QUIA OMNES
2400	B	04	01024	CONCEPTUS VEL ACTUS INTELLIGENDI SUNT DE EODEM GENERE, PUTA DE GENERE
2500	B	04	01025	QUALITATIS, UT ALIQUI DICUNT, VEL DE GENERE ACTIONIS VEL PASSIONIS,
2600	B	04	01026	UT ALIQUI DICUNT. I*GITUR NON DIFFERUNT ABINVICEM GENERE
2700	B	04	01027	GENERALISSIMO. S*ED CONSEQUENTIA PRINCIPALIS PROBATUR QUOD OBJECTA, SCILICET SUBSTANTIA,
2800	B	04	01028	QUALITAS DIFFERUNT GENERALISSIMO.
2900	B	04	01029	I*TEM EIUSDEM REI
3000	B	04	01030	OMNINO SIMPLICIS SUNT PLURES CONCEPTUS DIVERSI. D*EUS ENIM EST
3100	B	04	01031	OMNINO SIMPLEX ET TAMEN VALDE MULTA ET DIVERSA PRAEDICATA
3200	B	04	01032	SIBI ATTRIBUUNTUR, UT APPAREBIT IN X*I*I*. I*GITUR TALES CONCEPTUS
3300	B	04	01033	NON HABENT SUAM DIVERSITATEM EX PARTE OBJECTORUM.
3400	B	04	01034	I*TEM SI CONCEPTUS DISTINGUERENTUR SECUNDUM DISTINCTIONEM
3500	B	04	01035	OBJECTORUM, SEQUERETUR QUOD CONCEPTUS CONTRARIORUM, UT ALBEDENIS ET

2304	I	B	04	01023	ANTECEDENS, SCILICET CONSEQUENS
2804	I	I	04	01028	ANTECEDENS. F*ALSITAS CONSEQUENTIS
2402	I	B	04	01024	VEL
2803	I	I	04	01029	SIVE OMNES
2501	I	B	04	01025	QUALITATIS,
3006	I	I	04	01030	QUANTITATIS,
2602	I	B	04	01026	ALIQUI
3201	I	I	04	01032	ALII
2607	I	B	04	01026	ABINVICEM
3206	I	I	04	01032	ADINVICEM
2706	I	B	04	01027	QUOD
3306	I	I	04	01033	QUIA
2709	I	B	04	01027	SUBSTANTIA, QUANTITAS, QUALITAS DIFFERUNT
3403	I	I	04	01034	SUBJECTA QUANTITATIS, QUALITATIS DIFFERUNT GENERE
3004	I	B	04	01030	PLURES CONCEPTUS DIVERSI.
3604	I	I	04	01036	VALDE DIVERSI CONCEPTUS.
3205	I	B	04	01032	IN X*I*I*.
3903	I	I	04	01039	X*I*I* HUIUS.
3306	I	B	04	01033	PARTE
4006	I	I	04	01040	DIVERSITATE
3506	I	B	04	01035	UT ALBEDENIS
4302	I	I	04	01043	SCILICET ALBEDINIS

Example 8.6   Text and variants displayed by the program COLLATE.

```
B  04   01006    SPECIALISSIMAE. C*ONSEQUENTIA PATET I*I* % E*THICORUM% UBI DICITUR QUOD EX SIMILIBUS
B  04   01007    ACTIBUS GENERANTUR SIMILES HABITUS. S*ED ANTECEDENS PROBATUR
B  04   01008    QUIA ACTUS INTELLIGENDI NON POSSUNT HABERE DIFFERENTIAM SPECIFICAM EX PARTE INTELLECTUS
B  04   01009    CUM ILLE SIT UNUS ET IDEM. E*T IDEO SI DIFFERANT SPECIE, OPORTET
B  04   01010    QUOD ILLA DIFFERENTIA PROVENIAT EIS EX PARTE OBJECTORUM. I*DEO SI PROBATUM
B  04   01011    FUERIT QUOD EX IPSIS OBJECTIS NON HABENT DIFFERENTIAM SPECIFICAM.
B  04   01012    CONCLUDETUR QUOD NON DIFFERUNT SPECIE ET SIC ERUNT OMNES EIUSDEM
B  04   01013    SPECIEI SPECIALISSIMAE. E*T IDEO NUNC DESCENDO AD OSTENDENDUM QUOD
B  04   01014    OMNES ACTUS INTELLIGENDI NON DISTINGUUNTUR SECUNDUM DISTINCTIONES
B  04   01015    OBJECTORUM. E*T HOC PROBO MULTIPLICITER: PRIMO QUIA DIVERSORUM SECUNDUM
B  04   01016    SPECIEM. UT HOMINIS ET ASINI ET EQUI EST UNUS SIMPLEX CONCEPTUS',
B  04   01017    SCILICET SIMPLEX CONCEPTUS A QUO SUMITUR HOC NOMEN "ANIMAL" QUI APUD
B  04   01018    INTELLECTUM NUMERALITER EST UNUS ET INDIVISUS. ---- S*ECUNDO IDEM
B  04   01019    PROBATUR QUIA SI CONCEPTUS ESSENT DIVERSI SECUNDUM DIVERSITATES
B  04   01020    OBJECTORUM, SEQUERETUR QUOD CONCEPTUS SUBSTANTIAE ET CONCEPTUS

A  04   01010    E*RGO... SPECIALISSIMAE. % OM.% B*
B  04   01007    ACTIBUS> ACCIDENTIBUS F*
B  04   01007    ANTECEDENS  PROBATUR>  ARGUITUR C*.
B  04   01007    PROBATUR % OM.% C*
B  04   01009    OPORTET> IDEO E*
A  04   01019    PROBATUM % OM.% B*
B  04   01011    OBJECTIS % OM.% C*
B  04   01012    NON % OM.% E*
B  04   01013    DESCENDO...OMNES> OSTENDO QUOD D*, DESCENDO> DESCENDENDO A*C*
B  04   01013    OMNES % OM.% C*
B  04   01016    EST...SCILICET> ET VIRIS F*
B  04   01017    SIMPLEX % OM.% C*D*
B  04   01018    IDEM... QUIA- ETIAM QUIA PROPRIAS F*
B  04   01020    CONCEPTUS % OM.% D*
```

Example 8.7   COLLATE's display of text and variants in traditional style.

Among the best recent results of efforts to develop a collation program that can always keep its place is a program designed by Peter Shillingsberg. The program knows where each paragraph begins, so it can skip to the next paragraph if it has trouble finding matches in the two paragraphs it is comparing. It can also back up and look at preceding paragraphs, an important advance over most previous collation programs. Shillingsberg's program allows you to insert typesetting codes into your texts before they are collated. These codes can be ignored for normal collation, but it is often useful to know, for example, that a word was in italics in one text but not in another.

Still, the perfect collation program has not been invented yet, and it probably won't be until more research in the area of artificial intelligence enables computers to make the kinds of decisions editors make, rather than making mindless—but fast and accurate—comparisons. A good alternative to a program that goes through the entire text and gives you lists of variants to edit is an interactive program that lets you intervene each time the computer finds a difference between two texts. It is now possible for you to take such an approach (first described by Trevor Howard-Hill in 1973)[4] on a microcomputer, using programs such as URICA, which Thomas Sliker reported on at the ICCH 1985 conference. Such programs are more convenient to use and cheaper than programs that require a mainframe.

In an interactive program, the computer has one text as its base (it doesn't have to be the best text; you can have the computer create your copy text after it has found all the variants) and compares it to another, which it can read from a file or read as you type it in. Whenever it finds a discrepancy between the two texts, it asks you whether there is an error in one of the texts and gives you a chance to correct it if there is. If there isn't, the variant

186   Quaestiones super Metaphysicam

quidam negaverunt primum principium contra
quos ibidem disputavit Aristoteles et hoc
etiam dicit Aristoteles in II huius quod
multi negaverunt principia supposita in
scientia naturali propter consuetudinem   5
audiendi opposita.

Et similiter in VI Ethicorum (1) dicit
Aristoteles quod multi propter malitiam non
possunt principiis practicis assentire. Unde
malitia, ut dicit, corrumpit et mentiri facit   10
circa principia practica et sic bene apparet
falsitas illius consequentis principalis. Et
etiam ex praedicta auctoritate Commentatoris
fit ratio ad oppositum quia V Ethicorum (2)
dicitur quia naturale habet eandem vim apud   15
omnes, ut ignis consimiliter ardet hic et in

---

2 quos... disputavit] quod idem dispo-
nit E   3 Aristoteles] Commentator ACDEF | |
quod] scilicet AF   4 multi negaverunt]
multa E | | supposita] supponenda CDE
11 sic] tunc E 12 illius... principalis]
consequentis E   14 ad oppositum]
propositum A | | oppositum] propositum CDF | |
V] X E   15 quia] quod ACDEF | | eandem...
ut] vim causandi apud omnes unde ibi E

---

1 Aristot., Ethic. Nicom., VI, c. 6
(1140b 16-21).   2 Aristot., Ethic. Nicom.,
V, c. 7 (1134b 19).

Example 8.8   Sample page of published text and critical apparatus.

is written to a file. That file is later used to create textual lists, in conjunction with the base text and with others that have been collated against it.

The advantage of such an approach is that the user makes decisions about what is a variant and helps the computer find its place if it gets lost. Working this way is slower than having the computer do everything, but until the computer can perform flawlessly, it is just as quick to check the variants as they are found as it is to go over the complete list after the computer has gone through the whole text. In fact, it is a more efficient process, because the computer doesn't have to keep up with any spurious variants. You also avoid the step of transferring changes marked on paper to the computer file, but some editors find it tedious to do all the work at a computer screen.

Determining Relationships among Texts

Once you have all the variants, the computer can help you determine the relationships among the various texts and create stemmas. These relationships are almost always somewhat ambiguous, and neither the computer nor you can always come up with a definitive solution. Determining the relationships among texts is often extremely complex, but once you decide, what approach you want to use, it is usually possible to break the process down into steps that the computer can execute. Froger and Dearing,[5] for example, have developed programs to implement their methods, and Zarri has worked on implementing those of Quentin. What the computer can do better than you can is to find all the relationships that are possible, given the differences among the texts, and present them to you so you can decide which is the most likely. It can quickly take each text as an arbitrary base, compare it to the others, and construct all the genealogies (stemmas) that could account for the differences. It will still take your knowledge of the particular texts involved to determine which relationships make the most sense, but you won't have to go through the long process of looking at all the variants and deciding what might have come from where.

Compiling the Critical Apparatus

At this stage of your editing process you are ready to prepare the copy text, to which you can add the critical apparatus. In most cases, the provisional copy text that you used as a base against which to compare the other texts will be the basis of your text. If not, you still have the other texts in machine-readable form, and you have a record of how they differ from all the other texts. The process of constituting a copy text would not be substantially different.

You can make all substitutions and changes directly from what is already in the computer, in most cases just as you would with any text on a word processor. If there are words you need to change throughout the text, you can have the computer change them automatically via a global search and replace. For one-of-a-kind changes, you can search the text for each place you want to change and make the changes to your file. If there are only minor changes, you can key them in; if there are more substantive changes, such as blocks of text to add, you can make them by calling up the new text from the files that contain the variants from the other texts. You shouldn't have to enter any new material, so there shouldn't be any introduction of typographical errors.

Once your text is established, you can use other capabilities of the computer to check for errors you may not have caught while collating. You can have a concordance program prepare a list of all the words that occur in the text and thus tell easily whether there are any words that shouldn't be there or that are misspelled. You can also use a spelling checker to draw up a list of "suspicious" words.

Now you are ready to prepare the critical apparatus. You will of course have to write your own notes, but the textual lists can be constructed automatically from the files of variants. You will have discarded variants that were errors or that you don't want to include, such as differences in hyphenation or capitalization. Or you may have put what you consider less substantive variants in a separate file. Whatever decisions you make, you can have the computer list the variants and their sources in whatever format you choose.

Printing the Text and Apparatus

You now have the text and critical apparatus you need, as well as all sorts of details about the various texts and their relationships. You will need to print your edition, and this is where having used a computer really pays off. You've saved much time and effort by having the computer help in such tasks as collation and construction of the copy text, but you'll save much more by being able to print your edition directly from your machine-readable files. You won't have to hope the printer does a good job of typesetting your typescript and you won't have to spend countless hours reading several rounds of proofs, because you can send the printer either camera-ready copy or a file that can go directly into a typesetting machine. In either case, all you have to do is decide on a page format and give the computer the appropriate instructions.

Most of this process has already been described in the section on writing and publishing, but there are some details that should be mentioned here. You can do some very complex page formatting with a computer, including several different levels of text and notes. For example, you could have the main text, followed by textual lists in several categories (lexical and punctuation, for example), then notes to the text, and then notes to the lists. You could have each of these parts of the page in a different style of type and could even have sections in languages with different alphabets, whether they need to be printed from left to right or from right to left. You can also indicate authorship in a manuscript copy text by using different typefaces *(brother-in-law)*, *Jno. Henry Menton, solr, Martin Cunningham, John Power, .)eatondph 1/8 ador dorador douradora'* (must be where he called Monks the dayfather about Keyes's ad) *Thomas⸢ Kernan, Simon Dedalus, Stephen Dedalus B. A., Edw. J. Lambert, Cornelius T.° Kelleher, Joseph*

5 *M'C Hynes, L. Boom, CP M'Coy,* − ⸢[*Mackintosh°*] *M'Intosh°⸣ and several others.'*

  Nettled not a little by L.° Boom ⸢(B)(as it incorrectly stated)(B)⸣ and the line of bitched type but ⸢[amused] tickled to death⸣ simultaneously by C. P. M'Coy and Stephen Dedalus B. A. who were conspicuous, needless to say,

10 by their ⸢total⸣ absence ⸢(to say nothing of M'Intosh)⸣ L. Boom pointed it out to his companion B. A. engaged in stifling another yawn, half ⸢(H)[nervousness.] nervousness, not forgetting the usual crop of nonsensical ⸢howlers of⸣ misprints.(B)

  —Is that first epistle to the Hebrews, he asked as soon as his ^⟨lower⟩

15 bottom^ jaw would let him, in? Text: open thy mouth and put thy foot in it.
  —It is. Really, Mr Bloom said ⸢(though first he fancied he alluded to the archbishop till he added about foot and mouth with which there could be no possible connection)⸣ overjoyed ^to set his mind at rest^ and a bit flabbergasted at Myles Crawford's after all managing to.⸢ There.'

20 While the other was reading it on page two Boom ⸢(to give him for the nonce his new misnomer)⸣ whiled away a ^few odd^ leisure ^⟨moment⟩ moments^ in fits and starts with the account of the ⸢[race] third event at Ascot⸣ on page three, his side. Value 1000 sovs with 3000° sovs in specie added. For entire colts and fillies. ⸢Mr F. Alexander's⸣ ⸢[*Throwaway°*]

25 *Throwaway,°* b. h.⸣ by ⸢[*Rightaway-Thrale°*] *Rightaway-Thrale,°°* 5 yrs, 9 st 4 lbs'⸣ (W. Lane) 1, lord Howard de Walden's *Zinfandel°* (M. Cannon) 2, Mr W. Bass's *Sceptre°* 3. Betting 5 to 4 on *Zinfandel,°* 20 to 1 *Throwaway°* (off). *Sceptre°°* a shade heavier, 5 to 4 on *Zinfandel,°* 20 to 1 *Throwaway°* (off).' *Throwaway°* and *Zinfandel°* stood close order.

30 ^⸢[Then] It was anybody's race then the rank outsider⸣ drew to the ⸢[fore.] fore,° got long lead, beating lord Howard de Walden's chestnut colt and Mr W. Bass's bay filly *Sceptre°* on a 2½ mile ⟨course winner⟩ course. Winner trained by Braime° so that Lenehan's version of the business was

---

3-6 *Thomas--others.*] a4; ʍ aR   4 *T.*] aP *(ʍ)*; *ABSENT* aR   5 *Mackintosh*] *TD:* Mackintosh, tB   5 *M'Intosh*] e; M'Intosh, a2; *M'Intosh,* a4   7 L.] tB; L aR   19 to. There.] *STET* aR; *TD:* it. There tB; the thing, there. (aB)   23 3000] e; 300 aR; 3,000 tB 24 *Throwaway*] e; ʍ aR   25 *Throwaway,*] a2; ʍ a1   25 *Rightaway-Thrale*] e; ʍ aR; ←TN   25-26 *Rightaway-Thrale,--*9 st 4 lbs] e; *TD:* Rightaway. Thrale tB; Rightaway, 5 yrs, 9 st 4 lbs, Thrale a1   25 *Rightaway-Thrale,*] e; Rightaway, a1; *Rightaway,* a2

Example 8.9   Gabler edition of *Ulysses*, p. 1414 (Eumaeus episode).

for different authors, and you can indicate any changes an author made to a text. The computer can make all the decisions about what fits where, just as it does when it adds footnotes to your article or book.

An interesting example is the Gabler edition of Joyce's *Ulysses* (1984), which includes, on the left-hand pages, the text with all the different stages marked by special signs (Example 8.9). This impressive complexity and accuracy would hardly be possible without the aid of the computer, in this case Wilhelm Ott's program TUSTEP. The codes necessary to produce these formats can be included in your master text as it is prepared; this is much easier than going back in to add them later. You can have the computer ignore these codes when they are not needed, such as when running collation or concordance programs, or when you want a printout of just the text.

NOTES

1. For an outline of all the steps a journal publisher would go through, and of how a computer can fit in, see the MLA's *A Grin on the Interface: Word Processing for the Academic Humanist* (1984), pp. 50–51.
2. Ruth L. Widmann, "The Computer in Historical Collation: Use of the IBM 360/75 in Collating Multiple Editions of a Midsummer Night's Dream," *The Computer in Literary and Linguistic Research*, ed. R. A. Wisbey (Cambridge: Cambridge University Press, 1968), pp. 57–63.
3. Penny Gilbert, "The Preparation of Prose-Text Editions with the COLLATE System", *La Pratique des ordinateurs dans la critique des textes* (Paris: C.N.R.S., 1979), pp. 245–254; Peter L. Shillingsberg, "The Computer as Research Assistant in Scholarly Editing," *Literary Research Newsletter* 5:1 (Winter 1980):31–45.
4. T. H. Howard-Hill, "A Practical Scheme for Editing Critical Texts with the Aid of a Computer," *Proof* 3 (1973):335–356.
5. Jacques Froger, *La Critique des textes et son automatisation* (Paris: Dunod, 1967); Vinton A. Dearing, *Principles and Practice of Textual Analysis* (Berkeley: University of California Press, 1974).

APPENDIX I

Sources of Information

NETWORKS

There are two kinds of national networks: value-added and on-line networks. With a value-added network, the user calls a local telephone number for access and thus avoids long-distance charges. Usually there is no additional charge for these national information networks. The most common ones include DataPac (Transcanada), Telenet (GTE), and Tymnet.

An on-line network charges a registration fee and also a per-hour fee. CompuServe, out of Columbus, Ohio, can be accessed through any of the three value-added networks listed above. It includes, among others, the following data bases: College Press Service, Educational Products Information Exchange, Educators' Forum, Edutech, Foreign Language Education Forum, Grolier Academic American Encyclopedia, and Literary Forum. It does not, however, have a large scholarly clientele. CompuServe's starter kit costs $30 and includes some free access time. After 6 P.M., the charge is $6 an hour with a 300-baud modem and $12.50 an hour with a 1200-baud modem.

The Dow Jones/News Retrieval, out of Princeton, New Jersey, also uses the value-added networks listed above for access. It includes the Cineman Movie Reviews and Grolier Academic American Encyclopedia data bases. It requires a $30 registration kit and, after 6 P.M., costs $9 to $12 at 300 baud and $18 to $24 at 1200 baud.

The Source, out of McLean, Virginia, can be accessed not only with the three value-added networks already mentioned but also with SourceNet and Uninet. It includes the Education and Careers data bases and bulletin boards such as Library Forum. The cost is $49.95 for registration and, after 6 P.M., $7.75 an hour at 300 baud and $10.75 at 1200 baud.

If you are lucky, your institution already belongs to one of the two university networks. Bitnet is primarily for IBM mainframe systems and allows for electronic mail and file transfer but does not include a bulletin board. If you have access to Bitnet, you can speedily send large files such as a book-length manuscript or a substantial data base to a colleague at a member institution. Such an arrangement can be quite valuable for collaborative editing, research, and writing projects. Usenet is primarily for UNIX mainframe systems. It not only has electronic mail and file transfer capabilities but also offers bulletin boards for special interests.

BIBLIOGRAPHIC DATA BASES

The most useful for literary scholars is DIALOG Information Services, out of Palo Alto, California, which has, among others, the *MLA Bibliography* and ERIC (Educational Resources Information Center) available on-line. Most major research libraries now have access to Dialog, but you don't need a librarian to do a search. You can use almost any communications software and a modem. There is no registration fee, but there is an hourly charge after 6 P.M. For more information, call 800-334-2564.

For data bases in linguistics and CAI, try CALICO (acronym for Computer-Assisted Language Learning and Instruction Consortium). Call 801-378-6533 to apply for a password or write CALICO Data Base, 3078 JKHB, Brigham Young University, Provo, Utah 84602. There is no access fee, but the user must pay for the long-distance phone call required for the hookup.

Another bibliographic data base service is BRS After Dark, out of Latham, New York. Although it includes ERIC, Language and Language Behavior Abstracts, and Arts and Humanities Citation Index, its holdings in the humanities are not extensive. In fact, several years ago the MLA withdrew its file. It can be accessed through Telenet, DataPac, and Uninet for a $50 registration fee and $6 to $15 an hour.

MACHINE-READABLE TEXTS

The following repositories house major data bases of machine-readable literary texts and expository writing. For information on current holdings and policies governing access to the texts you need, write to them care of the address indicated.

English Texts

Brown Corpus
Department of Linguistics
Brown University
Providence, RI 02912

International Computer Archive of Modern English
Dr. Stig Johansson
University of Oslo
Oslo
Norway

Oxford Archive of English Literature
Oxford University Computing Service
13 Bambury Road
Oxford
England

French Texts

Institut National de la Langue Francaise
44 avenue de la Libération
54014 Nancy
France

ARTFL (American and French Research on the Treasury of the French
Language)
Department of Romance Languages and Literatures
University of Chicago
1050 East 59th Street
Chicago IL 60637

Italian Texts

CNUCE (Centro Nationale Universitario di Calcolo Eletronico)
Via Santa Maria 36
56100 Pisa
Italy

Greek Texts

Thesaurus Linguae Graecae
University of California at Irvine
Irvine, CA 92717

Latin and Greek Texts

LIBRI Archive
Kiewit Computation Centre
Dartmouth College
Hanover, NH 03755

PROFESSIONAL ORGANIZATIONS

Association for Computing Machinery, Special Interest Group on Language
Analysis and Studies in the Humanities, 11 West 42nd Street, Third Floor,
New York, NY 10036.

ACH (Association for Computers in the Humanities), Harry Lincoln, Music
Department, SUNY, Binghamton, New York 13201.

Association for Computational Linguistics; Dr. Donald E. Walker, Bell Communications Research, 445 South Street, Morristown, NJ 07960.

ALLC (Association for Literary and Linguistic Computing), J. P. G. Roper, ALLC Conference Secretariat, University of East Anglia, Computing Center, Norwich NR4 7TJ, United Kingdom.

ACL (Association for Computational Linguistics), Donald E. Walker, Bell Communications Research, 445 South Street, Morristown, NJ 07960.

EDUCOM, Interuniversity Communications Council, P.O. Box 364, Princeton, NJ 08540.

International Council for Computers in Education (ICCE), 1787 Agate Street, University of Oregon, Eugene, OR 97403.

Society for Conceptual and Content Analysis by Computer, Roy A. Boggs, Department of Computer Systems, The University of Toledo, 2801 West Bancroft Street, Toledo, Ohio 43606.

APPENDIX II

Selected Journals and Periodicals

ACH Newsletter
Association for Computers and the Humanities, University of Minnesota, 209
Lind Hall, Minneapolis, MN 55455

Apple Journal of Courseware Review
Apple Educational Foundation, 20525 Mariani Ave., Cupertino, CA 95014

Association for Literary and Linguistic Computing *Bulletin*
T. N. Corns, Dept. of English, UCNW, Bangor, Gwynedd LL57 2DG, Wales

British Journal of Educational Technology
Council for Educational Technology for the United Kingdom, 3 Devonshire
Street, London W1N 2BA, England

Byte
McGraw-Hill Publications, 70 Main St., Peterborough, NH 03458

C.A.C. Journal [Computer-Assisted Composition]
Methodist College, 5400 Ramsey St., Fayetteville, NC 28301

CALICO Journal
Computer-Assisted Language Learning and Instruction Consortium, Brigham
Young University, Provo, UT 84602

Callboard
Ealing College of Higher Education, St. Mary's Rd., London, England W5 5RF

Classroom Computer Learning
Pitman Learning Inc., 19 Davis Dr., Belmont, CA 94002

Collegiate Microcomputer
Rose-Hulman Institute of Technology, Terre Haute, IN 47803

Computers and Composition
Dept. of English, Colorado State University, Fort Collins, CO 80523

Computers and Education: An International Journal
Pergamon Press, Inc., Journals Division, Maxwell House, Fairview Park,
Elmsford, NY 10523

Computers and the Humanities
Paradigm Press, Box 1057, Osprey, FL 33559-1057

Computers and Translation
Paradigm Press, Box 1057, Osprey, FL 33559-1057

The Computing Teacher
International Council for Computers in Education, 1787 Agate St.,
University of Oregon, Eugene, OR 97403

Creative Computing
Ahl Computing, Inc., 39 E. Hanover Ave., Morris Plains, NJ 07950

Educational Computing
30–31 Islington Green, London N1, England

Educational Technology
140 Sylvan Ave., Englewood Cliffs, NJ 07632

Electronic Learning
902 Sylvan Ave., Box 2001, Englewood Cliffs, NJ 07632

English Microlab Registry
2513 61st St., Lubbock, TX 79413

ICAME NEWS
Newsletter of the International Computer Archive of Modern English,
Norwegian Computing Centre for the Humanities, Harald Hårfagres gate 31,
P.O. Box 53, N- 5014 Bergen–University, Norway

Instructional Innovator
Association for Education Communication and Technology, 1126 16th St. NW,
Washington, D.C. 20036

Journal of Computer-Based Instruction
Association for Development of Computer-Based Instructional Systems,
Western Washington University, Bellingham, WA 98225

Journal of Courseware Review
Box 28426, San Jose, CA 95159

Journal of Educational Computing Research
New Hampshire College, 2500 N. River Rd., Manchester, NH 03104.

Literary and Linguistic Computing
Oxford University Press, Walton St., Oxford OX2 6DP, UK.

Media and Methods
1511 Walnut St., Philadelphia, PA 19102

PC World
555 De Haro St., San Francisco, CA 94107

Personal Computing
Hayden Publishing Co., 50 Essex St., Rochelle Park, NJ 07662

Perspectives in Computing: Applications in the Academic and Scientific Community
IBM Corporation, 44 South Broadway, White Plains, New York 10601

Pipeline
CONDUIT, University of Iowa, Box 388, Iowa City, IA 52244

Research in Word Processing Newsletter
South Dakota School of Mines and Technology, Rapid City, SD 57701

SCOPE (Scholarly Communication: Online Publishing and Education)
Queens College of the City University of New York, Flushing, New York 11367

T.H.E. Journal
Technological Horizons in Education; free to qualified educators;
Information Synergy, Inc., Box 15126, Santa Ana, CA 92705-0126

APPENDIX III

Selected Bibliography

SUBJECT INDEX TO THE BIBLIOGRAPHY

The numbers below correspond to bibliographical items in the bibliography which follows.

Word Processing

18, 19, 46, 48, 53, 59, 60, 64, 87, 89, 90, 95, 96, 115, 131, 133, 148, 168, 186, 190, 209, 211, 214, 231, 242, 243, 250, 264, 268, 281, 286, 296, 303, 304, 319, 324, 333, 341, 368, 417, 423, 458, 465, 478, 487, 488, 489, 490, 491, 498, 513, 518, 522, 540, 543, 545, 552, 554, 569, 584, 621, 622, 669, 670, 717, 718, 746, 757, 777, 791, 796, 797, 799, 801, 834, 843, 847, 851, 875, 876

The Computer in the Writing Classroom

8, 13, 20, 21, 24, 25, 26, 27, 28, 29, 30, 31, 34, 36, 38, 41, 45, 49, 52, 62, 69, 74, 78, 82, 86, 91, 92, 93, 94, 100, 101, 108, 109, 110, 111, 112, 115, 120, 121, 123, 128, 132, 133, 144, 147, 151, 159, 163, 164, 166, 167, 171, 173, 183, 184, 185, 187, 205, 210, 222, 239, 240, 245, 254, 255, 261, 269, 271, 273, 275, 278, 280, 284, 286, 287, 292, 300, 308, 310, 311, 312, 318, 320, 322, 323, 329, 330, 340, 343, 349, 350, 355, 364, 370, 371, 372, 373, 389, 390, 396, 397, 402, 403, 408, 409, 414, 418, 425, 428, 431, 440, 443, 450, 451, 454, 455, 462, 463, 464, 466, 469, 473, 475, 476, 477, 479, 483, 484, 489, 492, 495, 497, 499, 503, 505, 506, 507, 508, 512, 513, 514, 523, 527, 538, 548, 551, 553, 556, 564, 567, 573, 575, 581, 586, 587, 593, 605, 608, 610, 611, 617, 618, 624, 630, 631, 647, 649, 660, 664, 665, 671, 678, 680, 682, 687, 688, 692, 693, 709, 713, 714, 715, 717, 718, 722, 723, 724, 727, 728, 729, 732, 734, 735, 736, 737, 738, 739, 749, 755, 761, 769, 772, 774, 775, 776, 777, 779, 780, 781, 782, 790, 791, 795, 796, 798, 799, 800, 806, 809, 810, 811, 814, 825, 826, 829, 836, 839, 841, 843, 845, 846, 847, 853, 865, 870, 871, 872, 873, 874, 877, 878, 879, 880, 881, 882, 896

Literary and Stylistic Analysis

1, 4, 10, 12, 14, 17, 33, 63, 66, 73, 79, 80, 81, 83, 84, 98, 115, 134, 141, 145, 150, 169, 200, 203, 207, 212, 218, 219, 221, 224, 225, 232, 246, 252, 263, 265, 266, 267, 270, 276, 282, 299, 338, 344, 345, 346, 356, 360, 376, 377, 378, 379, 392, 395, 401, 411, 413, 415, 419, 429, 445, 449, 453, 467, 468, 472, 480, 489, 511, 520, 524, 525, 526, 530, 531, 535, 536, 546, 549, 550, 558, 559, 560, 561, 571, 576, 577, 579, 597, 599, 607, 619, 639, 641, 642, 646, 672, 673, 674, 675, 676, 678, 685, 695, 711, 730, 731, 752, 756, 765, 766, 767, 768, 771, 793, 803, 804, 805, 807, 813, 816, 820, 835, 842, 855, 856, 857, 859, 861, 863, 864, 890

Data Bases, Networks, Bibliographies

4, 15, 22, 34, 54, 68, 88, 99, 115, 129, 192, 193, 194, 216, 220, 233, 234, 241, 247, 253, 258, 285, 301, 326, 337, 345, 346, 392, 410, 472, 489, 539, 541, 542, 544, 557, 570, 577, 585, 600, 607, 609, 612, 616, 617, 626, 648, 655, 659, 685, 697, 698, 699, 703, 710, 725, 726, 741, 756, 763, 764, 837, 863

Concordances

4, 14, 50, 55, 65, 67, 113, 114, 115, 172, 174, 195, 202, 226, 309, 344, 345, 346, 348, 381, 382, 392, 472, 489, 532, 577, 606, 607, 679, 685, 730, 862, 863

Second Language Learning

3, 6, 7, 22, 23, 38, 39, 40, 44, 47, 56, 58, 61, 70, 77, 85, 97, 103, 104, 105, 106, 115, 118, 124, 126, 135, 136, 138, 139, 140, 143, 149, 154, 155, 157, 158, 160, 161, 162, 170, 177, 178, 179, 180, 181, 188, 189, 191, 196, 197, 198, 201, 204, 208, 223, 229, 230, 236, 237, 244, 248, 249, 251, 257, 260, 262, 279, 294, 297, 307, 315, 316, 317, 325, 327, 334, 336, 339, 342, 352, 353, 354, 361, 362, 363, 374, 385, 386, 388, 393, 394, 397, 398, 399, 400, 404, 405, 406, 407, 412, 416, 420, 421, 430, 434, 435, 437, 438, 444, 447, 457, 459, 461, 474, 481, 482, 509, 515, 517, 521, 562, 563, 566, 574, 588, 589, 590, 603, 604, 623, 627, 629, 632, 633, 634, 635, 636, 637, 638, 644, 645, 650, 654, 658, 666, 667, 668, 681, 683, 684, 686, 689, 691, 696, 700, 701, 702, 704, 705, 706, 710, 720, 733, 740, 762, 770, 773, 789, 792, 794, 808, 812, 815, 817, 818, 819, 822, 823, 824, 830, 831, 832, 837, 838, 849, 850, 861, 867, 885, 886, 887, 888, 889, 891

Computer-Assisted Instruction in English

3, 7, 11, 22, 29, 30, 37, 38, 44, 51, 56, 57, 58, 61, 75, 76, 97, 102, 103, 104, 105, 106, 115, 122, 124, 125, 126, 137, 149, 153, 154, 155, 156, 165, 171, 191, 197, 199, 208, 215, 228, 236, 237, 248, 249, 251, 257, 260, 262, 279, 284, 294, 295, 297, 314, 316, 325, 335, 342, 363, 367, 369, 374, 387, 393, 398, 399, 404, 405, 407, 420, 421, 424, 430, 434, 435, 437, 444, 448, 452, 453, 456, 457, 458, 460, 482, 496, 499, 501, 502, 504, 509, 510, 519, 521, 528, 553, 555, 574, 580, 582, 583, 588, 602, 603, 608, 620, 622, 623, 627, 629, 634, 644, 650, 652, 654, 657, 658, 682, 683, 684, 686, 687, 688, 691, 696, 700, 704, 705, 707, 713, 716, 719, 720, 721, 733, 736, 740, 747, 748, 749, 750, 758, 773, 786, 810, 830, 832, 833, 837, 838, 858, 861, 868, 869, 872, 891

Linguistics, Lexicography, Translation

5, 9, 16, 18, 42, 43, 73, 115, 119, 259, 288, 293, 321, 375, 384, 442, 446, 500, 516, 520, 529, 561, 597, 601, 619, 625, 628, 651, 656, 708, 751, 813, 827, 828, 856, 861, 883

Textual Editing, Indices

4, 32, 35, 96, 107, 115, 116, 117, 142, 146, 175, 176, 241, 272, 277, 289, 290, 291, 319, 365, 366, 383, 391, 392, 423, 432, 433, 472, 485, 489, 533, 534, 547, 565, 577, 578, 594, 595, 596, 598, 607, 613, 690, 742, 743, 744, 745, 753, 785, 854, 863, 892, 893, 894

SELECTED BIBLIOGRAPHY

1   Abercrombie, John R. *Computer Programs for Literary Analysis.* Philadelphia: University of Pennsylvania Press, 1984. [With diskettes for IBM-PC (DOS 2.0), Apple Macintosh, and DEC Rainbow.]

2   *Academic's Guide to Microcomputer Systems.* Toronto, Canada: University of Toronto Computing Services, 1985.

3   Ahmad, Khurshid, et al., eds. *Computers, Language Learning, and Language Teaching.* New Directions in Language Teaching Series. Cambridge, MA: Cambridge University Press, 1985.

4   Aitken, A. J., R. W. Bailey, and N. Hamilton Smith, eds. *The Computer and Literary Studies.* Edinburgh, Scotland: Edinburgh University Press, 1973.

5   Akkerman, Erik. *Designing a Computerized Lexicon for Linguistic Purposes.* Atlantic Highlands, NJ: Rodopi-Humanities, 1985.

6   Alatis, James E. "The Application of Instructional Technology to Language Learning." *CALICO Journal* 1.1 (1983):9–12, 14.

7   Aleman-Centeno, Josefina R. "Computerized Audio-Visual Instructional Sequences (CAVIS): A Versatile System for Listening Comprehension in Foreign Language Teaching." *NALLD Journal* 17.3–4 (1983):24–26.

8   Alexander, John, and Fred Swartz. "The Dynamics of Computer-Assisted Writing Sample Measurements at Ferris State College." Annual Meeting of the Michigan Council of Teachers of English. Lansing, MI: October 29–31, 1982. ERIC Document ED 233 344.

9   Alford, M. H. T. "The Computer and Lexicography." *ALLC Bulletin* 1.3 (1973): 8–9.

10 Allais, Chr., and Cl. Allais. "A Method of Structural Analysis with an Application to *Les Liaisons dangereuses.*" *R.E.L.O. Revue* 2 (1968):13–33.

11 Allen, Brockenbrough S. "The Video-Computer Nexus: Towards an Agenda for Instructional Development." *Journal of Educational Technology Systems* 10.2 (1981):81–99.

12 Allen, John R. "Methods of Author Identification Through Stylistic Analysis." *French Review* 47 (1974):904–916.

13 Allen, O. Jane. "Professional Writing and Computer Programming: Some Parallels." In *Sixth International Conference on Computers and the Humanities,* edited by Sarah K. Burton and Douglas D. Short. New York: Computer Science Press, 1983, pp. 1–3.

14 Allen, Robert F. *Beyond Concordances: Stylo-Statistical Analysis of Literary Texts.* Paper presented at the convention of the Modern Language Association of America, 1984.

15 —, ed. *Data Bases in the Humanities and Social Sciences.* Osprey, FL: Paradigm Press, 1985.

16 Alterman, R. "A Dictionary Based on Concept Coherence." *Artificial Intelligence* 25.2 (February 1985):153–186.

17 Anderson, C. W., and G. E. McMaster. "Objective Analysis of Emotional Tone in Stories and Poems." *ALLC Journal* 3.2 (Autumn 1982):45–51.

18 Anderson, Lloyd. "Multi-lingual Word-Processing Systems: Desirable Features from a Linguist's Point of View." *Newsletter for Asian and Middle Eastern Languages on Computer* 1.1 (January 1985):28–30.

19 Anderson, Neil. "Writing-Process Software and the Individual Writer." *NCTE-ACE Newsletter* 1.2 (October–December 1985):11–12.

20 Anderson, Peter. "Classroom Publishing with Micros." *The Computing Teacher* 13.2 (October 1985):16–17.

21 Andrews, Deborah C. "Writer's Slump and Revision Schemes: Effects of Computers on the Composing Process." In *Collected Essays on the Written Word and the Word Processor,* edited by Thomas E. Martinez. Villanova, PA: Villanova University Press, 1984, pp. 243–250.

22 Arkwright, Thomas D. "Issues and Realities in Computer-Based Instruction: A Bibliography." *NALLD Journal* 17.3–4 (1983):15–21.

23 —. "Selected Videodisc Projects in Second Language Training at the Defense Language Institute." *Videodisc News* 1.6 (1980):1–5.

24 Arms, Valerie M. "Collaborative Writing on a Word Processor." Conference Record: The Many Facets of Computer Communications, IEEE Professional Communication Society, Atlanta, GA: October 19–21, 1983, pp. 85–86.

25 —. "The Computer and the Process of Composition." *Pipeline* 8 (Spring 1983): 16–18.

26 —. "Computers, Creativity, and Composition." In *Sixth International Conference on Computers and the Humanities,* edited by Sarah K. Burton and Douglas D. Short. Rockville, MD: Computer Science Press, 1983, pp. 4–7.

27 —. "Creating and Recreating." *College Composition and Communication* 24 (October 1983):355–358.

28 —. "A Dyslexic Can Compose on a Computer." *Educational Technology* 24 (January 1984):39–41.

29 Aronis, J. M., and S. Katz. "RICHARD: An Interactive Computer Program for Rhetorical Invention." *Educational Technology* 24.11 (November 1984): 26–30.

30 —. "INQUIRY: A Computer Program Based on Rhetorical Theory." *Educational Technology* 25.2 (February 1985):37–39.

31 Aschauer, Mary Ann, and Fred D. White. "Towards a Marriage of Two Minds: The Word Processor and Natural Habits of Thought in the 'Discovery' State of Composing." In *Collected Essays on the Written Word and the Word Processor,* edited by Thomas E. Martinez. Villanova, PA: Villanova University Press, 1984, pp. 188–204.

32 Association of American Publishers. *A Provisional Standard for Preparing and Processing Manuscripts on Computers.* Washington, DC: Association of American Publishers, 1986.

33 Austin, Warren B. "The Authorship of Certain Renaissance English Pamphlets." In *Proceedings: Computer Applications to Problems in the Humanities,* edited by Frederick M. Burelbach, Jr. Brockport, NY: SUNY College at Brockport, 1970, pp. 93–99.

34 Autrey, Ken. *Word Processing and Writing Instruction: An Annotated Bibliography.* Columbia: University of South Carolina English Dept., 1985.

35 Avery, Laurence G. "An Edition of Letters: The Computer in Textual Criticism." In *Sixth International Conference on Computers and the Humanities,* edited by Sarah K. Burton and Douglas D. Short. Rockville, MD: Computer Science Press, 1983, pp. 8–12.

36 Bacig Thomas, Donald Larmouth, and Kenneth Risdon. "A Comprehensive Computer-Aided Program in Writing." In *Computers and Composition: Selected Papers from the Conference on Computers in Writing: New Directions in Teaching and Research, University of Minnesota, April 1984,* edited by Lillian Bridwell, Donald Ross, Cynthia L. Selfe, and Kathleen E. Kiefer. Houghton, MI, and Fort Collins, CO: Michigan Technological University and Colorado State University, 1985, pp. 1–22.

37 Bacig, Thomas D., and Donald W. Larmouth. "Thinking and Writing: CAI in Teaching Composition." *SCCS: Proceedings of the 19th Annual Small College Computing Symposium,* edited by Dale Rognlie. Rapid City, SD: South Dakota School of Mines and Technology, April 11–12, 1986, pp. 1–11.

38 Baker, J. *Microcomputers in the Classroom.* Bloomington, IN: Phi Delta Kappa Foundation, 1982.

39 Baker, Robert L. "An Experience with Voice-Based Learning." *CALICO Journal* 1.4 (1984):17–19.

40 ——. "Foreign-Language Software: The State of the Art or Pick a Card, Any (Flash) Card." *CALICO Journal* 2.1 (September 1984):6–10, 27.

41 Balkema, Sandra J. "Studying the Composing Activities of Experienced Computer Writers." In *Computers and Composition: Selected Papers from the Conference on Computers in Writing: New Directions in Teaching and Research, University of Minnesota, April 1984,* edited by Lillian Bridwell, Donald Ross, Cynthia L. Selfe, and Kathleen E. Kiefer. Houghton, MI, and Fort Collins, CO: Michigan Technological University and Colorado State University, 1985, pp. 23–35.

42 Bara, Bruno G., and Giovanni Guida, eds. *Computational Models of Natural Language Processing.* New York: North-Holland, 1984.

43 Barden, William. "Speech Synthesis and Recognition." *Popular Computing* 1.11 (1982):129.

44 Barger, Robert Newton. "The Computer as a Humanizing Influence in Education." *T H E Journal* 10 (1983):109–11.

45 Barker, Thomas T. "The English Department Microlab: An Endangered Species?" *Research in Word Processing Newsletter* 3.9 (December 1985):2–5.

46 Barnet, Sylvan, and Marcia Stubbs. "From Subject to Essay Using a Word Processor." *Barnet and Stubbs's Practical Guide to Writing.* 5th ed. Boston: Little, Brown and Company, 1986, pp. 29–32.

47 Barson, J., *et al.* "University-Level CAI in French." *University-Level Computer-Assisted Instruction at Stanford: 1968–80,* edited by Patrick Suppes. Stanford, CA: Stanford University Press, 1981, pp. 685–706.

48 Bassler, Richard A. "Word Processing for Educators and Researchers Using Very-Low-Cost Microcomputers." In *Western Educational Computing Conference 1983* (California Education Computing Consortium). North Hollywood, CA: Western Periodicals, 1983, pp. 147–153.

49 Bates, Peter. "How to Turn Your Writing into Communication: Computer-Prompted Prose Doesn't Always Sing, But It Gets to the Heart of the Matter." *Personal Computing* 8.10 (October 1984):84–93.

50 Baudelaire, Charles. "Réflexions sur quelques-uns de mes contemporains: Théodore de Banville." In *Oeuvres complètes.* Paris, France: Seuil, 1968, pp. 481–483.

51 Baum, Joan, ed. *Computers in the English Class: With Particular Attention to CUNY.* Research Monograph Series 6 (October 1983).

52 Bean, John C. "Computerized Word-Processing as an Aid to Revision." *College English* 34.2 (May 1983):146–148.

53 Becker, Joseph D. "Multilingual Word Processing." *Scientific American* 251.1 (July 1984):96–107.

54 Becker, Lawrence. "Notebook II: A Database Manager for Text." *Computers and the Humanities* 19.1 (January–March 1985):53–56.

55 Bedford, Emmett G., and Robert Dilligan, eds. *A Concordance to the Poems of Alexander Pope.* Detroit, MI: Gale Research Co, 1974.

56 Behmer, Daniel Edward. "The Teacher/Pupil/Computer Partnership in Instructional Computing." *CALICO Journal* 1.5 (1984):9–11.

57 Bell, Kathleen. "The Computer and the English Classroom." *English Journal* 69 (December 1980):88–90.

58 Bell, T. H. "Effective Use of Computers in Schools Requires Coordinated Development." *T.H.E. Journal* 11.5 (1984):80–83.

59 Bencivenga, J. "Electronic Editing as a Tool." *English Journal* 71 (January 1982):91–92.

60 Bengel, Jane Walters. "Is Word-Processing Words-Worth It?" In *Collected Essays on the Written Word and the Word Processor,* edited by Thomas E. Martinez. Villanova, PA: Villanova University Press, 1984, pp. 301–312.

61 Berggren, Ruth. "The Road to Improved Software: Computer Literate Faculty." In *Computers and Composition: Selected Papers from the Conference on Computers in Writing: New Directions in Teaching and Research, University of Minnesota, April 1984,* edited by Lillian Bridwell, Donald Ross, Cynthia L. Selfe, and Kathleen E. Kiefer. Houghton, MI, and Fort Collins, CO: Michigan Technological University and Colorado State University, 1985, pp. 37–44.

62 Berlin, James A., and Rajesh Singha. "The Cincinnati Study: A Computerized Method for Evaluating a Freshman Writing Program." In *Sixth International*

Conference on Computers and the Humanities, edited by Sarah K. Burton and Douglas D. Short. Rockville, MD: Computer Science Press, 1983, p. 13.

63   Bernet, Charles. *Le Vocabulaire des tragédies de Jean Racine.* Paris/Geneva, Switzerland: Champion/Slatkine, 1983.

64   Bernhardt, Stephen A. "Seeing the Text." *College Composition and Communication* 37.1 (February 1986):66–67.

65   Berry-Rogghe, G. L. M. "COCOA—A Word Count and Concordance Generator." *ALLC Bulletin* 1.2 (1973):29–31.

66   —. "The Computation of Collocations and Their Relevance in Lexical Studies." In *The Computer and Literary Study,* edited by Aitken, Bailey, and Hamilton-Smith. Edinburgh, Scotland: Edinburgh University Press, 1973, pp. 103–112.

67   Bevan, E. Dean, ed. *A Concordance to the Plays and Prefaces of Bernard Shaw.* Detroit, MI: Gale Research Co, 1971.

68   "Bibliography Programs for Humanities Scholars." *MLA Newsletter* 15.3 (1983):6.

69   Bickel, Linda L. "Word Processing and the Integration of Reading and Writing Instruction." In *Writing On-Line: Using Computers in the Teaching of English,* edited by James L. Collins and Elizabeth A. Sommers. Upper Montclair, NJ: Boynton-Cook, 1985, pp. 39–45.

70   Blomeyer, Robert L. "Computer-Based Foreign Language Instruction in Illinois Schools." *CALICO Journal* 1.4 (1984):35–40, 42–44.

71   Bodmer, George R. "The Apple Ate My Paper." *College English* 46.6 (October 1984):610–611.

72   Bolter, J. David. "Information and Knowledge: The Computer As a Medium of Humanistic Communication." *Federation Reports: The Journal of the State Humanities Councils* 8.1 (January–February 1985):1–8.

73   Bolz, N., and G. Willee. "WISILB—A Computer Program Which Counts Syllables in English Words." *Sprache and Datenverarbeitung* 6.1–2 (1982):43–47.

74   Bonner, Paul. "Enter, the Powerful New Idea Tools." *Personal Computing* 8.1 (January 1984):70–79, 190–191.

75   Booth, Wayne C. "Catching the Overflow." *College English* 46 (February 1984): 140–142.

76   Bourque, Joseph H. "Understanding and Evaluating: The Humanist as Computer Specialist." *College English* 45.1 (January 1983):67–73.

77   Boyd, Gary, *et al.* "Remedial and Second Language English Teaching." *Computers and Education* 6.1 (1982):105–112.

78   Bradley, Virginia N. "Improving Students' Writing with Micro-Computers." *Language Arts* 59 (October 1982):732–743.

79   Brainerd, Bernard. "An Exploratory Study of Pronouns and Articles as Indices of Genre in English." *Language and Style* 5 (1972):239–259.

80.   —. "Statistical Analysis of Lexical Data Using Chi-Squared and Related Distributions." *Computers and the Humanities* 9 (1975):161–178.

81 —. *Weighing Evidence in Language and Literature: A Statistical Approach.* Toronto: University of Toronto Press, 1974.

82 Brandt, Ron. "On Reading, Writing, and Computers." *Educational Leadership* 39 (1981):60–64.

83 Bratley, Paul, and Paul A. Fortier. "Themes, Statistics and the French Novel." In *Sixth International Conference on Computers and the Humanities,* edited by Sarah K. Burton and Douglas D. Short. Rockville, MD: Computer Science Press, 1983, pp. 18–25.

84 Bratley, Paul, and Serge Lusignan. *Le Traitement des textes par ordinateur.* Montreal, Canada: University of Montreal Press, 1979.

85 Braun, Theodore E. D., and George M. Mulford. "Computer-Assisted Instruction as an Integral Part of a First Semester French Curriculum." *CHum* 18 (1984):47–56.

86 Brenner, Patricia A. "Software Applicable to the Needs of Student Writers." In *Sixth International Conference on Computers and the Humanities,* edited by Sarah K. Burton and Douglas D. Short. Rockville, MD: Computer Science Press, 1983, pp. 26–27.

87 Brent, Harry. "Word Processing in the Humanities: Advantages and Limitations." In *Collected Essays on the Written Word and the Word Processor,* edited by Thomas E. Martinez. Villanova, PA: Villanova University Press, 1984, pp. 8–14.

88 Brett, George. "The Electronic Newsletter." In *Sixth International Conference on Computers and the Humanities,* edited by Sarah K. Burton and Douglas D. Short. Rockville, MD: Computer Science Press, 1983, pp. 39–46.

89 Brewer, Daryln. "Word Processors: Do They Help Writers?" In *Humanizing the Computer: A Cure for the Deadly Embrace,* edited by Douglas Flahery. Belmont, CA: Wadsworth, 1986, pp. 120–124.

90 Bridwell, Lillian, and Ann Duin. "Looking In-Depth at Writers: Computers as Writing Medium and Research Tool." In *Writing On-Line: Using Computers in the Teaching of Writing,* edited by J. Collins and E. Sommers. New York: Boynton-Cook, 1985, pp. 115–121.

91 Bridwell, L., Parker Johnson, and Stephen Brehe. "Composing and Computers: Case Studies of Experienced Writers." In *Writing in Real Time: Modelling Production Processes,* edited by A. Matsuhashi. London: Longman, 1985.

92 Bridwell, L., Paula Reed Nancarrow, and Donald Ross. "The Writing Process and the Writing Machine: Current Research on Word Processors Relevant to the Teaching of Composition." In *New Directions in Composition Research,* edited by R. Beach and L. Bridwell. New York: Guildford Press, 1984.

93 Bridwell, L., and Donald Ross. "Integrating Computers Into a Writing Curriculum; or, Buying, Begging, and Building." In *The Computer in Composition Instruction,* edited by William Wresch. Urbana, IL: NCTE, 1984, pp. 107–119.

94 Bridwell, L., Geoffrey Sirc, and Robert Brooke. "Revising and Computing: Case Studies of Student Writers." In *The Acquisition of Written Language: Revision and Response,* edited by Sarah Freedman. Norwood, NJ: Ablex, 1985.

95   Brightman, Richard W., and Jeffrey M. Dimsdale. "Will Word Processing Take
      the 'Creative' Out of Creative Writing?" In *Using Computers in an Information
      Age.* New York: Delmar Publishers, 1986, pp. 371–372.

96   Brock, Thomas D. "Computers and Word Processors." In *Successful Textbook
      Publishing: the Author's Guide.* Madison, WI: Science Tech Publishers, 1985,
      pp. 137–157.

97   Brown, Peggy, ed. "Computer-Based Learning." *Forum for Liberal Education* 3.7
      (1981). ERIC Document ED 202 271.

98   Bruno, Agnes M. *Toward a Quantitative Methodology for Stylistic Analyses.* Berke-
      ley: University of California Press, 1974.

99   Budd, John. "The Uses of Online Bibliographic Searching in Literary Re-
      search." In *Sixth International Conference on Computers and the Humanities,* edited
      by Sarah K. Burton and Douglas D. Short. Rockville, MD: Computer Science
      Press, 1983, pp. 39–46.

100   Bullock, Richard H. "Basic Issues in Computer-Related Research in Writing."
      In *Collected Essays on the Written Word and the Word Processor,* edited by Thomas
      E. Martinez. Villanova, PA: Villanova University Press, 1984, pp. 348–358.

101   —. "The Lure of the Cursor, The Fear of the Byte: Affective Responses to
      Word Processors." In *Computers and Composition: Selected Papers from the Confer-
      ence on Computers in Writing: New Directions in Teaching and Research, University
      of Minnesota, April 1984,* edited by Lillian Bridwell, Donald Ross, Cynthia L.
      Selfe, and Kathleen E. Kiefer. Houghton, MI, and Fort Collins, CO: Michi-
      gan Technological University and Colorado State University, 1985, pp.
      45–55.

102   Burchard, Gina M. "Computer-Assisted Instruction in Technical Writing." In
      PCC 84: The Practical Aspects of Engineering Communication. Conference Record.
      New York: IEEE, 1984, pp. 65–66.

103   Burghardt, Wolfram. "Language Authoring with 'Comet.'" *CHum* 18 (1984):
      165–172.

104   Burke, Robert. *CAI with PILOT.* Englewood Cliffs, NJ: Prentice Hall, 1982.

105   —. *CAI Sourcebook.* Englewood Cliffs, NJ: Prentice Hall, 1982.

106   Burnett, J. Dale, and Larry Miller. "Computer-Assisted Learning and Reading:
      Developing the Product or Fostering the Process?" *Computers and Education*
      8.1 (1984):145–50.

107   Burns, Diane, and S. Venit. "PCs and Typesetters: A Mixed Marriage. Thanks
      to Front-end Software, PCs Can Now Drive Typesetters and Laser Printers
      Directly, Generating Both Reproduction-Quality Copy and Real Cost Sav-
      ings." *PC: The Independent Guide to IBM Personal Computers.* 4.25 (December
      10 1985):194–195, 202.

108   Burns, Hugh. "The Challenge for Computer-Assisted Rhetoric." *Computers
      and the Humanities* 18.3–4 (July–December 1984):173–181.

109   —. "Computer-Assisted Prewriting Activities: Harmonics for Invention." In
      Computers in Composition Instruction. Proceedings from the SWRL Educational
      Research and Development, Los Alamitos, CA, April 22–23, 1984, pp. 19–29.

110 —. "Computing as a Way of Brainstorming in English Composition." In *Proceedings of the NECC 1981 National Educational Computing Conference* (1981): 105–108.

111 —. "Recollections of First-Generation Computer-Assisted Prewriting." In *The Computer in Composition Instruction: A Writer's Tool,* edited by William Wresch. Urbana, IL: NTCE, 1984, pp. 15–33.

112 Burns, Hugh, and George H. Culp. "Stimulating Invention in English Composition Through Computer-Assisted Instruction." *Educational Technology* 20.8 (August 1980):5–10.

113 Burton, Delores M. "Automated Concordances and Word-Indexes: Machine Decisions and Editorial Revisions." *CHum* 16 (1982):195–218.

114 —. "Some Uses of a Grammatical Concordance." *CHum* 2 (1968):145–154.

115 Burton, Sarah K., and Douglas D. Short, eds. *Sixth International Conference on Computers and the Humanities.* Rockville, MD: Computer Science Press, 1983.

116 Busa, Roberto. "Computer Processing of Over Ten Million Words: Retrospective Criticism." In *The Computer in Literary and Linguistic Studies,* edited by Jones and Churchhouse. Cardiff, Wales: University of Wales Press, 1976, pp. 114–117.

117 —. *Index Thomisticus: Sancti Thomai Aquinatis Operum Omnium Indices et Concordantiae. . . .* 23 vols. Stuttgart, West Germany: Frommann-Holzboog, 1974.

118 Bush, Michael D., Gunther A. Mueller, and David M. Schrupp. "Klavier im Haus: An Interactive Video Experiment in Foreign Language Instruction." *CALICO Journal* 1.2 (1983):17–21.

119 Butler, Christopher. *Computers in Linguistics.* New York: Basil Blackwell, 1985.

120 Byrd, David G., Paula R. Feldman, and Phyllis Fleishel. *The Microcomputer and Business Writing.* New York: Random House, 1986.

121 Cacha, Frances B. "A Creative Writing Project in Logo and BASIC." *The Computing Teacher* 12.6 (March 1985):35–36.

122 Campbell, Jeremy. *Grammatical Man: Information, Entropy, Language, and Life.* Rockville, MD: Computer Science Press, 1983.

123 Campbell, John J., and Kathy J. Karlson. "Computers in Writing Instruction: A Model for Training." In *Computers and Composition: Selected Papers from the Conference on Computers in Writing: New Directions in Teaching and Research, University of Minnesota, April 1984,* edited by Lillian Bridwell, Donald Ross, Cynthia L. Selfe, and Kathleen E. Kiefer. Houghton, MI, and Fort Collins, CO: Michigan Technological University and Colorado State University, 1985, pp. 57–66.

124 Campanini, S. "Learning Characteristics of the Disadvantaged: Implications for CAI Design." In *Language Study and the PLATO System,* edited by Robert S. Hart. Studies in Language Learning 3.1. Urbana, IL: University of Illinois, 1981, pp. 214–224.

125 Candy, L. "User Interface Construction Software and the Computer-Aided Acquisition of Basic English Skills." *Interfaces in Computing* 2.1 (February 1984):69–80.

126   Carey, John. *An Economic Assessment of Electronic Texts for Higher Education.* Report 6. San Diego, CA: Electronic Text Consortium, San Diego State University, 1984.

127   —. *Electronic Text and Higher Education.* Report 1. San Diego, CA: Electronic Text Consortium, San Diego State University, 1984.

128   Carlson, Patricia Ann. "Computers and the Composing Process: Some Observations and Speculations." In *Proceedings, Sixth International Conference on Computers and the Humanities,* edited by Sarah K. Burton and Douglas D. Short. Rockville, MD: Computer Science Press, 1983, pp. 70–78.

129   Carney, T. F. *Personal Publishing: An Annotated Bibliography.* Windsor, ON: University of Windsor Department of Communication Studies, 1986.

130   —. "Personal Publishing on Microcomputers." *Research in Word Processing Newsletter* 4.4 (April 1986):2–11.

131   Case, Donald. "Processing Professorial Words: Personal Computers and the Writing Habits of University Professors." *College Composition and Communication* 36.3 (October 1985):317–322.

132   Castner, Bruce. "Composition and Literature: Learning to Write With Computers." In *Sixth International Conference on Computers and the Humanities,* edited by Sarah K. Burton and Douglas D. Short. Rockville, MD: Computer Science Press, 1983, pp. 79–82.

133   Catano, James V. "Computer-Based Writing: Navigating the Fluid Text." *College Composition and Communication.* 36.3 (October 1985):309–316.

134   Caulcott, Evelyn. *Significance Tests.* London: Routledge and Kegan Paul, 1973.

135   Cerri, Stefano, and J. Breuker. "A Rather Intelligent Language Teacher." In *Language Study and the PLATO System,* edited by Robert S. Hart. Studies in Language Learning 3.1. Urbana, IL: University of Illinois, 1981, pp. 182–192.

136   Chamberlain, Judith C. "Personalizing Your Latin Program." *Classical Outlook* 58.3 (1981):70–72.

137   Chandler, Daniel, ed. *Exploring English With Microcomputers.* London, England: Council for Educational Technology, 1983.

138   Chapelle, Carol. "Recognition of Student Input in Computer-Assisted Language Learning." *CALICO Journal* 1.3 (1983):7–9, 16.

139   Chapelle, Carol, and Joan Jamieson. "Language Lessons on the PLATO IV System." *System* 11.1 (1983):13–19.

140   Chardkoff, Joan Corb. "Index Cards: Computer-Assisted Instruction for Financially Deprived Schools." *Foreign Language Annals* 14.3 (1981):213–216.

141   Chatman, Seymour. "Stylistics: Quantitative and Qualitative." *Style* 1 (1976): 29–43.

142   Cheney, David R. "Advantages and Problems of Editing Letters on the Computer." In *Sixth International Conference on Computers and the Humanities,* edited by Sarah K. Burton and Douglas D. Short. Rockville, MD: Computer Science Press, 1983, pp. 89–93.

143   Cheng, Chin-Chuan, and B. Sherwood. "Technical Aspects of Computer Assisted Instruction in Chinese." In *Language Study and the PLATO System,*

edited by Robert Hart. Studies in Language Learning 3.1. Urbana, IL: University of Illinois, 1981, pp. 156–170.

144 Cherry, Lorinda L. "Computer Aids for Writers." *ACM SIGPLAN Notices* 16 (June 1981):62–67.

145 —, *et al.* "Computer Aids for Text Analysis." *Bell Laboratories Record* May–June 1983:10–16.

146 Chestnutt, David R. "Twentieth-Century Technology and Eighteenth-Century Letters: A Case Study of *The Papers of Henry Laurens.*" In *Sixth International Conference on Computers and the Humanities,* edited by Sarah K. Burton and Douglas D. Short. Rockville, MD: Computer Science Press, 1983, pp. 94–103.

147 Chew, Charles R., ed. *Computers in the English Program: Promises and Pitfalls.* New York State English Council. Urbana, IL: NCTE, 1984.

148 Clark, Michael. "Word Processing and the Academic Paper." In *Collected Essays on the Written Word and the Word Processor,* edited by Thomas E. Martinez. Villanova, PA: Villanova University Press, 1984, pp. 400–408.

149 Clement, Frank J. "Affective Considerations in Computer-Based Education." *Education Technology* 21.4 (1981):28–32.

150 Cluett, Robert. *Prose Style and Critical Reading.* New York: Columbia University Teachers College Press, 1976.

151 Coburn, Mark D. "Put a Poem on Your Screen: With These Activities, You Can Show Your Students That Poetry Is Much More Than Black Lines on a White Page. Poems Have Sound, Rhythm and Motion, Especially When They Appear on a Computer Screen." *Classroom Computer Learning* 6.5 (February 1986):48–49, 62.

152 Cohen, Gerald. "Can the Computer Tell You How Understandable Your Writing Is?" Conference Record: The Many Facets of Computer Communications, IEEE Professional Communication Society, Atlanta, GA: October 19–21, 1983, pp. 29–30.

153 Cohen, Michael E., and Richard A. Lanham. "HOMER: Teaching Style with a Microcomputer." In *The Computer in Composition Instruction: A Writer's Tool,* edited by William Wresch. Urbana, IL: NTCE, 1984, pp. 83–90.

154 Cohen, Vicki Blum. "Computer Courseware Development and Evaluation Criteria for the Evaluation of Microcomputer Courseware." *Educational Technology* 23.1 (1983):9–14.

155 —. "Utilizing Interactive Features in the Design of Videodisc Materials." *Educational Technology* 24.1 (1984):16–20.

156 Cole, Irad Dean. "The Roles of Rhetoric and Metaphor in Naturalized Programming: A Sample Microcomputer Application." In *Sixth International Conference on Computers and the Humanities,* edited by Sarah K. Burton and Douglas D. Short. Rockville, MD: Computer Science Press, 1983, pp. 111–117.

157 Cole, Peter, Robert Lebowitz, and Robert Hart. "A Computer-Assisted Program for the Teaching of Modern Hebrew." In *Language Study and the PLATO System,* edited by Robert S. Hart. Studies in Language Learning 3.1. Urbana, IL: University of Illinois, 1981, pp. 74–91.

158 —. "Teaching Hebrew with the Aid of Computers: The Illinois Program."
     CHum 18 (1984):87–100.

159 Coleman, Eve B. "Flowcharting as a Prewriting Activity." *Computers Reading,
     and Language Arts* 1.2 (Winter 1983):36–38.

160 Collett, John. "Getting in the Right Mood: A CAI Program on the Subjunctive
     in French." *CHum* 16 (1982):137–144.

161 —. "A Tenses Computer Program for Students of French." *Modern Language
     Journal* 66.2 (1982):170–179.

162 Collett, M. J. *Computers in Language Teaching.* Canterbury Monographs for
     Teachers of French 2. Christchurch, NZ: University of Canterbury, 1980.

163 Collier, Richard M. "The Word Processor and Revision Strategies." *College
     Composition and Communication* 34.2 (May 1983):149–155.

164 —. "Writing and the Word Processor: How Wary of the Gift-Giver Should We
     Be?" In *Computers and Composition: Selected Papers from the Conference on Comput-
     ers in Writing: New Directions in Teaching and Research, University of Minnesota,
     April 1984,* edited by Lillian Bridwell, Donald Ross, Cynthia L. Selfe, and
     Kathleen E. Kiefer. Houghton, MI, and Fort Collins, CO: Michigan Techno-
     logical University and Colorado State University, 1985, pp. 67–93.

165 Collins, Carmen. "Interactive Literacy: The Connection Between Reading and
     Writing and the Computer." In *Collected Essays on the Written Word and the
     Word Processor,* edited by Thomas E. Martinez. Villanova, PA: Villanova
     University Press, 1984, pp. 207–217.

166 Collins, James L., and Elizabeth A. Sommers, eds. *Writing On-Line: Using Com-
     puters in the Teaching of Writing.* Upper Montclair, NJ: Boynton-Cook, 1985.

167 Connors, Robert J., and Mark P. Haselkorn. "Computer Analysis of Reviewing
     and Revision: The RECOMP Project." In *Collected Essays on the Written Word
     and the Word Processor,* edited by Thomas E. Martinez. Villanova, PA: Vil-
     lanova University Press, 1984, pp. 267–279.

168 Conrad, Lora P., and Louis W. Bender. *Word Processing and Microcomputers in
     Small Two-Year Colleges: A National Study.* Tallahassee: Florida State Univer-
     sity (Institute for Higher Education), 1984.

169 Coppens-Ide, H. "Authorship Problems and the Computer." *R.E.L.O. Revue*
     3 (1971):187–194.

170 Cornick, Lisa. "Microcomputer Software for Teaching German: An Evalua-
     tion." Diss. Syracuse University, 1983. ERIC Document ED 234 752.

171 Covey, Preston K., Jr., and Michael G. Southwell. "Using Computers in Teach-
     ing Reasoning and Writing." *Collegiate Microcomputer* 1 (May 1983):141 ff.

172 Crennell, Kathleen M. "How to Use COCOA to Produce Indexes." *ALLC
     Bulletin* 3 (1975):190–196.

173 Crist, William. "Teaching Writing Through Word Processing and the Rheto-
     ric of Composition." In *Humanistic Perspectives on Computers in the Schools,*
     edited by Steven Harlow. New York: Haworth Press, 1985, pp. 77–83.

174 Crosland, Andrew T., ed. *A Concordance to F. Scott Fitzgerald's "The Great Gatsby."*
     Detroit, MI: Gale Research Co, 1975.

175   Cullen, Charles T. "The Jefferson Papers and the New Technology." In *The Challenge of Change: Critical Choices for Scholarly Publishing,* edited by Edward T. Cremmins. Washington, DC: Society for Scholarly Publishing, 1982, pp. 20–21.

176   —. "The Word Processor and Scholarly Editions." In *A Grin on the Interface: Word Processing for the Academic Humanist,* edited by Alan T. McKenzie. New York: The Modern Language Association of America, 1984, pp. 39–48.

177   Culley, Gerald R. "Two-Pronged Error Analysis from Computer-Based Instruction in Latin." In *The First Delaware Symposium on Language Studies,* edited by Di Pietro, Frawley, and Wedel. Newark, NJ: University of Delaware Press, 1983, pp. 197–200.

178   —. "When PLATO Knows Latin: Benefits of Letting the Computer Inflect the Forms." In *Proceedings of the Association for the Development of Computer-Based Instructional Systems.* Bellingham, WA: Western Washington University, 1980, pp. 237–40.

179   Culley, Gerald R., and George W. Mulford, eds. *Foreign Language Teaching Programs for Microcomputers: A Volume of Reviews.* Dover, DE: University of Delaware, 1983.

180   Curtin, Constance, and Stanley Shinall. "Computer-Assisted Reading Lessons." *CALICO Journal* 1.5 (1984):12–16.

181   Dahl, Rex C. "High Technology, Language Learning, and Nonverbal Cultural Literacy." *Unterrichtspraxis* 17.1 (1984):66–75.

182   Dahl, V., and P. Saint-Dizier. *Natural Language Understanding and Logic Programming.* New York: Elsevier, 1985.

183   Daiute, Colette A. "Can the Computer Stimulate Writers' Inner Dialogues?" In *The Computer in Composition Instruction,* edited by William Wresch. Urbana, IL: National Council of Teachers of English, 1984, pp. 131–139.

184   —. "The Computer as Stylus and Audience." *College Composition and Communication* 34 (May 1983):134–145.

185   —. "Word Processing: Can It Make Even Good Writers Better?" *Electronic Learning* March–April 1982:29–31.

186   —. *Writing and Computers.* Reading, MA: Addison-Wesley, 1985.

187   Daiute, Colette, and Robert Taylor. "Computers and the Improvement of Writing." In *Association of Computing Machinery '81 Conference Proceedings,* edited by Beth Levy. Los Angeles (9–11 November 1981):83–88.

188   Dalgish, Gerard M. "Computer-Assisted ESL Research and Courseware Development." *Computers and Composition* 2.4 (August 1985):45–62.

189   —. "Microcomputers and Teaching English as a Second Language." Office of Academic Affairs' Instructional Resource Center. New York: CUNY, 1984.

190   Danielson, Wayne A. "The Writer and the Computer." *Computers and the Humanities* 19.2 (April–June 1985):85–88.

191   Darrow, Marybeth, and Ed Obie. *Consumer Tips for School Districts for Microcomputer Hardware and Software.* NSBA Factsheet 1. Washington, DC: National School Board Assn., 1983.

192   *Data Base Directory.* White Plains, NY: American Society for Information Science, 1985.

193   *Datapro Directory of On-line Services.* 2 vols. Delran, NJ: Datapro Research, 1984.

194   Date, C. J. *Database: A Primer.* Reading, MA: Addison-Wesley, 1983.

195   Davidson, Hugh M. and Pierre Dubé, eds. *A Concordance to Pascal's* Pensées. Ithaca, NY: Cornell University Press, 1975.

196   Davies, Alan. "Computer-Assisted Language Testing." *CALICO Journal* 1.5 (1984):41–42, 48.

197   Davies, G., and J. Higgins. *Computers, Language and Language Learning.* London, England: Centre for Information on Language Teaching and Research, 1982.

198   Davies, Norman F. "Foreign/Second Language Education and Technology in the Future." *NALLD Journal* 16.3–4 (1982):5–14.

199   Davis, Ken, ed. *The Computerized English Class.* Urbana, IL: NTCE, 1983.

200   Davison, Ned J. "Aids to the Study of Rhymes and Sound Sequences." *MICRO* 1.2 (1980):3–12.

201   —. "From Research to Elementary Language Skills." *CALICO Journal* 2.1 (September 1984):14–19.

202   —. "An Interactive Concordance Program for the Small Computer." *CALICO Journal* 1.1 (1983):24–26.

203   —. "Literary Computing." *MICRO* 2.3 (1981):19–29.

204   Dawson, C., and N. Provenzano. "PLATO SITCOM Dialogs for Russian." In *Language Study and the PLATO System,* edited by Robert S. Hart. Studies in Language Learning 3.1. Urbana, IL: University of Illinois, 1981.

205   Day, John T. "Writing and Computers: The St. Olaf Experience." In *Computers and Composition: Selected Papers from the Conference on Computers in Writing: New Directions in Teaching and Research, University of Minnesota, April 1984,* edited by Lillian Bridwell, Donald Ross, Cynthia L. Selfe, and Kathleen E. Kiefer. Houghton, MI and Fort Collins, CO: Michigan Technological University and Colorado State University, 1985, pp. 95–111.

206   Dayton, Anne Harker. "Let's Stop Playing the Computer Con Game." *English Journal* 75.2 (February 1986):107–109.

207   Dearing, Vinton A. *Principles and Practice of Textual Analysis.* Berkeley, CA: University of California Press, 1974.

208   DeBloois, Michael, ed. *Videodisc/Microcomputer Courseware Design.* Englewood Cliffs, NJ: Educational Technology Publications, 1982.

209   Degnan, Sarah C. "Word Processing for Special Education Students: Worth the Effort." *T H E Journal* 12.6 (February 1985):80–82.

210   Delpino, Irene. *In the Context of a Course: Word Processing for Basic Writers.* Philadelphia, PA: Community College of Philadelphia, 1983.

211   Denley, Peter. *Word Processing and Publishing: Some Guidelines for Authors.* London, England: British Academy, 1985.

212 Derval, Bernard, and Michel Lenoble, eds. *La critique littéraire et l'ordinateur/Literary Criticism and the Computer*. Montreal, Canada: Association for Computers and the Humanities [ACH], 1985.

213 Devlin, Joe. "Desktop Publishing Is Breaking the Print Barrier: Desktop Publishing Offers the Potential for Any Personal Computer User to Become a Publisher. But There Are Some Caveats." *Computer Dealer* 9.3 (March 1986):28–33.

214 Dickinson, John, *et al.* "The Business of Words: Outlines. A New Type of Word Processor Tries to Help Us Organize Our Thoughts and Ideas by Providing a Variety of Logical Structures To Fit Them Into." *PC: The Independent Guide to IBM Personal Computers* 5.6 (March 25 1986):199–220.

215 Dimas, Chris. "A Strategy for Developing CAI." *Educational Technology* 18.4 (April 1978):26–29.

216 *Directory of United Nations Databases and Informations Systems-1985.* New York, NY/Geneva, Switzerland: UN Sales Section, 1985.

217 Ditlea, Steve. "Processing Your Ideas: New Programs Do for Thinking What Word Processing Did for Words." *Science Digest* 93.11 (November 1985): 84–85.

218 Doland, Virginia, M. "Computer Utilization in the Profession of Literature: A Systems Theory Analysis of a Revolution." Paper delivered at the 7th International Conference on Computers and the Humanities, 1985.

219 —. "The Literary Politics of Fielding's *Amelia:* Or, Can a TRS-80 Model II Find Happiness in Working With an 18th-Century Novel?" In *Sixth International Conference on Computers and the Humanities,* edited by Sarah K. Burton and Douglas D. Short. Rockville, MD: Computer Science Press, 1983, pp. 121–128.

220 Downes, Toni. "Using Data Bases in the Classroom." Proceedings of the 4th World Conference on Computers in Education, WCEE/85. 2 vols. eds. Karen Duncan and Diana Harris. Amsterdam: Elsevier Science, 1985, pp. 265–269.

221 Dowty, David R., Lauri Karttunen, and Arnold M. Zwicky, eds. *Natural Language Parsing: Psychological, Computational, and Theoretical Perspectives.* New York: Cambridge University Press, 1985.

222 Doyle, Claire. "Writing and Reading Instruction Using the Microcomputer." *T H E Journal* 2.1 (September 1983):144–145.

223 DuBrucq, Denyse C. "If the Tactilear Can Bring Hearing to the Deaf, What Can It Do for Those Learning a New Language?" *CALICO Journal* 1.5 (1984):27–30, 48.

224 Ducretet, Pierre R. "Quantitative Stylistics: An Essay in Methodology." *CHum* 4 (1970):187–191.

225 Ducretet, Pierre R., and M-P. Ducretet. Candide *de Voltaire: Etude Quantitative.* Toronto: University of Toronto Press, 1974.

226 Duggan, Joseph J. "The Value of Computer-Generated Concordances in Linguistic and Literary Research." *R.E.L.O. Revue* 4 (1966):51–60.

227   Dupre, Richard. "Writing Fiction With a Word Processor: The New Scriptorium." In *Collected Essays on the Written Word and the Word Processor,* edited by Thomas E. Martinez. Villanova, PA: Villanova University Press, 1984, pp. 372–378.

228   Dyer, Michael George. *In-depth Understanding: A Computer Model of Integrated Processing of Narrative Comprehension.* Cambridge, MA: MIT Press, 1983.

229   Dyer, Nancy Jo. "An Overview of Computing." *Hispania* 67 (1984):298–300.

230   E-Shi Wu, P. "Construction and Evaluation of a Computer-Assisted Curriculum in Spoken Mandarin." In *University-Level Computer-Assisted Instruction at Stanford: 1968–1980,* edited by Patrick Suppes. Stanford, CA: Stanford University, 1981, pp. 707–716.

231   Eagan, Ann, and M. A. Wilson. "Word Processing With Students: What Does the Teacher Need to Know?" *Pointer* 28 (Winter 1984):27–31.

232   Earp, Richard. "Using a Microcomputer for Parsing Text." Paper presented at the Seventh International Conference on Computers and the Humanities, 1985.

233   Eastman, Susan, and Terry Daugherty. "Using Compuserve to Write Research Papers." *ICCE Printout* 1.4 (November 1984):5–6.

234   Edelhart, Mike and Owen Davies. *Omni On-line Database Directory.* New York: Collier Books, 1983.

235   Edelman, Nathan. "Criticism in a Thousand Hard Lessons." In *The Eye of the Beholder,* edited by Jules Brody. Baltimore, MD: Johns Hopkins University Press, 1975, pp. 159–165.

236   Edelsky, Carole. "The Content of Language Arts Software: A Criticism." *Computers, Language, and Reading Arts* 1:4 (Spring 1984):8–11, 52.

237   *The Educational Software Selector.* New York: Teachers College Press, 1984.

238   Eisele, James E., *et al. Computer Assisted Planning of Curriculum and Instruction (How to Use Computer-Based Resource Units to Individualize Instruction).* Minneapolis, MN: ACH, 1985.

239   Elias, Richard. "Micros, Minis, and Writing: A Critical Survey." *Research in Word Processing Newsletter* 3.3 (March 1985):1–6.

240   —. "Will Computers Liberate the Comp Drudge?" In *Collected Essays on the Written Word and the Word Processor,* edited by Thomas E. Martinez. Villanova, PA: Villanova University Press, 1984, pp. 323–330.

241   Ellis, Edwin. "Computer Techniques Applied in the Compilation of a Bibliography With Index." In *Sixth International Conference on Computers and the Humanities,* edited by Sarah K. Burton and Douglas D. Short. Rockville, MD: Computer Science Press, 1983, pp. 131–138.

242   Elliston, Frank, and John Snapper. "Word Processors: Methodological and Moral Reflections." In *Sixth International Conference on Computers and the Humanities,* edited by Sarah K. Burton and Douglas D. Short. Rockville, MD: Computer Science Press, 1983, pp. 139–144.

243   Emmett, Arielle. "The Two Sides of a Word Processor: Front End and Back End Distinctions Give Structure to an Increasingly Complex Set of Software

Capabilities We Have Come to Know As Word Processing." *Personal Computing* 8.7 (July 1984):131–145.

244   Engel, F. L., and J. J. Andriessen. "Educational Technology Research: Computer-Aided Learning of a Foreign Vocabulary." *Educational Technology* 21.5 (1981):46–53.

245   Ennals, Richard. "Case Study Programs: Creative Writing Program." In *Artificial Intelligence: Applications to Logical Reasoning and Historical Research.* Chichester, England: Ellis Horwood, 1985, pp. 142–145.

246   Erdman, D. V., and E. G. Fogel, eds. *Evidence for Authorship: Essays on Problems of Attribution.* Ithaca, NY: Cornell University Press, 1966.

247   Erdt, Terrance. "Scholar Adventurers and the Electronic Library." In *Sixth International Conference on Computers and the Humanities,* edited by Sarah K. Burton and Douglas D. Short. Rockville, MD: Computer Science Press, 1983, p. 145.

248   *Evaluator's Guide for Microcomputer-Based Instructional Packages.* Eugene, OR: International Council for Computers in Education, 1982. ERIC ED 206 330.

249   Evans, James S. "Instructional Computing in the Liberal Arts: The Lawrence Experience." *T.H.E. Journal* 11.5 (1984):98–103.

250   Evans, John F. "Teaching Literature Using Word Processing." In *Writing On-Line: Using Computers in the Teaching of Writing,* edited by James L. Collins and Elizabeth A. Sommers. Upper Montclair, NJ: Boynton-Cook, 1985, pp. 83–88.

251   Evans, Richard W. "Primary and Secondary Stages in the Courseware Evaluation Process: An "Application to Computer-Aided Basic Skills Training." *Software Review* 1.1 (1982):58–69.

252   Farber, J. Joel, and David J. Zhu. "Metrical Analysis: Homer's *Odyssey.*" Paper presented at the Seventh International Conference on Computers and the Humanities, 1985.

253   Farina, L. F. "LDMS: A Linguistic Data Management System." *CHum* 17 (1983):99–120.

254   Feldman, Paula R. "Personal Computers in a Writing Course." *Perspectives in Computing* 4 (Spring 1984):4–9.

255   —. "A Review of Quintilian." *Research in Word Processing Newsletter.* 3.8 (November 1985):7–8.

256   —. "Using Microcomputers for College Writing—What Students Say." In *Collected Essays on the Written Word and the Word Processor,* edited by Thomas E. Martinez. Villanova, PA: Villanova University Press, 1984, pp. 116–124.

257   Fetter, Wayne R. "Guidelines for Evaluation of Computer Software (with an Evaluation Form)." *Educational Technology* 24.3 (1984):19–21.

258   Finkenstaedt, T., and D. Wolff. "France's Word Horde." *Times Literary Supplement* 13 September 1972:1229.

259   Firth, J. R. *Papers in Linguistics 1934–51.* Oxford, England: Oxford University Press, 1957.

260 Fisher, Glenn. "Where CAI Is Effective: A Summary of the Research." *Electronic Learning* 3.3 (1983):82, 84.

261 —. "Word Processing—Will It Make All Kids Love to Write?" *Instructor* 92 (February 1983):87–88.

262 Fleming, Malcolm. "Characteristics of Effective Instructional Presentation: What We Know and What We Need to Know." *Educational Technology* 21.7 (1981):33–38.

263 Flowers, Mary Lynn. *Sentence Structure and Characterization in the Tragedies of Jean Racine: A Computer Assisted Study.* Cranbury, NJ: Fairleigh Dickinson University Press, 1979.

264 Fluegelman, Andrew, and Jeremy Joan Hewes. *Writing in the Computer Age: Word Processing Skills for Every Writer.* New York: Anchor Press-Doubleday, 1983.

265 Fortier, Paul A. "Using the Computer for Literary Criticism: Theoretical Underpinnings and Cost Factors." In *Literary Criticism and the Computer,* edited by Bernard Derval and Michel Lenoble. Montreal, Canada: ACH, 1985.

266 Fortier, Paul, and J. C. McConnell. "Computer-Aided Thematic Analysis of French Prose Fiction." In *The Computer and Literary Studies,* edited by Aitken, Bailey, and Hamilton-Smith. Edinburgh, Scotland: Edinburgh University Press, 1973, pp. 167–182.

267 —. "Computer-Aided Thematic Analysis of French Prose Fiction, II. Analysis of text and Preparation Costs." In *The Computer in Literary and Linguistic Studies,* edited by Jones and Churchhouse. Cardiff, Wales: University of Wales Press, 1976, pp. 215–222.

268 Foster, Edward. "Outliners: A New Way of Thinking." *Personal Computing* 9.5 (May 1985):74–83.

269 Frase, Lawrence T. "Knowledge, Information, and Action: Requirements for Automated Writing Instruction." *Journal of Computer-Based Instruction* 11.2 (Spring 1984):55–59.

270 Frautschi, Richard L. "Recent Quantitative Research in French Studies." *CHum* 7 (1973):361–372.

271 Freese, C. Denny, and Larry Adams. "Word Processing in College Composition (or the Direct Use of the Microcomputer in Teaching College Composition)." In *Sixth International Conference on Computers and the Humanities,* edited by Sarah K. Burton and Douglas D. Short. Rockville, MD: Computer Science Press, 1983, pp. 202–203.

272 Friedberg, Jack. *Proofreading in the Word Processing Age.* New York: Irvington, 1985.

273 Friedman, Morton P. "WANDAH—A Computerized Writer's Aid." In *Computers and Composition: Selected Papers from the Conference on Computers in Writing: New Directions in Teaching and Research, University of Minnesota, April 1984,* edited by Lillian Bridwell, Donald Ross, Cynthia L. Selfe, and Kathleen E. Kiefer. Houghton, MI, and Fort Collins, CO: Michigan Technological University and Colorado State University, 1985, pp. 113–124.

274 Fries, Charles C. *The Structure of English.* New York: Harcourt, 1952.

275 Fritzler, M. "A Tentative Evaluation of the Software and Hardware Appropriate to a Word-Processor Assisted Writing Program." Manuscript. University of Minnesota Press, MN: The Program in Composition and Communication, 1985.

276 Froger, Jacques. *La Critique des testes et son automatisation.* Paris: Dunod, 1967.

277 Gabler, Hans Walter. "Computer-Aided Critical Edition of Ulysses." *Association for Literary and Linguistic Computing Bulletin* 8.3 (1981):232–248.

278 Gadomski, Kenneth E. "Another Chance Against the Terrors of Prose: Computers and the Writing Process." *Enquiry: Research at the University of Delaware* 4.4 (Summer 1984):15–18.

279 Gale, Larrie E. "Veni, Vidi, Vici via Videodisc: A Simulator for Instructional Conversations." *System* 11.1 (1983):41–46.

280 Gallagher, Brian. "Computers, Word Processing, and the Teaching of Writing." *Research in Word Processing Newsletter* 3.4 (April 1985):1–5.

281 —. *Microcomputer Word Processing Programs: An Evaluation and Critique.* New York: Instructional Resource Center of the City University of New York, 1985.

282 Galloway, Patricia. "Narrative Theories as Computational Models: Reader-Oriented Theory and Artificial Intelligence." *Computers and the Humanities* 17.4 (December 1983):169–174.

283 Garson, J. W., and B. Foorman. "Microcomputer Graphics and Visual Reasoning." In *NECC '84 Annual National Educational Computing Conference,* edited by Della T. Bonnette. Dayton, OH: University of Dayton, June 13–15, 1984, pp. 7–10.

284 Garvey, Ian. "Spelling Checkers: Can They Actually Teach Spelling?" *Classroom Computer Learning* 5.4 (November–December 1984):62–65.

285 Gaunt, Marianne I. "Rutgers Inventory of Machine-Readable Texts in the Humanities." In *Data Bases in the Humanities and Social Sciences,* edited by Robert F. Allen. Osprey, FL: Paradigm Press, 1985, pp. 283–290.

286 Geoiffrion, L. D. "Feasibility of Word Processing for Students with Writing Handicaps." *Journal of Education Technology Systems* 2 (1982–83):239–250.

287 Gerrard, Lisa. "From Wylbur to WANDAH: Designing Software for Student Writers." In *Computers and Composition: Selected Papers from the Conference on Computers in Writing: New Directions in Teaching and Research, University of Minnesota, April 1984,* edited by Lillian Bridwell, Donald Ross, Cynthia L. Selfe, and Kathleen E. Kiefer. Houghton, MI, and Fort Collins, CO: Michigan Technological University and Colorado State University, 1985, pp. 125–138.

288 Gevarter, William B. "An Overview of Computer-Based Natural Language Processing." Washington, DC: National Aeronautics and Space Administration, 1983. ERIC Document ED 244 607.

289 Gibson, Martin L. *Editing in the Electronic Era.* 2nd ed. Ames: Iowa State University Press, 1984.

290 Gilbert, Penny. "Automatic Collation: A Technique for Medieval Texts." *CHum* 7 (1973):139–147.

291   —. "The Preparation of Prose-Text Editions with the COLLATE System." *La Pratique des ordinateurs dans la critique des textes.* Paris: C.N.R.S., 1979, pp. 225–243.

292   Gingrich, Patricia S. "The UNIX Writer's Workbench Software: Results of a Field Study." *Bell System Technical Journal* 62.6.3 (July–August 1983): 1909–1921.

293   Goetschalckx, J., and L. Rolling. *Lexicography in the Electronic Age.* Amsterdam: North-Holland, 1982.

294   Gooding, Frank. "Software for Hardware: A Control Program for Electronic Speech Synthesis." *ALLC Bulletin* 13 (1985):1–4.

295   Goodman, Donald, and Sandra Schwab. "Computerized Testing for Readability." *Creative Computing* 6 (April 1980):46 ff.

296   Gonzales, Laurence. *Computers for Writers.* New York: Ballantine, 1984.

297   Gravander, Jerry W. "Beyond 'Drill and Practice' Programs." *Collegiate Microcomputer* 3.4 (November 1985):317–332.

298   Greenberger, Martin, ed. *Electronic Publishing Plus: Media for a Technological Future.* White Plains, NY: Knowledge Industry Publications, 1985.

299   Greenblatt, Daniel L. "Generative Metrics and the Authorship of 'The Expostulation.'" *Centrum* 1 (1973):87–104.

300   Greene, Wendy Tibbetts, Lynn Veach Sadler, and Emory W. Sadler. "Diagrammatic Writing Using Word Processing: Computer-Assisted Composition for the Development of Writing Skills." *The Computing Teacher* 12.7 (April 1985):62–64.

301   Grosch, Audrey N. "Personal Bibliographic System and Data Transfer System: Software Review." *Collegiate Microcomputer* 2.4 (Winter 1984):309–315.

302   Grout, Bill. *Desktop Publishing from A to Z.* Berkeley, CA: Osborne, McGraw-Hill, 1986.

303   Gula, Robert J. "Beyond the Typewriter: An English Teacher Looks at Word Processing." *Independent School* 42.3 (February 1983):44–46.

304   Gutsell, Jane Walters. "Is Word-Processing Words-Worth It?" *Collegiate Microcomputer* 3.4 (November 1985):307–311.

305   Haas, Christina, and John R. Hayes. *Effects of Text Display on Reading Tasks: Computer Screen vs. Hard Copy.* CDC Technical Report Series 3. Pittsburgh: Carnegie-Mellon University, 1985.

306   Haliday, M. A. K. "Categories of the Theory of Grammar." *Word* 17 (1961): 241–292.

307   Hall, Wendell H. "Microcomputer Simulations and Games for Foreign Language Learning." *MICRO* 1.4 (1980):8–11.

308   Halpern, Jeanne W., and Sarah Liggett. *Computers and Composing: How the New Technologies Are Changing Writing.* Carbondale, IL: Southern Illinois University Press, 1984.

309   Hamilton-Smith, Niel. *CONCORD.* Edinburgh, Scotland: Edinburgh Regional Computing Centre, 1972.

310 Hansen, Craig, and Lance Wilcox. "Adapting Microcomputers for Use in College Composition Courses." In *Collected Essays on the Written Word and the Word Processor,* edited by Thomas E. Martinez. Villanova, PA: Villanova University Press, 1984, pp. 106–115.

311 Hansen, C., and L. Wilcox. "An Authoring System for Use by Teachers of Composition." *Computers and Composition* 1.3 (1984):3–4.

312 Harris, Jeanette. "Student Writers and Word Processing: A Preliminary Evaluation." *College Composition and Communication* 36.3 (October 1985):323–330.

313 Harris, Mary Dee. *Introduction to Natural Language Processing.* Reston, 1985.

314 —. "Observations on Computers and Poetry." *Association for Computers and the Humanities Newsletter* 6.4 (Winter 1984):1, 6.

315 Harrison, John S. *Applications of Computer Technology in Foreign Language Teaching and Learning.* ERIC, 1982. ERIC Document ED 216 552.

316 Hart, Robert S., ed. *Language Study and the PLATO System.* Studies in Language Learning 3.1. Urbana, IL: University of Illinois, 1981.

317 Hart, Thomas Elwood. "The Computer-Tutor Metaphor and the Structure of German: Experimenting with a Microcomputer-Based Authoring System." *Unterrichtspraxis* 17.1 (1984):85–103.

318 Hartley, James. "The Role of Colleagues and Text-Editing Programs in Improving Text." *IEEE Transactions on Professional Communications* 27.1 (March 1984):42–44.

319 Haselkorn, Mark P., and Jim S. Borck. "The Word Processor and the Scholarly Journal." In *A Grin on The Interface: Word Processing for the Academic Humanist,* edited by Alan T. McKenzie. New York: The Modern Language Association of America, 1984, pp. 1–9.

320 Haselkorn, Mark P., and Robert J. Connors. "Computer Analysis of the Composing Process." In *Computers and Composition: Selected Papers from the Conference on Computers in Writing: New Directions in Teaching and Research, University of Minnesota, April 1984,* edited by Lillian Bridwell, Donald Ross, Cynthia L. Selfe, and Kathleen E. Kiefer. Houghton, MI, and Fort Collins, CO: Michigan Technological University and Colorado State University, 1985, pp. 139–158.

321 Healey, Antonette diPaolo. "The Dictionary of Old English and the Design of Its Computer System." In *Sixth International Conference on Computers and the Humanities,* edited by Sarah K. Burton and Douglas D. Short. Rockville, MD: Computer Science Press, 1983, p. 248.

322 Hedges, William, and Edward Turner. "The Cloze Test Becomes Practical for Use by the Classroom Teacher." *CRLA* 1 (Fall 1983):11–13.

323 Heidorn, G. E., *et al.* "The EPISTLE Text-Critiquing System." *IBM Systems Journal* 21 (1982):305–326.

324 Heilbrun, Carolyn. "Some Words for the Trepid." In *A Grin on the Interface: Word Processing for the Academic Humanist,* edited by Alan T. McKenzie. New York: The Modern Language Association of America, 1984, pp. 1–9.

325   Heines, Jessie M. "Text Editors." *Screen Design Strategies for Computer-Assisted Instruction.* Bedford, MA: Digital Press, 1984, pp. 116–121.

326   Henderson, M. M. T. "Microcomputers and Large Data Bases." *CHum* 16 (1982):219–222.

327   Hendricks, Harold, Junius L. Bennion, and Jerry Larson. "Technology and Language Learning at BYU." *CALICO Journal* 1.3 (1983):23–30, 46.

328   Herdan, Gustav. *Language as Choice and Chance.* Groningen, Netherlands: P. Noordhoff, 1956.

329   Hermann, Andrea W. "An Interim Report of an Ethnographic Study of Computers and a Writing Class: Collaborative Activities." In *Computers and Composition: Selected Papers from the Conference on Computers in Writing: New Directions in Teaching and Research, University of Minnesota, April 1984,* edited by Lillian Bridwell, Donald Ross, Cynthia L. Selfe, and Kathleen E. Kiefer. Houghton, MI, and Fort Collins, CO: Michigan Technological University and Colorado State University, 1985, pp. 159–173.

330   —. "Teaching Newspaper Writing Using the Computer." *Research in Word Processing Newsletter* 2.9 (December 1984):1–2.

331   Herrmann, Andrea W., and Brian Gallagher. *Using the Computer in the Classroom: Approaches and Issues.* Recorded Proceedings from 1984 NCTE Convention. Urbana, IL: NCTE, 1984. 60 minutes.

332   Hershey, William. "Idea Processors." *Byte* 10.6 (June 1985):337–350.

333   Hession, William, and Malcolm Rubel. *Performance Guide to Word Processing Software.* New York: McGraw-Hill, 1985.

334   Hertz, Robert M. *Microcomputers in Bilingual and Foreign Language Instruction: A Guide and Bibliography.* Los Alamitos, CA: National Center for Bilingual Research, 1983.

335   —. "Problems of Computer-Assisted Instruction in Composition." *Computing Teacher* 11.2 (1983):62–64.

336   —. "A Software Evaluation Guide for the Language Arts." *CALICO Journal* 1.5 (1984):21–23, 48.

337   Hewitt, Helen-Jo Jakusz. "Computer, Bibliography, and Foreign Language Typography." *Computers and the Humanities* 19.2 (April–June 1985):89–95.

338   Hidley, G. R. "Calculit: A Tool to Assist Literary Analysis." *Association for Literary and Linguistic Computing Bulletin* 11.1 (1983):9.

339   Higgins, John, and Tim Johns. *Computers in Language Learning.* Reading, MA: Addison-Wesley, 1984.

340   Hilligoss, Susan. "The History of Composing Tools and the Future of Word Processing." In *Sixth International Conference on Computers and the Humanities,* edited by Sarah K. Burton and Douglas D. Short. Rockville, MD: Computer Science Press, 1983, pp. 273–280.

341   Hinckley, Dan. *Writing with a Computer: Using Your Word Processor for a New Freedom and Creativity in Writing.* New York: Simon and Schuster (Computer Books), 1985.

342 Hinton, N. "CAI in Advanced Literature Classes." *Language Study and the PLATO System,* edited by Robert S. Hart. Studies in Language Learning 3.1. Urbana, IL: University of Illinois, 1981.

343 Hitchcock, Susan Tyler. "A Cautious View of Computers in Teaching Writing: Or, Computers Don't Teach Writing, People Do." *Research in Word Processing Newsletter* 3.7 (October 1985):7–9.

344 Hockey, Susan M. *Computing in the Arts at Oxford University.* Oxford, England: Oxford University Computing Services, 1977.

345 —. *A Guide to Computer Applications in the Humanities.* Baltimore: Johns Hopkins University Press, 1980.

346 —. "Literature and the Computer at Oxford University." In *Literary Criticism and the Computer,* edited by Bernard Derval and Michel Lenoble. Montreal, Canada: ACH, 1985.

347 —. *SNOBOL Programming for the Humanities.* Oxford: Oxford University Press, 1985.

348. Hockey, Susan M., and V. A. Shibayev. "The Bilingual Analytical Literary and Linguistic Concordance—BALCON." *ALLC Bulletin* 3 (1975):133–139.

349 Hocking, Joan. "The Impact of Microcomputers on Composition Students." Annual Meeting of the Conference on College Composition and Communication. Detroit, MI: March 17–19, 1983. ERIC Document ED 229 791.

350 Hoffer, William. "Books in the Information Age: The Librarian of Congress Argues That Computers and Books Are Allies." *Popular Computing* 5.1 (November 1985):20–21.

351 Holdstein, Deborah H. "Perception and Evaluation of Computers and Writing: Myths and Methods." In *Computers and Composition: Selected Papers from the Conference on Computers in Writing: New Directions in Teaching and Research, University of Minnesota, April 1984,* edited by Lillian Bridwell, Donald Ross, Cynthia L. Selfe, and Kathleen E. Kiefer. Houghton, MI, and Fort Collins, CO: Michigan Technological University and Colorado State University, 1985, pp. 175–184.

352 Holmes, Glyn. "A Contextualized Vocabulary Learning Drill for French." *Computers and the Humanities* 14 (1980):105–111.

353 —. "Second Language Learning and Computers." *Canadian Modern Language Review* 38.3 (1982):503–516.

354 Holmes, Glyn, and Marilyn E. Kidd. "The CLEF Project: Learning French on Color Micros." *ADCIS Conference Proceedings.* Bellingham, WA: Western Washington University, 1982, pp. 245–251.

355 Holmes, Leigh Howard. "Follow 2: A Theme Commentary Program." *The Computing Teacher* 12.5 (February 1985):38–39.

356 Holsti, Ole R. *Content Analysis for the Social Sciences and Humanities.* Reading, MA: Addison-Wesley, 1969.

357   Holtz, Herman. "Proposal Writing with a Computer." *The Consultant's Edge: Using the Computer as a Marketing Tool.* New York: John Wiley, 1985, pp. 41–74.

358   —. "Computer Aid in Newsletter Publishing." *The Consultant's Edge: Using the Computer as a Marketing Tool.* New York: John Wiley, 1985, pp. 189–204.

359   Holz, L. "Merge, and Merge Again: The Fine Art of Boilerplating." *Business Software* 3.4 (April 1985):26–28.

360   Holzer, Paul. "Machine Reading of Metric Verse." *Byte* 11.2 (February 1986): 224–225.

361   Hope, Geoffrey. "Elementary French Computer-Assisted Instruction." *Foreign Language Annals* 15.5 (1982):347–353.

362   Hope, Geoffrey, Heimy F. Taylor, and James P. Pusack. *Using Computers in Teaching Foreign Languages.* ERIC/CLL Language in Education 57. New York: Harcourt, 1984.

363   Hopmeier, George. "New Study Says CAI May Favor Introverts." *Electronic Learning* 1.1 (1981):16–17.

364   Horn, William Dennis. "The Effect of the Computer on the Written Word." In *Sixth International Conference on Computers and the Humanities,* edited by Sarah K. Burton and Douglas D. Short. Rockville, MD: Computer Science Press, 1983, pp. 282–286.

365   Howard-Hill, T. H. "Computer and Mechanical Aids to Editing." *Proof* 5 (1977):217–235.

366   —. "A Practical Scheme for Editing Critical Texts with the Aid of a Computer." *Proof* 3 (1973):335–356.

367   Hoye, Robert E., and Anastasia C. Wang, eds. *Index to Computer Based Learning.* Minneapolis, MN: ACH, 1985.

368   Huelskamp, Allen. "Word Processed Papers and a Positive Shift in Priorities." *Writing as a Liberating Activity Newsletter* 1.22 (1984):3–4.

369   Hughes, David R. "Teaching Electronic English Via Telecommunications." In *Sixth International Conference on Computers and the Humanities,* edited by Sarah K. Burton and Douglas D. Short. Rockville, MD: Computer Science Press, 1983, pp. 287–298.

370   Hull, Glynda A. "Computer-Assisted Instruction and Basic Writing: A Proposal." In *Collected Essays on the Written Word and the Word Processor,* edited by Thomas E. Martinez. Villanova, PA: Villanova University Press, 1984, pp. 125–136.

371   —. "The Use of Microcomputers in Basic Writing." In *Computers and Composition: Selected Papers from the Conference on Computers in Writing: New Directions in Teaching and Research, University of Minnesota, April 1984,* edited by Lillian Bridwell, Donald Ross, Cynthia L. Selfe, and Kathleen E. Kiefer. Houghton, MI, and Fort Collins, CO: Michigan Technological University and Colorado State University, 1985, pp. 185–193.

372 Hult, Christine. "The Effects of Word Processing on the Correctness of Student Writing." *Research in Word Processing Newsletter* 3.8 (November 1985): 1–5.

373 Humes, Ann. "Research on the Composing Process." *Review of Educational Research* 53 (Summer 1983):213.

374 Huntington, John F. *Computer-Assisted Instruction Using BASIC.* Minneapolis, MN: ACH, 1985.

375 Hutchins, W. J. "Machine Translation and Machine-Aided Translation." *Translation: Literary, Linguistic and Philosophical Perspectives.* Newark: University of Delaware Press, 1984, pp. 59–129.

376 Hymes, Dell. "Phonological Aspects of Style: Some English Sonnets." In *Style in Language,* edited by Thomas A. Sebeok. Cambridge, MA: M.I.T. Press, 1960, pp. 33–53.

377 Iker, Howard P. "SELECT: A Computer Program to Identify Associationally Rich Words for Content Analysis. I. Statistical Results." *CHum* 8 (1974): 313–9.

378 —. "SELECT: A Computer Program to Identify Associationally Rich Words for Content Analysis. II. Substantive Results." *CHum* 9 (1975):3–12.

379 Iker, Howard P., and R. Klein. "WORDS: A Computer System for the Analysis of Content." *Behavior Research Methods and Instrumentation* 6 (1974):430–438.

380 Ingle, Schuyler. "Who Needs a Mainframe." *Pro/Files* (November–December 1983):38, 40–41, 86, 91.

381 Ingram, William. "Concordances in the Seventies." *CHum* 8 (1974):273–277.

382 Jacobson, Sibyl C., Robert J. Dilligan, and Todd K. Bender, eds. *Concordance to Joseph Conrad's "Heart of Darkness."* Carbondale, IL: Southern Illinois University Press, 1973.

383 Jacobson, Sibyl C., and Todd K. Bender. "Computer Assisted Editorial Work on Conrad." *Conradiana* 5.3 (1973):37–47.

384 Jakobson, Roman. "Linguistics and Poetics." *Style in Language,* edited by Thomas A. Sebeok. Cambridge, MA: M.I.T. Press, 1960, pp. 350–377.

385 James, Charles J. "Experimenting with Voice Recognition in German." *Unterrichtspraxis* 17.1 (1984):140–141.

386 Jansen, Louise M. "Using a Computer in the Production of German Teaching Materials." *Unterrichtspraxis* 17.1 (1984):142–144.

387 Jarchow, Elaine McNally. "Teaching Literature with the Help of Microcomputers." *The Computing Teacher* 11.4 (November 1983):35–37.

388 Jarvis, Stan. "Language Learning Technology and Alternatives for Public Education." *CALICO Journal* 1.4 (1984):11–16

389 Jensen, Karen, and George E. Heidorn. "First Aid to Authors: The IBM EPISTLE Text-Critiquing System." In *Digest of Papers, COMPRON,* Spring 1984. [IEEE Computer Society Conference.] Silver Spring, MD: IEEE Computer Society Press, 1984, pp. 462–464.

390   Jobst, Jack. "Computers and Essay Grading." In *Sixth International Conference on Computers and the Humanities,* edited by Sarah K. Burton and Douglas D. Short. Rockville, MD: Computer Science Press, 1983, pp. 309–310.

391   Jonassen, David. "Producing an Index with Your Microcomputer Database Manager." *Collegiate Microcomputer* 3.4 (November 1985):375–381.

392   Jones, Alan, and R. F. Churchhouse, eds. *The Computer in Literary and Linguistic Studies. Proceedings of the Third International Symposium.* Cardiff, Wales: University of Wales Press, 1976.

393   Jones, Nancy Baker, and Lary Vaughan. *Evaluation of Educational Software: A Guide to Guides.* Chelmsford, England: Northeast Regional Exchange; Austin, TX: Southwest Educational Development Lab, 1983.

394   Jorgensen, Peter A. "Versatility in the Design of Foreign-Language Computer-Assisted Instruction." *Unterrichtspraxis* 17.1 (1984):104–108.

395   Joyce, James. "Networks of Sound: Graph Theory Applied to Studying Rhymes." In *Computing in the Humanities. Proceedings of the Third International Conference on Computing in the Humanities,* edited by Lusignan and North. Waterloo, Ontario: University of Waterloo Press, 1977, 307–316.

396   —. "UNIX Aids for English Composition Courses." In *Computers in the Humanities,* edited by Richard W. Bailey. Amsterdam: North Holland Publishing: ICCH/5, 1982, pp. 33–38.

397   Kachru, Y., C. Nelson, and R. Hart. "Computer-Based Instruction in Elementary Hindi." In *Language Study and the PLATO System,* edited by Robert S. Hart. Studies in Language Learning 3.1. Urbana, IL: University of Illinois, 1981, pp. 54–73.

398   Kearsley, Gregory. "Instructional Videodisc." *Perspectives* 34.6 (1983): 417–423.

399   Kearsley, Gregory, Beverly Hunter, and Robert J. Seidel. "Two Decades of Computer-Based Instruction Projects: What Have We Learned?" *T. H. E. Journal* 10 (January 1983):90–94; 10 (February 1983):88–96.

400   Keller, Howard H. "Vocabulary Flashcards on the Microcomputer." *Russian Language Journal* 35.1 (1981):7–9.

401   Kemp, Kenneth W. "Personal Observations on the Use of Statistical Methods in Quantitative Linguistics." In *The Computer in Literary Linguistic Studies,* edited by Jones and Churchhouse. Cardiff, Wales: University of Wales Press, 1976, pp. 59–77.

402   Kiefer, Kathleen E., and Charles R. Smith. "Improving Students' Revising and Editing: The Writer's Workbench System." In *The Computer in Composition Instruction: A Writer's Tool,* edited by William Wresch. Urbana, IL: NCTE, 1984, pp. 65–82.

403   —. "Textual Analysis with Computers: Tests of Bell Laboratories' Computer Software." *Research in the Teaching of English* 17 (October 1983):201–214.

404   Kenning, M. J., and M.-M. Kenning. *Introduction to Computer-Assisted Language Teaching.* Oxford, England: Oxford University Press, 1983.

405   Kidd, Marilyn E. "The Computer and Language Remediation." *Programmed Learning and Educational Technology* 19.3 (1982):234–39.

406   —. "Realizing the Potential of the Computer in the Learning of Modern Languages." In *Proceedings of the Third Canadian Symposium on International Technology.* Ottawa, Canada: National Research Council of Canada, 1980, pp. 264–268.

407   Kidd, Marilyn E., and Glyn Holmes. "CAL Evaluation: A Cautionary Word." *Computers and Education* 8.1 (1984):77–84.

408   King, Barbara, June Birnbaum, and Jane Wageman. "Word Processing and the Basic College Writer." In *Collected Essays on the Written Word and the Word Processor,* edited by Thomas E. Martinez. Villanova, PA: Villanova University Press, 1984, pp. 251–266.

409   Kind, Patricia. *Mind to Disk to Paper: Business Writing on a Word Processor.* New York: Franklin Watts, 1985.

410   Kinmonth, Earl H. "BIBLIOFILE: Humanizing the UNIX System." *CHum* 18 (1984):71–86.

411   Kjetsaa, Geir. "Storms on the Quiet Don: A Pilot Study." *Scando-Sclavica* 22 (1967):5–24.

412   Klier, Betje. "Microcomputer Assisted Foreign Language Instruction: An Example in French Culture and Civilization." *French Review* 57.2 (1983): 163–167.

413   Kline, Edward A. "Computational Stylistics." In *Proceedings of the Second Indiana University Computer Network Conference on Instructional Computer Applications.* Bloomington, IN: Office of Information and Computer Services, Indiana University, 1975, pp. 11–17.

414   Knapp, Linda Roehrig. *The Word Processor and the Writing Teacher.* Englewood Cliffs, NJ: Prentice-Hall, 1986.

415   Kolin, Philip C. "Shakespeare and the Computer: A Checklist of Scholarship." *The Shakespeare Newsletter* 31.3 (May 1981):22; 31.4–5 (September–November 1981):28; 31.6 (December 1981):36.

416   Kossuth, Karen C. "Suggestions for Comprehension-Based Computer-Assisted Instruction in German." *Unterrichtspraxis* 17.1 (1984):109–115.

417   Krasnoff, Barbara, *et al.* "The Word on Word Processors." *PC Magazine* 3.17 (September 4 1984):112–119, 151–152, 159–182.

418   Kreiter-Kurylo, Carolyn. "Computers and Composition." *The Writing Instructor* 2.4 (Summer 1983):174–182.

419   Krippendorff, K. *Content Analysis: An Introduction to its Methodology.* Beverly Hills, CA: Sage, 1980.

420   Kuchinskas, G. "Interactive Language Experiences Between Students and Computers." In *AEDS Twenty-First Annual Convention Proceedings: Frontiers in Educational Computing.* Portland, OR: May 9–13, 1983. Washington, DC: Association for Educational Data Systems, pp. 181–184.

421   Kurshan, Barbara. "Computer Technology and Instruction: Implications for Instructional Designers." *Educational Technology* 21.8 (1981):28–30.

422 Labuz, Ronald. *How to Typeset from a Word Processor: An Interfacing Guide.* New York: Bowker, 1984.

423 Lacy, Allen. "What Becomes of Manuscripts When Words Are 'Processed'?" *The Chronicle of Higher Education* 29.3 (September 12 1984):38.

424 Lacy, Dan. "Print, Television, Computers, and English." *ADE Bulletin* 72 (Summer 1982):34–38.

425 Lake, Daniel. "Beyond Word-Processing: All of Your Favorite Writing Activities Take on New Appeal When Mixed with Modems and the Class Computer." *Computer Classroom Learning* 6.3 (November–December 1985):37–39.

426 Langenscheidt, Florian, and Constance Putnam. "A Publisher's Perspective on Software Development." *Unterrichtspraxis* 17.1 (1984):56–65.

427 Lanning, Gerald W. "Simplifying Documentation." *Computerworld* 19.4 (January 28 1985):37–38.

428 Lannon, John M. "Writing for Computer Users." *Technical Writing.* 3rd ed. Boston: Little, Brown, 1985, pp. 590–593.

429 *La Pratique des ordinateurs dans la critique des textes.* Paris, France: Centre National de la Recherche Scientifique, 1979.

430 Larsen, Mark D. "Persistent Problems of Computer-Assisted Instruction." *CALICO Journal* 1.5 (1984):31–34.

431 Larsen, R. B. "The Impact of Computers on Composition: A Polemic." *Educational Technology* 24.12 (December 1984):22–26.

432 Last, R. W. "Publishing Computer Output of Processed Natural Language Texts, I." *ALLC Bulletin* 1.3 (1973):5–7.

433 —. "Publishing Computer Output of Processed Natural Language Texts, II." *ALLC Bulletin* 2.2 (1974):38–41.

434 Last, Rex. *Language Teaching and the Microcomputer.* New York: Basil Blackwell (Harper & Row), 1984.

435 Lathrop, Ann. "The Terrible Ten in Educational Programming: My Top Ten Reasons for Automatically Rejecting a Program." *Educational Computer Magazine* September–October, 1982.

436 Lathrop, Ann, and Bobby Goodson. "How to Start a Software Exchange." *Recreational Computing* 10.2 (1981):24–26.

437 Lavine, Roberta. "Humanizing Computer-Assisted Instruction." *MICRO* 2.1 (1981):5–10.

438 Lavine, Roberta, Z. Fechter, and Sharon Ahern Fechter. In *Computer-Assisted Instruction in the ESL Curriculum,* 1981. ERIC Document ED 214 391.

439 Law, A. G., *et al.* "Computer Voice Support for Visually-Handicapped Students." *Computers and Education* 8.1 (1984):35–39.

440 Lawler, J., ed. *Computers in Composition Instruction.* Los Alamitos, CA: SWRL Educational Research and Development, 1982.

441 Lawrence, John Shelton. *The Electronic Scholar: A Guide to Academic Microcomputing.* Norwood, NJ: Ablex, 1985.

442 Lawson, Veronica, ed. *Practical Experience of Machine Translation: Proceedings of a Conference.* London, 5–6 November 1981. Amsterdam, Netherlands: North-Holland, 1982.

443 Leahy, Ellen K. "A Writing Teacher's Shopping and Reading List for Software." *English Journal* 73 (January 1984):62–65.

444 LeClercq, Angie. "Videodisc Technology: Equipment, Software, and Educational Applications." *Library Technology Report* 17.4 (1981):293–334.

445 Leed, Jacob, ed. *The Computer and Literary Style.* Kent, OH: Kent State University Press, 1966.

446 Lehmann, W. P., and Winfield S. Bennett. "Human Language and Computers." *Computers and the Humanities* 19.2 (April–June 1985):77–83.

447 Leiblum, M. D. "Factors Sometimes Overlooked and Underestimated in the Selection and Success of CAL as an Instructional Medium." *AEDS Journal* 15.2 (Winter 1982):67–77.

448 Leibowicz, J. "ERIC/RCS Report: CAI in English." *English Education* 14 (December 1982):241–247.

449 Leighton, Joseph. "Automatic Analysis of Simple Rhetorical Devices in 17th Century German Sonnets." In *The Computer in Literary and Linguistic Studies,* edited by Jones and Churchhouse. Cardiff, Wales: University of Wales Press, 1976, 246–254.

450 Lees, Elaine O. "Proofreading With the Ears: A Case Study of Text-to-Voice Performance of a Student's Writing." In *Collected Essays on Computers and the Humanities,* edited by Thomas E. Martinez. Villanova, PA: Villanova University Press, 1984, pp. 218–230.

451 —. "Using a Text-to-Voice System to Assist Poor Editors." In *Computers and Composition: Selected Papers from the Conference on Computers in Writing: New Directions in Teaching and Research, University of Minnesota, April 1984,* edited by Lillian Bridwell, Donald Ross, Cynthia L. Selfe, and Kathleen E. Kiefer. Houghton, MI, and Fort Collins, CO: Michigan Technological University and Colorado State University, 1985, pp. 195–211.

452 Leidy, Judy, *et al.* "Using Computer-Assisted Instruction in an ESL Program." *NALLD Journal* 15.1 (1980):13–24.

453 Leonard, Rosemary. *The Interpretation of English Noun Sequences on the Computer.* New York: North-Holland, 1984.

454 Levin, J. A. *Microcomputer-Based Environments for Writing: A Writer's Assistant.* San Diego, CA: Laboratory of Comparative Human Cognition, University of California, San Diego, 1981.

455 Levin, Robert L. "Computer-Assisted Writing." In *New Directions for Community Colleges: Microcomputer Applications in Administration and Instruction,* edited by Donald A. Dellow and Lawrence H. Poole. San Francisco, CA: Jossey-Bass, 1984.

456 Levin, Robert, and Claire Doyle. "The Microcomputer in the Writing/Reading/Study Lab." *T.H.E. Journal* 10.4 (February 1983): 77–79, 100.

457   Levin, Will. "Interactive Video: The State-of-the-Art Teaching Machine." *Computing Teacher* 11.2 (1983):11–17. EJ 290–130.

458   Levy, Myrna. "Using a Simple Word Processing Program With Special Education Students." *Creative Word Processing in the Classroom* (Fall 1984):11–13.

459   Lewis, Derek R. "Computer-Assisted Language Learning at the University of Dundee." *CALICO Journal* 1.3 (1983):10–12, 46.

460   Lindenau, Suzanne E. "The Teacher and Technology in the Humanities and Arts." *Modern Language Journal* 68.2 (1984):119–124.

461   Lines, Vardell, and Dennis Martin. "CAI TOOLKIT: A New Authoring System for Teaching Languages." *CALICO Journal* 1.3 (1983):43–45.

462   Lippey, Gerald. *Computer Assisted Test Construction.* Minneapolis, MN: ACH, 1985.

463   Littlefield, Patti. "Teaching Writing With a Word Processor." *Creative Word Processing in the Classroom* (Fall 1984):13–15.

464   —. "Word Processors in the Classroom: Two Views." *Computers, Reading, and Language Arts* 1 (Fall 1983):38–39.

465   Lockwood, Russ. "Choosing and Using a Word Processor," "Word Processor Comparison Chart." *Creative Computing* 10.12 (December 1984):126–142.

466   Lofgreen, Charlotte D. "Computers and College Composition." *CALICO Journal* 1.1 (1983):47–50.

467   Logan, Harry M. "The Computer and Metrical Scansion." *The Association for Literary and Linguistic Computing Journal* 3.1 (Spring 1982):9–14.

468   Logan, Harry M., and Barry W. Miller. "A Case for *The Book of the Duchess:* A Semantic Analysis of Sentence Structure." In *Sixth International Conference on Computers and the Humanities,* edited by Sarah K. Burton and Douglas D. Short. Rockville, MD: Computer Science Press, 1983, pp. 384–390.

469   Loheyde, K. M. J. "Computer Use in the Teaching of Composition: Considerations for Teachers of Writing." *Computers in the Schools* 1.2 (Summer 1984): 81–86.

470   Longo, Stephen A. "Similarities Between a Computer Language and a Natural Language." In *Collected Essays on the Written Word and the Word Processor,* edited by Thomas E. Martinez. Villanova, PA: Villanova University Press, 1984, pp. 148–155.

471   Lozy, Mohamed El. *Editing in a UNIX Environment: The vi/ex Editor.* Englewood Cliffs, NJ: Prentice-Hall, 1985.

472   Lusignan, Serge, and John S. North, eds. *Computing in the Humanities. Proceedings of the Third International Conference on Computing in the Humanities.* Waterloo: University of Waterloo Press, 1977.

473   Lutz, Jean Ann. "A Study of Professional and Experienced Writers Revising and Editing at the Computer with Pen and Paper." Unpublished dissertation, Rensselaer Polytechnic Institute, 1983.

474   Lyman, Elisabeth R., and Deborah S. Postlewait. *Lessons on Line: English, ESL.* C.E.R.L. PLATO Lesson Catalog: Curricular and Utility Programs. Urbana, IL: University of Illinois, 1980.

475 Lyons, Thomas R. "Computer-Assisted Instruction in English Composition." *Pipeline* 6.2 (1981):13–14.

476 Macdonald, Nina H. "The UNIX Writer's Workbench Software: Rationale and Design." *Bell System Technical Journal* 62.6, pt. 3 (July–August 1983): 1891–1908.

477 Macdonald, Nina H, *et al.* "The Writer's Workbench: Computer Aids for Text Analysis." *Educational Psychologist* 17.3 (1982):172–179.

478 McAllister, Carole H. "The Effects of Word Processing in the Quality of Writing: Fact or Illusion?" *Computers and Composition* 2.4 (August 1985): 36–44.

479 McCole, Moira. "Technical Writing and Word Processing." In *Collected Essays on the Written Word and the Word Processor,* edited by Thomas E. Martinez. Villanova, PA: Villanova University Press, 1984, pp. 394–399.

480 McConnell, J. C., and Paul Fortier. *THEME: A System for Computer-Aided Theme Searches of French Texts.* Winnipeg, Canada: University of Manitoba, Department of French and Spanish, 1975.

481 McCoy, Ingeborg M., and David M. Weible. "Foreign Languages and the New Media: The Videodisc and the Microcomputer." In *Practical Applications in Foreign Language Teaching,* edited by Charles J. James. Skokie, IL: National Textbook, 1983, pp. 105–152.

482 McCulloch, D. W. "Computer Software Exchange: Some Economic Considerations." *Educational Technology* 21 (May 1981):34–35.

483 McDaniel, Ellen. "Software for Text Analysis and Writing Instruction." *Research in Word Processing Newsletter* 3.9 (December 1985):7–13.

484 —. "Using Computers to Write About Computers and Writing: A Lesson in Comparative Literacies." In *Computers and Composition: Selected Papers from the Conference on Computers in Writing: New Directions in Teaching and Research, University of Minnesota, April 1984,* edited by Lillian Bridwell, Donald Ross, Cynthia L. Selfe, and Kathleen E. Kiefer. Houghton, MI, and Fort Collins, CO: Michigan Technological University and Colorado State University, 1985, pp. 213–231.

485 McFarlane, James. "Indexing by Microcomputer: An Easy Way to Put the Finishing Touches on Your Literary Masterpiece." *Creative Computing* 10.12 (December 1984):168, 171.

486 McGarvey, Jack. "Is It Time to Boot Out Cursive Writing?" *Classroom Computer Learning* 6.6 (March 1986):36–37.

487 —. "Search-and-Replace: Developing an Editor's Eye." *Computer Classroom Learning* 5.7 (March 1985):46–48.

488 McGovern, Edmond. *Wordprocessing: A Writer's Guide.* Exeter, England: Globefield Press, 1985.

489 McKenzie, Alan T., ed. *A Grin on the Interface: Word Processing and the Academic Humanist.* New York: Modern Language Association, 1984.

490 —. "The Word Processor and the Typing Chores of the Academic Department." In *A Grin on the Interface: Word Processing for the Academic Humanist,*

edited by Alan T. McKenzie. New York: The Modern Language Association of America, 1984, pp. 25–38.

491 —. "The Word Processor and the Work Habits of the Academic Humanist." In *A Grin on the Interface: Word Processing for the Academic Humanist,* edited by Alan T. McKenzie. New York: The Modern Language Association of America, 1984, pp. 10–24.

492 McKenzie, Jamieson. "Accordion Writing—Expository Composition With the Word Processor." *English Journal* 73 (September 1984):56–58.

493 McSherry, James E. *Computer Typesetting: A Guide for Authors, Editors, and Publishers.* Arlington, VA: Open-Door Press, 1984.

494 Mace, Scott. "Novelists Inspire Games: Science-Fiction Authors Lend Their Talents to 'Interactive Fiction.'" *Infoworld* 6.25 (June 18 1984):42–45.

495 Mackey, Kevin. "Electronic Mail in the Writing Class." *Classroom Computer Learning* 5.3 (October 1984):32–33.

496 Madian, Jon. "Curriculum Strategies Through Word Processing." *Creative Word Processing in the Classroom* Winter–Spring 1984:v1–v6.

497 Madigan, Chris. "The Tools That Shape Us: Composing by Hand vs. Composing by Machine." *English Education* 16 (October 1984):143–150.

498 Maloney, Eric. "Word Processors Don't Improve Writing." *80 Micro* August 1985:8.

499 Marchesano, Louis. "Process CAI: A Bridge Between Theory and Practice in Writing Instruction." *Collegiate Microcomputer* 4.1 (February 1986):83–87.

500 Marchuk, Yu. N. "Machine Translation in the U.S.S.R." *CHum* 18 (1984):23–38.

501 Marcus, Stephen. "COMPUPOEM: A Computer Writing Activity." *English Journal* 71 (February 1982):96–99.

502 —. "Computers and the Poetic Muse." In *Sixth International Conference on Computers and the Humanities,* edited by Sarah K. Burton and Douglas D. Short. Rockville, MD: Computer Science Press, 1983, pp. 406–408.

503 —. "Computers in the Curriculum: Writing." *Electronic Learning* (October 1984):54–56.

504 —. "The Host in the Machine: Decorum in Computers Who Speak." In *Proceedings of the American Educational Research Association.* New Orleans, LA: April 1984, 3 pp.

505 —. "The Muse and the Machine." In *Handbook for Planning an Effective Writing Program;* rev. ed. Sacramento, CA: California State Department of Education, 1983, pp. 59–62.

506 —. "Real-Time Gadgets with Feedback: Special Effects in Computer-Assisted Writing." In *The Computer in Composition Instruction: A Writer's Tool,* edited by William Wresch. Urbana, IL: NCTE, 1984, pp. 120–130. [Reprinted from *The Writing Instructor* 2.4 (Summer 1983):156–164.]

507 Marcus, Stephen, and Sheridan Blau. "Not Seeing Is Relieving: Invisible Writing with Computers." *Educational Technology* 23 (April 1983):12–15.

508 Marius, Richard, and Harvey S. Weiner. "Writing With Word Processors." In *The McGraw-Hill College Handbook.* New York: McGraw-Hill, 1985, pp. 572–574.

509 Markosian, L., and T. Ager. "Applications of Parsing Theory to Computer-Assisted Instruction." *System* 11.1 (1983):65–77.

510 Marling, William. "Grading Essays on a Microcomputer." *College English* 46.8 (December 1984):797–810.

511 Martindale, Colin. "Evolutionary Trends in Poetic Style: The Case of English Metaphysical Poetry." *CHum* 18 (1984):3–22.

512 Martinez, Thomas. "Apples and Pears: Use of Apple Computers To Aid Secondary School Writing." In *Collected Essays on the Written Word and the Word Processor,* edited by Thomas E. Martinez. Villanova, PA: Villanova University Press, 1984, pp. 70–87.

513 —, ed. *Collected Essays on the Written Word and the Word Processor* (from the Delaware Valley Writing Council's Spring Conference, 25 February 1984. Villanova, PA: Villanova University Press).

514 —. "Using the Bank Street Writer As an Aid for Freshman English Writing." *Collegiate Microcomputer* 3.4 (November 1985):291–294.

515 Marty, Fernand. "Reflections on the Use of Computers in Second Language Learning Acquisition." In *Language Study and the PLATO System,* edited by Robert Hart. Studies in Language Learning 3.1. Urbana, IL: University of Illinois, 1981, pp. 25–53.

516 Melby, Alan K. "The Translation Profession and the Computer." *CALICO Journal* 1.1 (1983):55–57.

517 Melendez, Gloria S. "Interactive Instruction in Spanish Interfacing the Microcomputer and the Videodisc." *MICRO* 1.1 (1980):11–12.

518 Mendelson, Edward. "Word Processing: A Guide for the Perplexed." *The Yale Review.* 74.4 (Summer 1985):615–640.

519 Meredith, J. C. *The CAI Author/Instructor: An Introduction and Guide to the Preparation of Computer Assisted Instruction Materials.* Minneapolis, MN: ACH, 1985.

520 Meunier, Jean G., Serge Boivert, and François Denis. "The Lemmatisation of Contemporary French." In *The Computer in Literary and Linguistic Studies,* edited by Jones and Churchhouse. Cardiff, Wales: University of Wales Press, 1976, pp. 208–214.

521 Michalski, Ryszard S., *et al.,* eds. *Machine Learning: An Artificial Intelligence Approach.* Palo Alto, CA: Tioga Publishing Co., 1983.

522 Microcomputer Support Group. "Word Processing Packages." *Academic's Guide to Microcomputer Systems.* Toronto, ON: University of Toronto Computing Services, 1985, pp. 62–109.

523 Mikelonis, Victoria, and Vicki Gervickas. "Using Computers in the Technical Writing Classroom: A Selected Bibliography (1978–84)." *The Technical Writing Teacher* 12.2 (Fall 1985):161–176.

524 Milic, Louis T. *Style and Stylistics: An Analytical Bibliography.* New York: The Free Press, 1967.

525 —. *A Quantitative Approach to the Style of Jonathan Swift.* The Hague, Netherlands: Mouton, 1967.

526 —. "The Annals of Computing: Stylistics." *CHum* 16 (1982):19–24.

527 Miller, Lance A., *et al.* "Text-Critiquing with the EPISTLE System: An Author's Aid to Better Syntax." In *AFIPS Proceedings, National Computer Conference.* May 4–7, 1981. (Arlington, VA: AFIPS Press, 1981):649–655.

528 Milner, Joseph O., ed. *Micro to Main Frame Computers in English Education.* Urbana, IL: NCTE, 1982.

529 Mirza, J. S. "Vowels' Extraction Using a Microcomputer for Acoustical Investigations." *ALLC Bulletin* 13 (1985):39–42.

530 Misek, Linda D. *Automated Contextual Analysis of Thematic Structure in Natural Languages.* Cleveland, OH: Case Western Reserve, 1970.

531 —. "Computing a Context: Style, Structure, and the Self-Image of Satan in *Paradise Lost.*" Unpublished dissertation, Case Western Reserve University, 1972.

532 —. *Context Concordance to John Milton's "Paradise Lost."* Cleveland: Case Western Reserve University, 1971.

533 Misek-Falkoff, Linda D. "Computing, Text Markup, and 'Speech Acts': From Outline to Published Book with Authorial Ease." Yorktown Heights, NY: Thomas J. Watson Research Center (IBM), 1983. [Paper presented at Sixth International Conference on Computers and the Humanities, June 6–8, 1983. North Carolina State University at Raleigh.]

534 —. "Using Text Processors To Create Finished Books and Rhetorically Indexed Data-Bases." Yorktown Heights, NY: Thomas J. Watson Research Center (IBM), 1984. [Paper presented to New York Special-Interest Group in Computers and the Humanities. (January 18, 1984). IBM, New York City.]

535 Mitchel, J. L., and Kellen C. Thornton. "Computer-Aided Analysis of Old English Manuscripts." *Computing in the Humanities,* edited by Peter C. Patton *et al.* Lexington, MA: Lexington Books, 1981, pp. 105–112.

536 Mitchell, J. L., ed. *Computers in the Humanities.* Edinburgh, Scotland: Edinburgh University Press, 1974.

537 Mitchell, Catherine C. "Computers Are Only Machines." *The Chronicle of Higher Education* 39.18 (January 16 1985):40.

538 Moberg, Goran G. *Writing on Computers in English Comp.* New York: The Writing Consultant, 1986.

539 Modern Language Association. "Bibliography Programs for Humanities Scholars." *MLA Newsletter* 15.3 (Fall 1983):6.

540 —. "Multilingual Word-Processing Equipment." *MLA Newsletter* 16.1 (Spring 1984):15.

541 —. "New Software for Bibliographic Search." *MLA Newsletter* 17.1 (Spring 1985):5.

542 —. "On-Line with the MLA." *MLA Newsletter* 16.2 (Summer 1984):4.

543 —. "Update on Multilingual Word-Processing." *MLA Newsletter* 16.2 (Summer 1984):13–14.

544 —. "User-Friendly On-Line Searching." *MLA Newsletter* 16.4 (Winter 1984): 5–6.

545 —. "Word Processing for the Scholar." *MLA Newsletter* 17.2 (Summer 1985):2.

546 Moe, A. J. "Analyzing Text With Computers." *Educational Technology* 20.7 (July 1980):29–31.

547 Moffett, John B., and S. J. De Amicis. "Computer-Assisted Editing." In *Conference Record: The Many Facets of Computer Communications.* IEEE Professional Communication Society. Atlanta, Georgia (October 19–21 1983):35–43.

548 Monahan, Brian D. "Computing and Revising." *English Journal* 71 (1982): 93–94.

549 Montgomery, J. "Cloze Procedure: A Computer Application." *The Computing Teacher* 11.9 (May 1984):16–18, 20.

550 Moorman, Charles. "Computing Housman's Fleas: A Statistical Analysis of Manly's Landmark Manuscripts in the General Prologue to *The Canterbury Tales.*" In *Sixth International Conference on Computers and the Humanities,* edited by Sarah K. Burton and Douglas D. Short. Rockville, MD: Computer Science Press, 1983, pp. 431–446.

551 Moran, Charles. "Word Processing and the Teaching of Writing." *English Journal* 72 (March 1983):113–115.

552 Morgan, Bradford A. "Communication Feedback with a Word Processor." Conference Record: The Many Facets of Computer Communication. IEEE Professional Communication Society, Atlanta, GA: October 19–21, 1983. 95–98.

553 —. "Evaluating Student Papers With a Word Processor." In *Collected Essays on the Written Word and the Word Processor,* edited by Thomas E. Martinez. Villanova, PA: Villanova University Press, 1984, pp. 233–242. Partially republished in *Research in Word Processing Newsletter* 2 (September 1984):1–6.

554 —. "Setting up a Word Processing Microlab." *Research in Word Processing Newsletter* 3.2 (February 1985):1–3.

555 —. "Stack Crunching: Use a Standalone To Process Student Papers." *Research in Word Processing Newsletter* 2.2 (February 1984):1–5.

556 Morgan, Charles. "Word Processors and the Teaching of Writing." *English Journal* 72.3 (March 1983):113–115.

557 Morrisey, Robert, and Claude Del Vigna. "A Large Natural Data Base: American and French Research on the Treasury of the French Language." In *Data Bases in the Humanities and Social Sciences,* edited by Robert F. Allen. Osprey, FL: Paradigm Press, 1985, pp. 17–21.

558 Morton, A.Q. *Literary Detection: How to Prove Authorship and Fraud in Literature and Documents.* New York: Scribners, 1978.

559   Morton, A. Q., and James McLeman. *Christianity and the Computer*. London: Hodder and Stoughton, 1964.

560   Mosteller, Frederick, and David L. Wallace. *Inference and Disputed Authorship: The Federalist*. Reading, MA: Addison-Wesley, 1964.

561   Muller, Charles. *Initiation aux méthodes de la statistique linguistique*. Paris, France: Hachette, 1973.

562   Murray, Janet *et al.* "M.I.T.'s Athena Language Learning Project." *Northeast Conference on the Teaching of Foreign Languages Newsletter* 18 (1985):46–48.

563   Mydlarski, Donna, and Dana Paramskas. "PROMPT: A Template System for Second Language Reading Comprehension." *CALICO Journal* 1.5 (1984): 3–7.

564   Nancarrow, Paula Reed, Donald Ross, and Lillian Bridwell, eds. *Word Processors and the Writing Process: An Annotated Bibliography*. Westport, CT: Greenwood Press, 1984.

565   Negus, Kenneth C. "Self-Publishing German Texts With Microcomputers." In *Sixth International Conference on Computers and the Humanities*, edited by Sarah K. Burton and Douglas D. Short. Rockville, MD: Computer Science Press, 1983, pp. 454–455.

566   Nelson, Robert J. "Electronic Media in Foreign Language Education: A Report on Applications." *French Review* 46.2 (1982):330–41.

567   Neuwirth, Christine M. "Toward the Design of a Flexible, Computer-Based Writing Environment." *The Computer in Composition Instruction: A Writer's Tool*, edited by William Wresch. Urbana, IL: NCTE, 1984, pp. 191–205.

568   Newman, John Henry. *The Idea of a University*. London, England: 1907.

569   Newman, Michael. "Poetry Processing: The Concept of Artistic Freedom Takes on New Meaning When Text Processing Handles the Mundane Tasks of Prosody." *Byte* 11.2 (February 1986):221–228.

570   Nievergelt, Juge, *et al. Document Processing Systems: A Collection of Survey Articles*. Amsterdam: North-Holland Publishing Company, 1982.

571   Nisenholtz, M., and E. M. Morphos. "Information Technology and New Forms of Participation in the Narrative." In *Information Processing 83: Proceedings of the IFIP 9th World Computer Congress*. Paris, France: September 19–23, 1983, pp. 727–731.

572   Nissan, Ephraim. *Advances in Computing and the Humanities*. vol 1. Greenwich, CT: JAI Press, 1985.

573   Noble, David F., and Virginia Noble. *Improve Your Writing With Word Processing*. Indianapolis, IN: Que, 1985.

574   Nugent, Gwen., P. J. Peters, and Lee Rockwell. *Instructional Development for Videotex: Flowcharts and Scripting*. Report 3. San Diego, CA: Electronic Text Consortium, San Diego State University, 1984.

575   Nydahl, Joel. "Writing Instruction Software with HBJ WRITER." *Research in Word Processing Newsletter* 4.4 (April 1986):12–16.

576 Oakman, Robert L. "Carlyle and the Machine: A Quantitative Analysis of Syntax in Prose Style." *ALLC Bulletin* 3 (1975):100–114.

577 —. *Computer Methods for Literary Research.* 2nd ed. Athens: University of Georgia Press, 1984.

578 —. "Textual Editing and the Computer." *Costerus* 4 (1975):79–106.

579 —. "Using the Computer in Literary Research: Reflections on the State of the Art." *Literary Research Newsletter* 5.1 (Winter 1980):3–14.

580 Oates, W. "An Evaluation of Computer-Assisted Instruction in English Grammar Review." *Language Study and the PLATO System,* edited by Robert S. Hart. Studies in Language Learning 3.1. Urbana, IL: University of Illinois, 1981.

581 O'Brien, P. "Using Microcomputers in the Writing Class." *The Computing Teacher* 11.9 (May 1984):20–21.

582 O'Connor, Rory J. "Outline Processors Catch On." *Infoworld* 6.27 (July 2 1984):30–31.

583 Ohanian, Susan. "IBM's 'Writing to Read' Program: Hot New Item or Same Old Stew?" *Classroom Computer Learning* 4.8 (March 1984):30–33.

584 Olds, Henry F. "A New Generation of Word Processors." *Computer Classroom Learning* 5.7 (March 1985):22–25.

585 Olds, Henry F., Jr., and Anne Dickenson. "Move Over, Word Processors— Here Come the Databases." *Computer Classroom Learning* 6.2 (October 1985):46–49.

586 Oliver, Lawrence J. "Monster, Not Mentor: A Comment on 'Monsters and Mentors.' " *College English* 46 (April 1984):410–416 (with response by Helen J. Schwartz; see #716).

587 —. "Pitfalls in Electronic Writing Land." *English Education* 16 (May 1984): 94–100.

588 Olsen, Solveig, ed. *Computer-Aided Instruction in the Humanities.* New York: The Modern Language Association of America, 1985.

589 —. "Foreign Language Departments and Computer-Assisted Instruction: A Survey." *Modern Language Journal* 64.3 (1980):341–349.

590 —. "The Prospects of CAI in Foreign Language Studies." *MICRO* 1.3 (1980): 4–6.

591 O'Malley, Christopher. "Going Beyond Word Processing: Spelling Checkers, Thesauruses, Outliners, and Style Analyzers Pick Up Where Word Processing Software Leaves Off to Help You Sidestep Embarassing Mistakes." *Personal Computing* 9.12 (December 1985):113–121.

592 Ong, Walter J. *Orality and Literacy: The Technologizing of the Word.* New York: Methuen, 1982.

593 Oreovicz, Frank S. "A Writing Instructor's Best Friend: The Word Processor." *Engineering Education* (February 1983):376–377.

594 Ott, Wilhelm. "Bibliographie: Computer in der Editionstechnik." *ALLC Bulletin* 2.1 (1974):73–80.

595   —. "Computer Applications in Textual Criticism." *The Computer and Literary Studies,* edited by Aitken, Bailey, and Hamilton-Smith. Edinburgh, Scotland: Edinburgh University Press, 1973, pp. 199–223.

596   —. "The Emancipated Input/Output." *The Computer and Linguistic Studies,* edited by Jones and Churchhouse. Cardiff, Wales: University of Wales Press, 1976, pp. 27–37.

597   —. *Materialen zu Metrik und Stilistik.* 15 vols. Tuebingen: Max Niemeyer Verlag, 1970.

598   Packard, David. "Can Scholars Publish Their Own Books?" *Scholarly Publishing* 5 (1973):65–74.

599   —. "Metrical and Grammatical Patterns in the Greek Hexameter." In *The Computer in Literary and Linguistic Studies,* edited by Jones and Churchhouse. Cardiff, Wales: University of Wales Press, 1976, pp. 85–91.

600   Paijmans, J. J. "Natural Language Databases on Microcomputers." In *Data Bases in the Humanities and Social Sciences,* edited by Robert F. Allen. Osprey, FL: Paradigm Press, 1985, pp. 341–346.

601   Paikeday, Thomas M. "The Joy of Lex." *Creative Computing* (November 1983): 240–245.

602   Palmer, Al, *et al.* "Changing Teacher and Student Attitudes Through Word Processing." *The Computing Teacher* 11.9 (May 1984):45–47.

603   Paramskas, Dana M. "Courseware-Software Interfaces: Some Designs and Some Problems." *CALICO Journal* 1.3 (1983):4–6.

604   Park, William M. "Computer-Assisted Instruction: The View from the Language Lab." *Unterrichtspraxis* 17.1 (1984):53–55.

605   Parris, P. B. "Building the Perfect Beast: Pre-Writing Fiction Without Special Software." In *SCCS: Proceedings of the 19th Annual Small College Computing Symposium,* edited by Dale Rognlie. Rapid City, SD: South Dakota School of Mines and Technology, April 11–12, 1986, pp. 231–237.

606   Parrish, Stephen M. "Concordance-Making by Computer: Its Past, Future, Techniques and Applications." In *Proceedings: Computer Applications to Problems in the Humanities,* edited by Frederick M. Burelbach, Jr. Brockport, NY: Suny College at Brockport, 1970, pp. 16–33.

607   Patton, Peter C., and Renee A. Holoien, eds. *Computing in the Humanities.* Lexington, MA: D.C. Heath, 1981.

608   Paul, Terri, and Don Payne. "Computer-Assisted Instruction: Teaching and Learning from Basic Writers." *The Writing Instructor* 2.4 (Summer 1983): 193–199.

609   Pearlman, Dara. "Throw Out Your Index Cards: Here's How To Use Your Editing System To Take Notes, Keep Files, and Build a Database for Research or Writing Projects. It's a Lot More Efficient Than Shuffling Index Cards." *PC: The Independent Guide to IBM Personal Computers* 4.4 (February 19, 1985):331–332.

610   Pedersen, Elray L. "TICCIT Will Gladly Learn and Gladly Teach Composition Skills." In *Computers and Composition: Selected Papers from the Conference on*

Computers in Writing: New Directions in Teaching and Research, University of Minnesota, April 1984, edited by Lillian Bridwell, Donald Ross, Cynthia L. Selfe, and Kathleen E. Kiefer. Houghton, MI, and Fort Collins, CO: Michigan Technological University and Colorado State University, 1985, pp. 233–241.

611 —. "Computer-Assisted Evaluation of Student Papers: I Can Write Anything You Can Write—Faster and Better." *CALICO Journal* 1.2 (1983):39–42.

612 Petrick, Stanley R. "Natural Language Based Information Management Systems." In *Science, Computers, and the Information Onslaught: A Collection of Essays,* edited by Donald M. Kerr *et al.* New York: Academic Press, 1984, pp. 173–208.

613 Petty, George, and W. M. Gibson. *Project OCCULT: The Ordered Computer Collation of Unprepared Literary Texts.* New York: New York University Press, 1970.

614 Pfaehler, Brenda. "Electronic Text: The University of Wisconsin Experience." *Technological Horizons in Education Journal* 13.1 (August 1985):67–70.

615 Pfaffenberger, Bryan. *The Scholar's Personal Computing Handbook: A Practical Guide.* Boston, MA: Little, Brown, 1986.

616 —. "A Scholar's Typology of Database Management Programs." *Research in Word Processing Newsletter* 3.1 (January 1985):1–6.

617 —. "Taking Notes," "Studying Notes," "Researching Papers," "Writing Papers," and "Revising Papers." In *The College Student's Personal Computer Handbook.* Berkeley, CA: Sybex, 1984, pp. 58–162.

618 —. "Word Processing in Composition Instruction: Achievements and Prospects." In *SCCS: Proceedings of the 19th Annual Small College Computing Symposium,* edited by Dale Rognlie. Rapid City, SD: South Dakota School of Mines and Technology, April 11–12, 1986, pp. xii–xx.

619 Picchi, E., *et al.* "A Morphosyntactic Analyzer for Italian." In *Sixth International Conference on Computers and the Humanities,* edited by Burton and Short. Rockville, MD: Computer Science Press, 1983, pp. 512–20.

620 Pickett, Nell Ann, and Ann A. Laster. "Computer Graphics." *Technical English: Writing, Reading and Speaking.* 4th ed. New York: Harper & Row, 1984, pp. 496–497.

621 Piper, Karen L. "The Electronic Writing Machine: Using Word Processors with Students." *The Computing Teacher* 11.5 (December 1983–January 1984): 82–83.

622 —. "Separating Wheat from Chaff: Evaluating Word Processing Programs for Language Arts Instruction." *Computers, Reading and Language Arts* 1 (Winter 1983):9–14.

623 Pogue, Richard E. "The Authoring System: Interface between Author and Computer." *Journal of Research and Development in Education* 14 (1980):57–68.

624 Pollitt, A. H. "Warming to the Wonder of the Word Processor." *The Computing Teacher* 11.9 (May 1984):48–49.

625 Porter, Martin. "Oxford Goes On-Line: As the Editors of the Huge and Authoritative *Oxford English Dictionary* Put All 17 Volumes On-Line, IBM Is

Providing Funds and PCs for the Project." *PC: The Independent Guide to IBM Personal Computers* 4.4 (February 29 1985):233–238.

626   Potter, Rosanne G. "BIBOUT: MLA Style from a Bibliographic Data Base." In *Sixth International Conference on Computers and the Humanities,* edited by Sarah K. Burton and Douglas D. Short. Rockville, MD: Computer Science Press, 1983, pp. 525–532.

627   Priven, Judith S. "Authoring vs. Programming: Computer Software from the Educator's Point of View." *Media and Methods* 18 (November 1982):10–13.

628   *Proceedings of the First International Workshop on Natural Language Understanding and Logic Programming.* Rennes, France. 18–20 September, 1984. New York: Elsevier Science Publishers, 1985.

629   "Public Domain Software Listings." *Computing Teacher* 11.7 (1984):46–59.

630   Pufahl, John. "Response to Richard M. Collier, 'The Word Processor and Revision Strategies.' " *College Composition and Communication* 34 (May 1983): 49–55.

631   Purvis, Dale, Mimi Schwartz, and Faye Vowell. "Computers, Word Processors, and the Teaching of Writing." Cassette. 1983 NCTE Convention Speech. Urbana IL: NCTE, 1983, 65 minutes.

632   Pusack, James P. "Answer-Processing and Error Correction in Foreign Language CAI." *System* 11.1 (1983):53–64.

633   —. "Computer-Assisted Instruction in Foreign Languages." *Pipeline* 6.2 (1981):5–8, 10. EJ 255 507.

634   —. *DASHER: A Natural Language Answer Processor.* Iowa City: CONDUIT, 1982.

635   Pusack, James P., and Sue K. Otto. "Stringing Us Along: Programming for Foreign Language CAI." *CALICO Journal* 1.2 (1983):26–33.

636   —. "Blueprint for a Comprehensive Foreign Language CAI." *CHum* 18 (1984):195–204.

637   Putnam, Constance E. "Foreign Language Instructional Technology: The State of the Art." *CALICO Journal* 1.1 (1983):35–41.

638   Quinn, Robert A. "Teaching Spanish Poetry Via Microcomputer: A Creative, Integral Approach to Becquer's RIMAS." In *Sixth International Conference on Computers and the Humanities,* edited by Sarah K. Burton and Douglas D. Short. Rockville, MD: Computer Science Press, 1983, pp. 551–555.

639   Raben, Joseph. "A Computer-Aided Study of Literary Influence: Milton to Shelley." In *Proceedings of a Literary Data Processing Conference, September 9–11, 1964,* edited by Jess B. Bessinger, Jr., Stephen M. Parrish, and Harry F. Arader. New York: Modern Language Association, 1964, pp. 230–274.

640   —. "Computer Applications in the Humanities." *Science* 228 (April–June 1985):434–438.

641   —. "Text Comparison: Principles and a Program." *The Computer and Linguistic Studies,* edited by Jones and Churchhouse. Cardiff, Wales: University of Wales Press, 1976, pp. 297–308.

642   Radday, Yehuda T. *The Unity of Isaiah in Light of Statistical Linguistics.* Hildesheim: Gerstenberg, 1973.

643 Radencich, Marguerite C., and Jeanne S. Schumm. "To Byte or Not to Byte." *Media and Methods* 20 (September 1984):9–12.

644 Ragsdale, Ronald G. *Evaluation of Microcomputer Courseware.* Toronto, Canada: Ontario Institute for Studies in Education, 1982.

645 Rangel, Dianne Kerr, Ludmilla P. Mercado, and Danny B. Daniel. "Aspects of Developing CAI for English as a Second Language." In *NECC '84: 6th Annual Educational Computing Conference,* edited by Della T. Bonnette. Dayton, OH: University of Dayton, June 13–15, 1984, pp. 282–285.

646 Ranson, Nicholaas, and Jean Knepley. "Edmund Ironside: A Reappraisal Appraised." Paper presented at the Seventh International Conference on Computers and the Humanities, 1985.

647 Raye, Carol L. "Writer's Workbench System: Heralding a Revolution in Textual Analysis." In *Sixth International Conference on Computers and the Humanities,* edited by Sarah K. Burton and Douglas D. Short. Rockville, MD: Computer Science Press, 1983, pp. 569–572.

648 Razik, T. A., ed. *The Educational Technology Bibliography Series.* 1. Minneapolis, MN: ACH, 1985.

649 Redman, Timothy, Deborah H. Holdstein, and L. DeCelles. "Evaluating Computer-Assisted Instruction for Writing: A First Glance." *Collegiate Microcomputer* 2.2 (May 1984):101–106.

650 Reed, Mary Jac M., and Lynn H. Smith. "Developing Large CAI Packages." *CALICO Journal* 1.3 (1983):13–16.

651 Reichman, Rachel. *Getting Computers to Talk Like You and Me: Discourse Context, Focus, and Semantics.* Cambridge, MA: MIT Press, 1985.

652 Reid, Joy, *et al.* "Computer-Assisted Text-Analysis for ESL Students." *CALICO Journal* 1.3 (1983):40–42, 46.

653 Rich, Elaine. "Natural-Language Interfaces." *Computer* 17:9 (September 1984):39–47.

654 Ridgway, Jim, *et al.* "Conclusions from CALtastrophies." *Computers and Education* 8.1 (1984):93–100.

655 Riedl, Richard. "CompuServe in the Classroom: A Journalism Class Uses This Information Utility as a News Resource." *The Computing Teacher* 13.6 (March 1986):62–64.

656 Ritchie, Graeme D. *Computational Grammar: An Artificial Intelligence Approach to Linguistic Description.* New York: Barnes and Noble, 1980.

657 Robertson, Barbara. "Page Making on Your Micro: Design Typeset, and Paste Up Electronically with Powerful New Software." *Popular Computing* 5.1 (November 1985):60–62, 134, 137.

658 Robyler, M. D. "When Is It 'Good Courseware'? Problems in Developing Standards for Microcomputer Courseware." *Educational Technology* 21.10 (1981):47–54.

659 Roddy, Kevin P. "Project Rhetor: An Encyclopedia in the History of Rhetoric." In *Sixth International Conference on Computers and the Humanities,* edited by

Sarah K. Burton and Douglas D. Short. Rockville, MD: Computer Science Press, 1983, pp. 579–587.

660   Rodrigues, Dawn. "Computers and Basic Writers." *College Composition and Communication* 36.3 (October 1985):336–339.

661   Rodrigues, Dawn, and Raymond J. Rodrigues. "Computer-Based Creative Problem Solving." *The Computer in Composition Instruction: A Writer's Tool,* edited by William Wresch. Urbana, IL: NCTE, 1984, pp. 34–46.

662   —. "Computer-Based Invention: Its Place and Potential." *College Composition and Communication* 35 (February 1984):78–87.

663   Rodrigues, Raymond J. "The Computer-Based Writing Program from Load to Print." *English Journal* 73 (January 1984):27–30.

664   —. "Creating Writing Lessons with a Word Processor." *The Computing Teacher* 13.5 (February 1986):41–43.

665   —. "The Computer-Based Writing Program from Load to Print." *English Journal* 23 (January 1984):27–30.

666   Rogers, Raymond A. "Pinyin for the PC: Designing a Chinese Word Processor Is No Easy Task." *PC World* 2.6 (June 1984):285–289.

667   "Ronald Cole on Voice-Recognition Technology and Personal Computing." *Personal Computing* 7.7 (1983):47–53.

668   Roseberry, Robert L. "Two Computer Programs for the Language Student." *CALICO Journal* 1.4 (1984):20–24.

669   Rosen, Arnold. *Getting the Most Out of Your Word Processor.* Englewood Cliffs, NJ: Prentice-Hall, 1983.

670   Rosenbaum, Nina J. "Issues and Problems with Research Involving Word Processing: A Teacher's Experience." In *Collected Essays on the Written Word and the Word Processor,* edited by Thomas E. Martinez. Villanova, PA: Villanova University Press, 1984, pp. 331–347.

671   Rosenthal, Steve. "Prose with Style: An Overview of Writer's Workbench." *UNIX Review* 2.5 (August 1984):46–56.

672   Ross, Donald. "Beyond the Concordance: Algorithms for Description of English Clauses and Phrases." *The Computer and Literary Studies,* edited by Aitken, Bailey, and Hamilton-Smith. Edinburgh, Scotland: Edinburgh University Press, 1973, pp. 85–99.

673   —. *Description and User's Instructions for EYEBALL.* Minneapolis, MN: University of Minnisota Department of English, 1974.

674   —. "EYEBALL: A Computer Program for Description of Style." *CHum* 6 (1972):213–221.

675   —. "EYEBALL and the Analysis of Literary Style." In *Computing in the Humanities,* edited by Peter C. Patton and Renée A. Holoien. Lexington, MA: D.C. Heath, 1981, pp. 85–103.

676   —. "An EYEBALL View of Blake's *Songs of Innocence and of Experience.*" *Computers in the Humanities,* edited by J. L. Mitchell. Edinburgh, Scotland: Edinburgh University Press, 1974, pp. 94–108.

677 —. "Humanists' Control of Emerging Technologies." Paper delivered at the University of Minnesota Symposium on Technology in a Humane Society February 1985.

678 —. "Realities of Computer Analysis of Compositions." In *Writing On-Line: Using Computers in the Teaching of Writing,* edited by J. Collins and E. Sommers. New York: Boynton-Cook, 1985.

679 Rosslyn, Wendy. "COCOA as a Tool for the Analysis of Poetry." *ALLC Bulletin* 3 (1975):15–18.

680 Roth, Audrey J. "From a Computer Writer's Log." *Writing As a Liberating Activity Newsletter* 122 (1984):1–2, 10.

681 Rowe, A. Allen. *Fifty-Four Kiloframes Equals Two Semesters of Language? The Defense Language Institute—Air Force Academy Videodisc Research Project Report No. 1: Origins and Objectives.* Presidio of Monterey: Defense Language Institute Foreign Language Center, 1983.

682 Rubin, Andee, and Bertram Bruce. "QUILL: Reading and Writing With a Microcomputer." Reading Education Report No. 48. Washington, DC: National Institute of Education, 1984, 44 pp.

683 Rubin, Joan. "Using the Educational Potential of Videodisc in Language Learning." *CALICO Journal* 1.4 (1984):31–34.

684 Rubin, Philip. *A Primer on Electronic Text Technology for College Administrators.* Report 4. San Diego, CA: Electronic Text Consortium, San Diego State University, 1984.

685 Rudall, B. H. *Computers and Literature: A Practical Guide.* Tunbridge Wells, Kent: Abacus Press, 1986.

686 Ruschoff, Bernd. "The Integration of CALL Materials into the Overall Curriculum." *CALICO Journal* 1.4 (1984):26–28.

687 Russ-Eft, D., and D. McLaughlin. *Needs and Development Opportunities for Educational Computer Software in Reading, Writing, and Communication Skills.* Washington: Department of Education, 1983. No. 0400-82-0021.

688 Russ-Eft, D., D. McLaughlin, and A. Elman. *Issues for the Development of Reading and Writing Software.* Palo Alto, CA: American Institute for Research in the Behavioral Sciences, 1983.

689 Russell, John R. "Computers and Foreign Language Instruction." *NALLD Journal* 16.3–4 (1982):17–23.

690 Ryan, Vincent, and V. A. Dearing. "Computerized Manuscript and Index Processing." *Scholarly Publishing* 4 (1974):333–350.

691 Sadler, Chris, and Sue Eisenbach. "Selecting Microcomputers for Schools." *Computers and Education* 8.1 (1984):165–171.

692 Sadler, Lynn Veach, and Wendy Tibbetts Greene. "Computer-Assisted Composition at Bennett College." In *Computers and Composition: Selected Papers from the Conference on Computers in Writing: New Directions in Teaching and Research, University of Minnesota, April 1984,* edited by Lillian Bridwell, Donald Ross, Cynthia L. Selfe, and Kathleen E. Kiefer. Houghton, MI, and Fort Collins, CO: Michigan Technological University and Colorado State University, 1985, pp. 243–256.

693 Sadler, Lynn Veach, Wendy Tibbets Greene, and Emory W. Sadler. "The Computer-Assisted Research Paper." In *Proceedings of the 4th World Conference on Computers in Education, WCEE/85.* 2 vols, edited by Karen Duncan and Dianna Harris. Amsterdam, Netherlands: Elsevier Science, 1985, pp. 193–197.

694 —. "Diagrammatic Writing Using Word Processing: 'Larger Vision' Software." *Research in Word Processing Newsletter* 4.1 (January 1986):2–7.

695 Sainte-Marie, Paule, Pierre Robillard, and Paul Bratley. "An Application of Principal Component Analysis to the Works of Molière." *CHum* 7 (1973):- 131–137.

696 Salisbury, David F. "How to Decide When and Where to Use Microcomputers for Instruction." *Educational Technology* 24.3 (1984):22–24.

697 Salton, Gerard. Automatic Information Organization and Retrieval. New York: McGraw-Hill, 1968.

698 —. *Dynamic Information and Library Processing.* Englewood Cliffs, NJ: Prentice-Hall, 1975.

699 —, ed. *The SMART Retrieval System: Experiments in Automatic Document Processing.* Englewood Cliffs, NJ: Prentice-Hall, 1971.

700 Sanders, David, and Roger Kenner. "Whither CAI? The Need for Communicative Courseware." *System* 11.1 (1983):33–39.

701 Sanders, Ruth H. "Artificial Intelligence and Foreign Language Learning." In *Sixth International Conference on Computers and the Humanities,* edited by Sarah K. Burton and Douglas D. Short. Rockville, MD: Computer Science Press, 1983, pp. 595–599.

702 —. "PILOT SPION: A Computer Game for German Students." *Unterrichtspraxis* 17.1 (1984):123–29.

703 Satterwhite, Robb. "Subject Indexing and Creation of a Controlled Vocabulary: The MLA Bibliography and the MLA Thesaurus." In *Data Bases in the Humanities and Social Sciences,* edited by Robert F. Allen. Osprey, FL: Paradigm Press, 1985, pp. 209–217.

704 Savitsky, David. "A Guide to Producing Educational Software." *Computing Teacher* 11.7 (1984):26–27.

705 Scanlan, Richard T. "Computer-Assisted Instruction in Latin and English Vocabulary Development." In *Language Study and the PLATO System,* edited by Robert S. Hart. Studies in Language Learning 3.1. Urbana, IL: University of Illinois, 1981, pp. 113–122.

706 Schaeffer, Reiner H. "Meaningful Practice on the Computer: Is It Possible?" *Foreign Language Annuals* 14.2 (1981):133–137.

707 Schank, Roger C. "English for Computers." In *The Cognitive Computer: On Language, Learning, and Artificial Intelligence.* Reading, MA: Addison-Wesley, 1984, pp. 90–109.

708 Schank, Roger C., and Kenneth Mark Colby, eds. *Computer Models of Thought and Language.* New York: W. H. Freeman, 1973.

709 Schantz, L. M. "The Computer As Tutor, Tool, and Tutee in Composition." *The Computing Teacher* 11.3 (October 1983):60–62.

710 Scherr, Barry P., and Lawrence W. Robinson. "Creating Computer-Assisted Drills for Russian: The Structure of the Data Base." *Russian Language Journal* 34.118 (1980):21–36.

711 Schneider, Ben Ross, Jr. "Using the Computer in Literary Research: The Basic Advantages." *Literary Research Newsletter* 5.1 (Winter 1980):15–20.

712 Schneider, Edward W., and Junius L. Bennion. "Veni, Vidi, Vici via Videodisc: A Simulator for Instructional Conversation." *System* 11.1 (1983):41–46.

713 Schrader, Vincent E. "Teaching Journalism on the Micro." *English Journal* 73 (April 1984):93–94.

714 Schwartz, Helen J. "But What Do I Write? Literary Analysis Made Easier." *Computing Teaching* 11.1 (1983):16–18.

715 —. "Computer Aids for Individualizing Instruction Throughout the Writing Process." Annual Meeting of the Conference on College Composition and Communication. Detroit, MI: March 17–19, 1985. ERIC Document ED 245 225.

716 —. "Hypothesis Testing with Computer-Assisted Instruction." *Educational Technology* 23 (October 1983):26–27.

717 —. *Interactive Writing: Composing With a Word Processor.* New York: Holt, 1985. [Includes a useful instructor's manual and textfile disks for IBM or Apple microcomputers.]

718 —. "Introducing Word Processing to Students." *Research in Word Processing Newsletter* 3.7 (October 1985):1–5.

719 —. "Keeping CAI Humane in the Humanities." Proceedings of the AFIPS Conference. Arlington: AFIPS, 1981.

720 —. "Monsters and Mentors: Computer Applications for Humanistic Education." *College English* 44.2 (1982):141–152. EJ 257 857.

721 —. "SEEN: A Tutorial and User Network for Hypothesis Testing." *The Computer in Composition Instruction: A Writer's Tool,* edited by William Wresch. Urbana, IL: NCTE, 1984, pp. 47–62.

722 —. "Teaching Organization With Word Processing." *Computers, Reading, and Language Arts* 1 (Winter 1983):34–35.

723 —. "Teaching Writing With Computer Aids." *College English* 46.3 (March 1984):239–247.

724 Schwartz, Helen J., and L. Bridwell. "Selected Bibliography on Computers in Composition." *CCC* 35.1 (1984):71–77.

725 Schwartz, James M. "Database Management for Teachers and Researchers." *Research in Word Processing Newsletter* 2.7 (October 1984):1–3.

726 —. "Databases & Bygone Days: Computers in Composition Instruction." *Research in Word Processing Newsletter* 2.3 (March 1984):1–3.

727 Schwartz, Lillian. "Teaching Writing in the Age of the Word Processor and Personal Computer." *Educational Technology* 23 (June 1983):33–35.

728 Schwartz, Mimi. "Computers and the Teaching of Writing." *Educational Technology* 22 (November 1982):27–29.

729 Scotchmoor, Judith. "Order Out of Chaos: Making a Mess Out of Stories Can Actually Help Your Students Learn Word Processing and Sentence-Sequencing Skills." *Classroom Computer Learning* 4.8 (March 1984):69.

730 Sedelow, Sally. "The Use of the Computer for Stylistic Studies of Shakespeare." *CSHVB* 4 (1973):33–36.

731 — and Walter Sedelow, Jr. "Stylistic Analysis." *Automated Language Processing: The State of the Art,* edited by Harold Borko. New York: John Wiley and Sons, 1976, pp. 201–203.

732 Segall, Jeffrey. "The Uses of the Word Processor As an Aid in the Revision Process." In *Collected Essays on the Written Word and the Word Processor,* edited by Thomas E. Martinez. Villanova, PA: Villanova University Press, 1984, pp. 291–298.

733 Seidel, Steven R. "The Software Crisis: Its Impact in the Classroom in the 1990's." *Educational Technology* 22 (July 1982):22–23.

734 Selfe, Cynthia L. "Beyond Bandaids and Bactine: Computer-Assisted Instruction and Revision." ERIC Document ED 232 182.

735 —. "The Electronic Pen: Computers and the Composing Process." In *Writing On-Line: Using Computers in the Teaching of Writing,* edited by James L. Collins and Elizabeth A. Sommers. Upper Montclair, NJ: Boynton-Cook, 1985, pp. 55–66.

736 —. "Software for Hardnoses: CAI for College Composition Teachers." *Educational Technology* 24.9 (September 1984):25–29.

737 —. "Wordsworth II: New Wave CAI for College Composition Teachers." November, 1982. ERIC Document ED 225 151.

738 —. "Wordsworth II: Process-Based CAI for College Composition Teachers." In *The Computer in Composition Instruction: A Writer's Tool,* edited by William Wresch. Urbana, IL: NCTE, 1984, pp. 174–190.

739 Selfe, Cynthia L., and Billie J. Wahlstrom. "The Benevolent Beast: Computer-Assisted Instruction for the Teaching of Writing." *The Writing Instructor* 2.4 (Summer 1984):183–192.

740 Sheridan, James. "Software Should Be Written by Writers." *CALICO Journal* 1.3 (1983):17–19.

741 Sherman, D. "A Computer Archive of Language Materials." In *Computing in the Humanities,* edited by Lusignan and North. Waterloo: University of Waterloo Press, 1977, pp. 283–294.

742 Shillingsburg, Miriam J. "Computer Assistance to Scholarly Editing," *Bulletin of Research in the Humanities* (Winter 1978):448–463.

743 —. "Relying on the Weird: Dangers in Editing by Computer." In *Sixth International Conference on Computers and the Humanities,* edited by Sarah K. Burton and Douglas D. Short. Rockville, MD: Computer Science Press, 1983, pp. 654–658.

744 Shillingsburg, Peter L. "The Computer as Research Assistant in Scholarly Editing." *Literary Research Newsletter* 5.1 (Winter 1980):31–45.

745 Shipley, Linda J., and James K. Gentry. "How Electronic Editing Equipment Affects Editing Performance." *Journalism Quarterly* 58 (1981):371–374, 387.

746 Shneiderman, B., *et al.* "An Empirical Comparison of Two PLATO Text Editors." *Journal of Computer-Based Instruction* 10:1–2 (Summer 1983):43–50.

747 Shostak, Robert. "Computers and Teaching English: Bits 'n' Pieces." *Computing Teacher* 9 (November 1981):49–51.

748 Shuman, R. Baird., ed. *Computer-Assisted English Instruction.* Education in the 80's: English. Washington: National Education Assn., 1981.

749 ——. "A Dozen Ways for English Teachers to Use Microcomputers." *English Journal* 74.6 (October 1985):37–39.

750 Signer, Barbara. "How Do Teacher and Student Evaluations of CAI Software Compare?" *Computing Teacher* 11.3 (1983):34–36.

751 Sigurd, Bengt. "Commentator: A Computer Model of Verbal Production." *Linguistics* 20 (1982):611–632.

752 Sillery, Bob. "Scholars with Computers Dig into the Classics." *Personal Computing* 9.12 (December 1985):29–30.

753 Silva, Georgette, and Harold Love. "The Identification of Text Variants by Computer." *Information Storage and Retrieval* 5 (October 1969):89–108.

754 Simonsen, Redmond. "Bring the Power of Publishing to Your PC: New Options Let You Produce Professional-Looking Documents on Your Computer." *Popular Computing* 5.1 (November 1985):56–59, 129–130.

755 Sirc, G. "A Computer Tool for Analyzing the Composing Process." Paper delivered at the 1984 annual Meeting of the MLA, Washington, December 1984.

756 Siskin, H. Jay. "A Data Storage and Retrieval Program for Text Analysis." In *Sixth International Conference on Computers and the Humanities,* edited by Sarah K. Burton and Douglas D. Short. Rockville, MD: Computer Science Press, 1983, pp. 662–671.

757 Sivin, Jay P., *et al.* "EPIE Reports: Some Notes on Word Processing in the Classroom." *Computers, Language, and Reading Arts* 1:4 (Spring 1984):53–55.

758 Skellings, E. "Rhyming to Reason." *Perspectives in Computing* 3.4 (December 1983):12–19.

759 Smith, Charles R., and Kathleen E. Kiefer. "Computer-Assisted Editing in Expository Writing." In *Proceedings of the Second Annual Role of Computers in Education Conference.* Palantine, IL: Micro-Ideas and William Rainey Harper College, 1982, pp. 87–90.

760 ——. "Using the Writer's Workbench Programs at Colorado State University." In *Sixth International Conference on Computers and the Humanities,* edited by Sarah K. Burton and Douglas D. Short. Rockville, MA: Computer Science Press, 1983, pp. 672–684.

761   Smith, Charles R., Kathleen E. Kiefer, and Patricia S. Gingrich. "Computers Come of Age in Writing Instruction." *Computers and the Humanities* 18:3–4 (July–December 1984):215–224.

762   Smith, Donald Edwin. "Focuser: A Strategic Interaction Paradigm for Language Acquisition." Unpublished dissertation, Rutgers University, 1982.

763   Smith, Joan M. "Transmitting Text: A Standard Way of Communicating Characters." *ALLC Bulletin* 11 (1983):31–8.

764   —. "Transmitting Text: A Standard Way of Communicating Characters." *ALLC Bulletin* 11 (1983):63–68.

765   Smith, John B. "Arras and Literary Criticism." *Literary Criticism and the Computer,* edited by Bernard Derval and Michel Lenoble. Montreal, Canada: ACH, 1985.

766   —. "Computer Criticism." *Style* 12 (Fall 1978):326–356.

767   —. "A New Environment for Literary Analysis." *Perspectives in Computing* 4.2–3 (1984):20–31.

768   —. "Thematic Structures and Complexity." *Style* 9 (1975):32–54.

769   Smith, John B., and Catherine F. Smith. "Spatial Thinking and Top-Down Writing." In *Computers and Composition: Selected Papers from the Conference on Computers in Writing: New Directions in Teaching and Research, University of Minnesota, April 1984,* edited by Lillian Bridwell, Donald Ross, Cynthia L. Selfe, and Kathleen E. Kiefer. Houghton, MI and Fort Collins, CO: Michigan Technological University and Colorado State University, 1985, pp. 257–270.

770   Smith, Kim L. "Using Microcomputer Word Processors for Foreign Languages." *CALICO Journal* 1.4 (1984):45–47.

771   Smith, M. W. A. "Recent Experience and New Developments of Methods for the Determination of Authorship." *ALLC Bulletin* 11 (1983):73–82.

772   Smith, R., K. E. Kiefer, and P. S. Gingrich. "Computers Come of Age in Writing Instruction." *CHum* 18 (1984):215–224.

773   Sokoloff, Harris. "Finding Support for Computer Program Development." *Media and Methods* 17 (October 1981):16–26.

774   Solomon, Gwen. "The Reading-Writing Connection: Four Word Processing Activities." *Electronic Learning* 5.1 (September 1985):46–47.

775   —. *Teaching Writing with Computers: The Power Process.* Englewood Cliffs, NJ: Prentice-Hall, 1986.

776   Sommers, Elizabeth A. "Integrating composing and Computing." In *Writing On-Line: Using Computers in the Teaching of Writing,* edited by James L. Collins and Elizabeth A. Sommers. Upper Montclair, NJ: Boynton-Cook, 1985, pp. 3–10.

777   —. "Classroom Research on Word Processing and the Writing Process." In *Computers and Composition: Selected Papers from the Conference on Computers in Writing: New Directions in Teaching and Research, University of Minnesota, April 1984,* edited by Lillian Bridwell, Donald Ross, Cynthia L. Selfe, and Kath-

leen E. Kiefer. Houghton, MI and Fort Collins, CO: Michigan Technological University and Colorado State University, 1985, pp. 271–276.

778 Sommers, Elizabeth A., and James L. Collins. "Microcomputers and Writing." *Computers and Composition* 2.4 (August 1985):27–35.

779 Southwell, Michael G. "The COMP-LAB Writing Modules: Computer-Assisted Grammar Instruction." In *The Computer in Composition Instruction: A Writer's Tool,* edited by William Wresch. Urbana, IL: NCTE, 1984, pp. 91–104.

780 —. "Computer Assistance for Teaching Writing: A Review of Existing Programs." *Collegiate Microcomputer* 2.3 (August 1984):193–206.

781 —. "Computer-Assisted Instruction in Composition at York College/CUNY: Composition for Basic Writing Students." *The Writing Instructor* 2.4 (Summer 1983):165–172.

782 —. Using Computer-Assisted Instruction for Developmental Writing." *AEDS Journal* 15 (1982):80–91.

783 Sowa, John. *Conceptual Structures: Information Processing in Man and Machine.* Reading, MA: Addison Wesley, 1983.

784 Spezzano, Charles. "Unconventional Outliners." *PC World* (March 1986):168–175.

785 Spisak, James W. "The New Technology: An Author's Perspective." In *The Challenge of Change: Critical Choices for Scholarly Publishing,* edited by Edward T. Cremmins. Washington, DC: Society for Scholarly Publishing, 1982, pp. 26–38.

786 Standiford, Sally N., Kathleen Jaycox, and Anne Auten. *Computers in the English Classroom: A Primer for Teachers.* Urbana, IL: National Council of Teachers of English, 1983.

787 Stanko, Jim. "Using Your Spreadsheet As a Thought Processor." *Lotus: Computing for Managers and Professionals* 1.6 (October 1985):83–85.

788 Steinberg, Esther R. *Teaching Computers to Teach.* Urbana-Champaign, IL: University of Illinois Press, 1984.

789 Stevens, Vance. "A Report of a Project Illustrating the Feasibility of Video/Computer Interface for Use in ESL." *CALICO Journal* 1.1 (1983):27–30, 50.

790 Stewart, George. "The Text Scanner: Program Your Computer to Test the Readability of Any Writing Sample." *Popular Computing* 3.9 (July 1984): 199–203.

791 Stibravy, John A., and Chuck Beck. "Errors Caused by the Use of Word Processing in Reports by Beginning Technical Writing Students." *Research in Word Processing Newsletter* 3.4 (April 1985):9–11.

792 Stolurow, L., and E. Cubillos. *Needs and Development Opportunities for Educational Software for Foreign Language Instruction in Schools.* Washington: Dept. of Education, 1983. No. 0400-82-0021.

793 Stone, Philip. J., *et al. The General Inquirer: A Computer Approach to Content Analysis.* Cambridge, MA: M.I.T. Press, 1966.

794   Strei, Gerry. "Format for the Evaluation of Courseware Used in Computer-Assisted Language Instruction (CALI)." *CALICO Journal* 1.2 (1983):43–46.

795   Strickland, James. "Prewriting and Computing." *Writing On-Line: Using Computers in the Teaching of Writing,* edited by James L. Collins and Elizabeth A. Sommers. Upper Montclair, NJ: Boynton-Cook, 1985, pp. 67–74.

796   Stromberg, Linda, and Ruth J. Kurth. "Using Word Processing to Teach Revision in Written Composition." Annual Meeting of the National Reading Conference. Austin, TX: November 29–December 3, 1985. ED 241 953.

797   Strommer, John. "Subversive Word Processors: Too Much Computer Power Can Undermine a Writer's Efforts." *Popular Computing* 4.7 (May 1985): 160.

798   Stuart, Ann. *Writing and Analyzing Effective Computer System Documentation.* New York: Holt, 1984.

799   Sudol, Ronald A. "Applied Word Processing: Notes on Authority, Responsibility, and Revision in a Workshop Model." *College Composition and Communication* 36.3 (October 1985):331–335.

800   Suhy, Andrew M. "Computers and Clear Writing: A Symbiotic Relationship." In *Collected Essays on the Written Word and the Word Processor,* edited by Thomas E. Martinez. Villanova, PA: Villanova University Press, 1984, pp. 139–147.

801   Sullivan, David R., *et al.* "Advanced Word Processing." In *Computing Today: Microcomputer Concepts and Applications.* Boston, MA: Houghton Mifflin, 1985, pp. 135–155.

802   Swartz, Theodore F. "Finding Funding for Your Computer Project." *Classroom Computer Learning* 4.8 (March 1984):36–41.

803   Swigger, Boyd K. "PROVIDE—A Preliminary Program for Text Analyses." *SIGLASH Newsletter* 6.5 (1973):3.

804   Tallentire, D.R. "The Mathematics of Style (Thinking by Numbers, 2)." *Times Literary Supplement* (August 13, 1971):973–974.

805   Tambovtsev, Yuri A. "The Relations of Some Siberian Languages from the Phonostatistical Viewpoint." In *Sixth International Conference on Computers and the Humanities,* edited by Sarah K. Burton and Douglas D. Short. Rockville, MD: Computer Science Press, 1983, p. 687.

806   Tamplin, John. "Word Processing—Does It Work? Penn State Enjoys Success with On-Line Editor." *Electronic Education* 5.4 (January 1986):10, 16.

807   Tankard, Jim. "The Literary Detective: Use Your Computer To Identify an Unknown Author." *Byte* 11.2 (February 1986):231–238.

808   Taylor, Heimtraut F., and Lillian Pennington. "A Self-Evaluation of the Individualized Instruction Program in German at the Ohio State University." *Unterrichtspraxis* 15.1 (1982):4–13.

809   Thiesmeyer, John. "Some Boundary Considerations for Writing-Software." In *Computers and Composition: Selected Papers from the Conference on Computers in Writing: New Directions in Teaching and Research, University of Minnesota, April 1984,* edited by Lillian Bridwell, Donald Ross, Cynthia L. Selfe, and Kathleen E. Kiefer. Houghton, MI, and Fort Collins, CO: Michigan Technological University and Colorado State University, 1985, pp. 277–291.

810 —. "Teaching With the Text Checkers." In *Collected Essays on the Written Word and the Word Processor,* edited by Thomas E. Martinez. Villanova, PA: Villanova University Press, 1984, pp. 280–290.

811 Thomas, Jean. "Introducing Students to Free Verse on the Word Processor." *NCTE-ACE Newsletter* 1.2 (October–December 1985):10.

812 Thrush, Jo Ann P., and Randolph S. Thrush. "Microcomputers in Foreign Language Instruction." *Modern Language Journal* 68.1 (1984):21–27.

813 Tollenaere, F. de. "The Problem of the Context in Computer-Aided Lexicography." In *The Computer and Literary Studies,* edited by Aitken, Bailey and Hamilton-Smith. Edinburgh, Scotland: Edinburgh University Press, 1973, pp. 25–35.

814 Tracey, Richard. "The Word Processor and the Writing Process." *Teaching English in the Two-Year College* 10.1 (1983):27–33.

815 Trescares, Pierre. *Possible Pedagogical Applications of a Talking Computer Terminal for the French-Speaking Blind to Foreign Language Teaching,* 1980. ERIC Document ED 202, 227.

816 Turner, Kathleen, and Matthew Marino. "Beyond Word Crunching." In *Sixth International Conference on Computers and the Humanities,* edited by Sarah K. Burton and Douglas D. Short. Rockville, MD: Computer Science Press, 1983, pp. 717–724.

817 Tuttle, Harry Grover. "Computers in the Modern Language Classroom." *NYSAFLT Language Association Bulletin* 37.5 (1981):1–5.

818 —. "Programming/Evaluating Second Language CAI." *Foreign Language Annals* 16.1 (1983):35–39.

819 Twarog, Leon I., and E. Garrison Walters. "Mastery-Based, Self-Paced Instruction in Foreign Languages at Ohio State University: A Report to the Profession on a Four Year Experiment in Individualized Instruction in Six Foreign Languages." *Modern Language Journal* 65.1 (1981):1–23. EJ 251 170.

820 Ule, L. A. "The Use of CONSTAT in Authorship Investigations." *ALCC Bulletin* 3 (1975):211–25.

821 Underwood, John H. *Linguistics, Computers, and the Language Teacher: A Communicative Approach.* Rowley, MA: Newbury House, 1984.

822 —. "Simulated Conversation as a CAI Strategy." *Foreign Language Annals* 15.3 (1982):209–12.

823 —. "Using PILOT for Conversational Foreign Language Programs." *Educational Computer* 1.4 (1981):33, 50.

824 Van Campen, Joseph A. "A Computer-Assisted Course in Russian." *University-Level Computer-Assisted Instruction at Stanford: 1968–1990,* edited by Patrick Suppes, Stanford, CT: Stanford University, 1981, pp. 603–646.

825 Van Pelt, William V. "Another Approach to Using Writer's Workbench Programs: Small Class Applications." In *Sixth International Conference on Computers and the Humanities,* edited by Sarah K. Burton and Douglas D. Short. Rockville, MD: Computer Science Press, 1983, pp. 725–729.

826   Vazulik, Johannes W. "The Personal Computer: An Adjunct to FL Instruction." *MICRO* 1.2 (1980):13–16.

827   Venezky, Richard L. "Computer Applications in Lexicography." In *Lexicography in English,* edited by Raven I. McDavid, Jr. and Audrey R. Duckert. New York: New York Academy of Sciences, 1973, pp. 287–292.

828   Von Alten, Judith Walters. "Translators Gain Fluency: Multilingual Word Processors Point to Universal Communication." *Infoworld* 6.33 (August 13 1984):35–37.

829   Von Blum, Ruth, and Michael E. Cohen. "WANDAH: Writing Aid AND Author's Helper." In *The Computer in Composition Instruction: A Writer's Tool,* edited by William Wresch. Urbana, IL: NTCE, 1984, pp. 154–173.

830   Wager, Walter. "Design Considerations for Instructional Computing Programs." *Journal for Educational Technology Systems* 10 (1982):261–70.

831   Wagers, William D. "Voice-Based Learning." *CALICO Journal* 1.5 (1984):35–38.

832   Wagers, William D., and Karin Horn. *The VBLS: Voice-Based Learning System.* Denton, OH: Scott Instruments Corporation, 1982.

833   Waggoner, Michael. "The New Technologies versus the Lecture Tradition in Higher Education: Is Change Possible?" *Educational Technology* 24.3 (1984): 7–12.

834   Wagner, W. G., *et al.* "Learning Word Processing Skills with Limited Instruction: An Exploratory Study with College Students." *Educational Technology* 25.2 (February 1985):26–28.

835   Waite, Stephen V. F. "Word Position in Plautus: Interplay of Verse Ictus and Word Stress." In *The Computer in Literary and Linguistic Studies,* edited by Jones and Churchhouse. Cardiff, Wales: University of Wales Press, 1976, pp. 92–105.

836   Waldo, Mark L. "Computers and Composition: A Marriage Made in Heaven?" In *Collected Essays on the Written Word and the Word Processor,* edited by Thomas E. Martinez. Villanova, PA: Villanova University Press, 1984, pp. 313–322.

837   Walker, David D. "Towards a National Software Library." *Educational Media International* 3 (1981):20–24.

838   Walker, Richard A., and Chris Sherman. "Evaluating Educational Software." *PC Magazine* 2.6 (1983):519–521, 525.

839   Wall, Shavaun M., and Nancy E. Taylor. "Using Interactive Computer Programs in Teaching Higher Conceptual Skills: An Approach to Instruction in Writing." *Educational Technology* 22.2 (1982):13–17.

840   Wallace, Ivan. "Text-Editing Equipment: Alternatives in Teaching Word Processing." *Business Education Forum* 37.7 (April 1983):8–11.

841   Wallace, M. Elisabeth. "A Computer Writing Project at a Liberal Arts College." *T.H.E. Journal* 12.3 (October 1984):111–115.

842   Waltman, Franklin M. "C.L.A.S. and the Cantar de Mio Cid." *CHum* 10 (1976):145–152.

843   Wanderman, Richard. "Bridge to Clarity: The Computer As Compensatory Writing Tool." *Softalk for the IBM Personal Computer* 3 (June 1984): pp. 25–30.

844   Wang, William S-Y. Introduction. *Language, Writing, and the Computer: Readings from Scientific American.* New York: W. H. Freeman, 1986.

845   Warden, Roseann. "Word Processing in the Contemporary Composition Class." *Writing As a Liberating Activity Newsletter* 1.22 (1984):7–8, 6.

846   Watt, Daniel. "Word Processors and Writing." *Independent School* 42 (February 1983):41–43.

847   —. "Word Processors and Writing, Using Interactive Computer Programs in Higher Conceptual Skills: An Approach to Instruction in Writing." *Educational Technology* (February 1982):13–17.

848   *Webster's New World Dictionary of Computer Terms.* Compiled by Laura Darcy and Louise Boston. New York: Simon and Schuster, 1983.

849   Weible, David M. "The Foreign Language Teacher as Courseware Author." *CALICO Journal* 1.1 (1983):62–64.

850   Weischedel, R. M., W. Voge, and M. James. "An Artificial Intelligence Approach to Language Instruction." *Artificial Intelligence* 10 (1978):225–240.

851   Weisman, Herman M. "Automating the Writing Process." *Basic Technical Writing.* 5th ed. Columbus, OH: Charles E. Merrill, 1985, pp. 51–60.

852   Welsch, Lawrence A. "Using Electronic Mail as a Teaching Tool." *Communications of the ACM* 25 (February 1982):105–108.

853   Wessel, David. "Computer Software for Writers: Helping the Bad, Hurting the Good." *The Wall Street Journal* (July 7, 1986):17.

854   Widmann, R. L. "Computer Collation." *SCHVB* 4 (1973):45–51.

855   —. "Computers and Literary Scholarship." *CHum* 6 (1971):3–14.

856   —. "Recent Scholarship in Literary and Linguistic Studies." *CHum* 7 (1972): 3–27.

857   —. "Trends in Computer Applications to Literature." *CHum* 9 (1975): 231–235.

858   Wilcox, Lance. "The Usefulness of Computer Materials Created by Teachers: Answer to Bork." In *Computers and Composition: Selected Papers from the Conference on Computers in Writing: New Directions in Teaching and Research, University of Minnesota, April 1984,* edited by Lillian Bridwell, Donald Ross, Cynthia L. Selfe, and Kathleen E. Kiefer. Houghton, MI and Fort Collins, CO: Michigan Technological University and Colorado State University, 1985, pp. 293–305.

859   Williams, C. B. *Style and Vocabulary: Numerical Studies.* London, England: Griffin, 1970.

860   Wilson, N., and W. Wright. "Computers and Poetry." In *Proceedings of the 4th Symposium on Small Computers in the Arts* Philadelphia. 25–28 October, 1984. Silver Spring, MD: IEEE Computing Society Press, 1984, pp. 76–88.

861   Winograd, Terry. "Computer Software for Working With Language." *Scientific American* 251.3 (September 1984):130–145.

862   Wisbey, Roy A., ed. *A Complete Concordance to the Vorau and Strassburg "Alexander."* Leeds, England: W. S. Maney and Son, Ltd., 1968.

863   —, ed. *The Computer in Literary and Linguistic Research.* Cambridge: Cambridge University Press, 1971.

864   Wishart, David, and S. Leach. "A Multivariate Analysis of Platonic Prose Rhythm." *CSHVB* 3 (1970):90–99.

865   Withey, Margaret M. "The Computer and Writing." *The English Journal* (November 1983):24–31.

866   Wittig, Susan. "The Computer and the Concept of Text." *Computers and the Humanities* 11.4 (1977):211–215.

867   Wohlert, Harry S. "Voice Input/Output Speech Technologies for German Language Learning." *Unterrichtspraxis* 17.1 (1984):76–84.

868   Womble, Gail G. "Do Word Processors Work in the English Classroom?" *English Journal* 73 (January 1984):34–37.

869   —. "Process and Processor: Is There Room for a Machine in the English Classroom?" *English Journal* 73 (January 1984):34–37.

870   —. "Revising and Computing." In *Writing On-Line: Using Computers in the Teaching of Writing,* edited by James L. Collins and Elizabeth A. Sommers. Upper Montclair, NJ: Boynton-Cook, 1985, pp. 75–82.

871   Woodruff, Earl. "Computers and the Composing Process: An Examination of Computer-Writer Interaction." In *Computers in Composition Instruction,* edited by Joseph Lawlor. Los Alamitos, CA: Southwest Regional Laboratories, 1982, pp. 31–45.

872   Woodruff, Earl, *et al.* "On the Road to Computer-Assisted Compositions." *Journal of Educational Technology Systems* 10 (1981–82):133–148.

873   Woolston, Donald C. "Incorporating Microcomputers into Technical Writing Instruction." *Engineering Education* 75.2 (November 1984):88–90.

874   "Word Processing: How Will It Shape the Student as a Writer?" *Classroom Computer News* 3 (November–December 1982):24–27, 74–76.

875   "Word Processing in the Classroom." *ATARI Teachers' Network* 1.2 (July 1983):2.

876   "Word Processing Throughout the Curriculum." *Electronic Learning* 3 (May–June 1984):46.

877   Worley, Lloyd. "Using Word Processing in Composition Classes." Annual Meeting of the Conference on College Composition and Communication. New York, NY: March 29–31, 1984. ERIC Document ED 243 127.

878   Wresch, William, ed. Computers in English Class: Finally beyond Grammar and Spelling Drills." *College English* 44 (1982):483–490.

879   —. "Computer Essay Generation." *The Computing Teacher* 10 (March 1983): 63–65.

880 —. *The Computer in Composition Instruction.* Urbana, IL: National Council of Teachers of English, 1984.

881 —. "Essay Writer: A Program To Help Students Through the Writing Process." *Collegiate Microcomputer* 1.3 (August 1983):281–287.

882 —. "Questions, Answers, and Automated Writing." In *The Computer in Composition Instruction: A Writer's Tool,* edited by William Wresch. Urbana, IL: NCTE, 1984, pp. 143–153.

883 Wright, William. "Programs That Understand Language: How They Do It—Syntax-Directed Methods/Part 2." *Creative Computing.* 11.11 (November 1985):76–80.

884 Wyatt, David, ed. *Computer-Assisted Language Instruction.* New York: Pergamon Press, 1984.

885 —. *Computers and ESL.* ERIC/CLL Language in Education 56. New York: Harcourt, 1984.

886 —. "Computer-Assisted Language Instruction: Present State and Future Prospect." *System* 11.1 (1983):3–11.

887 —. "ESL Applications of the Computer-Controlled Videodisc Player." *CHum* 18 (1984):243–250.

888 —. *Language Learning and Computers: a Practical Sourcebook.* New York: Regents Publishing, 1984.

889 —. "Three Major Approaches to Developing Computer-Assisted Language Learning Materials for Microcomputers." *CALICO Journal* 1.2 (1983):34–38.

890 Yule, G. Udny. *The Statistical Study of Literary Vocabulary.* Cambridge: Cambridge University Press, 1944.

891 Zaharias, Jane Ann. "Computers in the Language Arts Classroom: Promise and Pitfalls." *Language Arts* 60 (1983):990–996.

892 Zarri, G. P. "Algorithms, *stemmata codicum* and the Theories of Dom H. Quentin." In *The Computer and Literary Studies* Ed. Aitken, Bailey and Hamilton-Smith. Edinburgh, Scotland: Edinburgh University Press, 1973, pp. 225–237.

893 —. "A Computer Model for Textual Criticism?." In *The Computer in Literary and Linguistic Studies,* edited by Jones and Churchhouse. Cardiff, Wales: University of Wales Press, 1976, pp. 133–155.

894 —. "Il metodo per la 'recensio' di Dom H. Quentin esaminato criticamente." *Lingua e Stile* 4 (1969):161–182.

895 Zingle, Henri. "Synthèse vocale en allemand à partir du texte." *ALLC Bulletin* 13 (1985):5–7.

896 Zurek, Jerome. "Computers and the Writing Process: A Report of Students With Two Years' Experience." In *Collected Essays on the Written Word and the Word Processor,* edited by Thomas E. Martinez. Villanova, PA: Villanova University Press, 1984, pp. 156–164.

APPENDIX IV

Glossary of Computer Terms

Artificial Intelligence: the capacity of machines to perform tasks most people would say require human intelligence, for example, learning from experience, solving problems, comprehending natural language, recognizing and responding to auditory patterns, or analyzing a poem. The computer in the film "War Games" demonstrated artificial intelligence. However, such high levels of computer "thinking" have not yet been achieved and await more advanced technology to be realized.

Applications Generator: software that enables a user with no technical knowledge of programming to write computer programs.

ASCII: an acronym for American Standard Code for Information Interchange. See page 16.

Authoring Language: a programming language especially designed for the creation of CAI. PILOT is the best known of these authoring languages.

Authoring System: a program that allows a teacher to create her own CAI without learning a programming language. The teacher writes lessons or interactive exercises that fit into a set of formats provided by the authoring system. Examples of such systems include VBLS, FLIP/ISAAC, CAP, DASHER, Teaching Assistant, and COMET.

Backup: a copy of a file. Some programs automatically make backup files, but if yours doesn't, it's a good idea to create your own as a safeguard against anything happening to the original. This is especially important if you are working on a mainframe, working with a hard disk, or transporting a floppy disk between home and school. Mainframe files are usually backed up on magnetic tape, and hard-disk files on tape, on floppies, or on another hard disk.

BASIC: a programming language created in 1963 at Dartmouth in which instructions are written in standard English. The acronym stands for Beginner's All-purpose Symbolic Instruction Code. Today it is the most popular microcomputer programming language and exists in a number of dialects.

Bit: the smallest unit of data computers recognize—a binary digit. There are only two possible values, expressed as zero and one, or, in terms of electrical impulses, on and off. The computer translates all information, including complex mathematical problems, essays, and graphics, into various combinations of bits in order to manipulate it. This process is called digitizing. A byte equals eight bits.

Boilerplate: prefabricated text for documents used many times. You might use a boilerplate, for example, for the text of a letter accepting papers for a conference. With mail merge programs, computers can disguise boilerplates by inserting personalizing material—for instance, the name of the paper accepted.

Booting (Up): getting the computer up and running. The term comes from the notion of tugging at one's boot-straps. With most microcomputers, one boots up by flipping the "on" switch after inserting a start-up disk. Thus the computer transfers a program into its memory. If your program for some reason does not then run, the computer has failed to boot. [Note: In such cases, check the autoexec file, if there is one.]

Branching: a program's ability to vary its sequence depending on input. This concept is an important one in CAI. A student demonstrating a high ability level may breeze through the lesson, whereas one who is having difficulty can receive more instruction and additional practice.

Bug: usually a software mistake or problem. Programmers can often be found muttering about bugs. The term comes from the early years of computer development when computers were built with tubes and intricate webs of wires. Insects, crawling into the mechanism, could cause it to malfunction. Today, when bugs occur in the hardware, it's most often a problem in the electrical system or in the design of the unit. In most cases, though, the bugs you will find are in the software—errors in the logic of the program. Because modern software is so complex, it is rarely bug-free. If the bugs interfere with the successful or smooth operation of the software, it should be debugged; that is, the errors should be found and corrected. Updates of popular software programs are often created to do just that. The difference between a bug and an "error message" is that in the latter case, the user has probably goofed. Your monitor will display an error message if you've keyed in something that defies the rules of either the program, the computer, or the language. The computer will refuse to go on until you correct the error. Bugs are not so neatly identified, and it is common for bug-infested programs to run.

Byte: the basic unit of measurement for describing memory capacity. Most characters, such as a letter or symbol, may be stored in one byte of memory. 1,024 bytes equal one K or Kilobyte. One million bytes equal a megabyte. See *bit*.

CAI: acronym for "computer-aided instruction" or "computer-assisted instruction"; that is, software designed to help students learn by allowing them to interact with a computer.

CALI: acronym for "computer-assisted language instruction," or CAI for students of foreign languages.

CALL: acronym for "computer-assisted language learning." Many people mistakenly use this term as a synonym for CAI or CALI, but it has a more specialized meaning that depends on the linguistic distinction between language learning and language acquisition.

Card: a board containing chips and circuits.

Cathode Ray Tube: see CRT.

CAVI: acronym for "computer-assisted video instruction." Videodisks or cassettes work in conjunction with computer software to give the instruction a more exciting visual element.

Central Processing Unit (CPU): The computer's "brain," the component containing the circuitry inside the machine where all the computing or "thinking" takes place—that is to say, where all instructions are recognized and executed.

Chip: or IC, short for "integrated circuit." A small piece of semiconducting material, usually silicon, embedded with microscopic integrated circuits that contain coded information and help to control the computer's functions or to store its data. The development of the chip made microcomputers (and credit card calculators) possible. Much current computer research centers on creating a more sophisticated chip.

CMI: acryonym for "computer-managed instruction." Software that enables a teacher to use a computer to design, administer, and evaluate instruction. CMI was a term used in the past to refer to self-paced computer instruction.

Command: an instruction keyed into the computer by the user of a program.

Compatibility: the ability of a program to work on a computer different from the one for which it was originally developed. Also referred to as "transportability" or "transferability."

Computer: a programmable electronic device capable of storing, retrieving, and processing data.

Computer language: see *programming language.*

Concordance: an alphabetical listing of words in a literary text, including a certain amount of the context. Concordances used to take scholars a lifetime to compile. Now, with the help of software designed for the purpose, computers help speed the task immeasurably.

Control Character: a symbol that appears on the monitor but does not print. It indicates a special function of some programs—for example, the marking of a block of text.

Control Key: a key used for sending commands. On most keyboards, it is located to the left of the traditional typewriter keys. The usual method for sending a command using the control key is to hold it down while pressing another key.

Courseware: instructional software.

CPU: see *central processing unit.*

CRT: cathode ray tube, otherwise known as a monitor screen. It looks like a TV set and visually displays input and output from the computer. In choosing a CRT, look for one with good resolution. (If you want to see what poor resolution looks like, hook your TV set up to your computer.) CRT's come in monochrome and color. Amber screens are generally considered easier on the eyes than green screens.

Cursor: a marker that appears on the monitor screen to indicate where you are working in your file or where your next command will be executed. This pointer sometimes appears as a blinking line, a block, or a triangle, depending on your program.

Daisy Wheel: the part of certain letter-quality printers that corresponds to a typewriter ball. Its name comes from its shape—circular with print characters arranged around a central spindle, like the petals of a daisy. Daisy wheels are available in many type fonts, and the wheels can be easily interchanged. Laser printers, which produce higher-quality copy more quickly and more quietly, are gradually supplanting the daisy-wheel printer.

Data Base: a central depository of information. Data base searching, or the ability of the computer to provide quick access to information in large data bases, is one of the most important applications of computers in research.

Data File: a file containing records for the program to manipulate. The records must be entered in a specially structured form dictated by the program. In word processing, a text file, or document file, is a data file that contains the text being composed or edited. Text files differ from other sorts of data files because the text of a document need not follow a fixed form. It is easy to explain the concept of a text file to students by drawing a parallel between it and the contents of a folder in a filing cabinet. The file name, displayed on a directory, can be likened to the label on the file folder. Opening a file is like pulling out the file folder and looking at its contents.

Debug: see bug.

Defaults: preset but changeable directions to the computer that are imbedded in the program. Defaults save the user time by indicating, for example, a standard page length or margin width, so that these directions do not have to be given each time the program is run. Many programs build in a way to customize the defaults.

Dictionary: a word list used in spelling checkers and in some text analysis programs.

Directory: the list of files on the logged disk. In MS-DOS, the command DIR will give you a directory of all files on a disk.

Disk: a storage medium for computers. There are three basic kinds: floppy disks, otherwise known as diskettes or floppies, hard disks, and CD-ROM (Compact Disk Read Only Memory). Floppy disks, which store information on circular, magnetic tape, come in various physical sizes. The size you need depends on the computer. Unlike floppies, hard disks are usually installed as a permanent part of the computer and are made of aluminum or hard plastic. They have a much larger memory and work faster than floppy disks. CD-ROM uses laser technology to store vast amounts of material on a disk similar to those used on compact disk audio equipment. Also spelled *disc.*

Disk Drive: the mechanism in the computer that spins the disk to store information on it and to retrieve information.

Disk-Full Error: this error occurs when the memory capacity of your disk has been exceeded and there is no more room left for writing a file to disk. Improper handling of this error can cause you to lose all the data you have keyed in since last saving the file. Avoid this problem by keeping strict tabs on how much of a disk's memory is still free.

Documentation: the manual that comes with hardware or software. In the early days, documentation was notorious for being poorly written, but recently, manufacturers have tried to make it more user friendly—that is, intelligible. Still, much documentation is far from satisfactory. One often feels, as Byron once said of Coleridge, "I wish he would explain his explanation."

DOS: short for "disk operating system," or the set of master commands to which a computer is built to respond. Different computers have different operating systems that are not interchangeable. Before purchasing software, make sure it runs on your computer's disk operating system.

Dot Commands: see *embedded commands.*

Dot-Matrix Printer: a printer that uses a matrix of dots to form characters. In the early days, dot matrix printing was always easily recognizable as "computer printing" because spaces between dots were not filled in and characters were typically crude in appearance. However, because the technology has improved and these printers now use matrixes with more dots spaced closer together, it sometimes takes an attentive eye to distinguish the print from that produced by a daisy wheel or laser jet. The advantage of dot-matrix printers is that they are relatively inexpensive and quick and can print almost any character.

Down, or Downtime: results when the computer will not work because of some sort of failure. Guard against permanent loss of data caused by the computer suddenly going down by making frequent backup copies of your files and by printing out your documents at intervals. Mainframe users are more incapacitated by downtime than microcomputer users, who, assuming that they have their data stored on floppies, need only move to another computer to continue their work.

Editor: a program used to revise the contents of a computer file.

EDP: acronym for "electronic data processing." Refers to a computer's manipulation of electrical impulses.

Embedded Command: a command that you can place in the text of a document and that gives a word processing program special formatting information. Sometimes such commands are used to change temporarily the defaults in a program. In other cases, they are required because there are no defaults. They often begin with a period that appears in the leftmost column on the screen. The dot instructs the program to treat what follows as a command rather than as material to be printed.

Fatal Error: the program's suddenly terminating in midstream and causing you to lose your data. This error is caused by a hardware failure, an operating system failure, or a bug in the program. The results of a fatal error vary: Your keyboard may lock up—that is, become completely unresponsive; you may see garbage or some curious, nonmeaningful pattern on the monitor; or, without warning, you may find yourself thrown out of your program back into the operating system. If you get a fatal error, try rebooting the system.

Field: in nontext files, a category used to define or "map" the location and length of items in a record for a program to manipulate. Files are made up of records and records are made up of fields.

File: Any entry that shows up on your directory listing, such as programs, records, or documents. See *data file.*

Flowchart: a diagram of a program's logic, showing the steps in its design.

Form Feed: the process in printing of moving from one page to the next. When the printer finds itself at the end of the text on one page, no matter how many lines from the bottom of the page it is, it moves to the top of the next page, before beginning to print again.

Formatting Features: in word processing, the computer must be told how to format text in a word processing program. The directions concerning such matters as right justification, proportional spacing, and boldfacing are called formatting features.

Function Keys: keys that activate preprogrammed commands. In a word processing program, for example, function keys mark the beginning or end of a block of text, move the cursor to the top or bottom of the screen, and so on. Software is available which enables you to redefine and thus customize preprogrammed function keys.

Garbage: unintelligible symbols or patterns of characters displayed on the screen, resulting from a fatal error.

Graphics: computer-generated illustrations displayed on a monitor (either still or animated) or produced on paper with a printer. Good graphics are illustrations of high resolution.

Hard Copy: a computer printout rather than a CRT screen display.

Hard Disk: See *disk*.

Hardware: the machinery of the computer, including such physical equipment as the CPU, the keyboard, the disk drives, the monitor screen, and the printer. The part of the computer, both mechanical and electronic, that you can touch, unlike the software.

Input: information or commands entered into the computer. Also used as a verb to mean the process of feeding information into the computer. Input can be entered from a keyboard or a mouse, or it can be read in by such means as magnetic tape, disk, or optical scanner.

Install Program: customizes a program for a particular computer or printer.

Interactive Program: a program that allows for some semblance of dialogue between a user and the program. Part of the appeal of much CAI is its interactiveness, in which the student receives immediate feedback. Good interactive software responds quickly and in a meaningful way, giving the impression of a two-way conversation taking place. Some interactive programs will not continue until the user responds. In fact, many people believe that only software having this latter characteristic deserves to be called interactive.

Interface: to exchange data. May also refer to the device enabling such an exchange to take place among computer components.

Justification: a formatting feature of word processing that brings text up flush with both right and left margins, as in a newspaper column. Text with a ragged right margin is called unjustified.

K: short for kilobyte, or 1,024 bytes. You generally need 128 K of RAM (random access memory) to run a word processing program. See *byte* and *memory*.

Keyboard: the device that controls the electronic signals enabling a user to key in commands, records, and documents. Many of the keys on a computer keyboard are the same and have the same configuration as those on a typewriter. However, there are additional keys (such as a control key and an enter key) not found on conventional typewriters. Some keyboards are more elaborate than others, with numeric keypads, special programmable function keys, delete keys, and the like.

Laser Printer: a high speed, nonimpact letter-quality printer that enables you to mix different type fonts and to use graphics and foreign-language characters. See *daisy wheel* and *dot-matrix printer.*

Letter-Quality Printer: computer-driven machinery that produces on paper copy closely resembling that of an electric typewriter. See *dot-matrix printer* and *daisy wheel.*

Loading: the process of transferring either a program or data from some information storage device, such as a disk or tape, into the computer's central memory.

Logged Disk Drive: The disk drive the computer has been directed to spin in order to store or retrieve information on the disk it contains. A computer with more than one disk drive requires you or the program to tell it which one to read or log onto.

Macro: one command that tells the computer to execute a predetermined string of commands.

Mainframe Computer: a computer capable of handling more than 45 terminals simultaneously. Unlike a microcomputer, it is too physically large to fit on top of a desk and usually runs on a proprietary operating system —that is, a system used only by the company that developed that particular mainframe, rather than on MS-DOS, PC-DOS, or XENIX. Recent technological advances have resulted in microcomputers with memories larger than those of many early mainframe computers. One either uses a terminal to input into a mainframe computer or uses a MODEM to hook a microcomputer up to a mainframe.

Main Memory: the computer's working space. Like a desk to a scholar, it is the area in which the computer performs its tasks.

Memory: space used for storing data and commands. Computer memory is described in terms of its size and is measured in K or kilobytes. One K of memory is equivalent to 1,024 bytes (which, if printed out double-spaced with one-inch margins on each side, takes up slightly less than half a sheet of 8½″ × 11″ paper).

Menu: in some programs, the menu consists of commands available to the user and listed on the screen for reference. In others, it is the table of contents of a program or a list of options.

Microcomputer: a computer that fits on top of a desk. It contains a microprocessor and may work independently of any other computer or may be connected to a mainframe via a modem. Microcomputers generally have at least 64 K of RAM. Outfitted with hard disks, they may store as much as 160 megabytes or more of data. Its operating system is some variation of PC-DOS, MS-DOS, or UNIX. Also called a *micro* or a *microprocessor.*

Microjustification: a formatting feature that automatically inserts spaces between words in increments smaller than characters in order to bring text up flush with both right and left margins, as in a newspaper column. Microjustified text is easier to read than justified text in which only full character-sized spaces are inserted between words, which sometimes results in large or different-sized gaps.

Microprocessor: a miniaturized CPU on a silicon chip.

Microspacing: available only on certain printers, microspacing is what makes boldfacing possible. The printer must to be able to print horizontally in increments as short as 1/120th of an inch.

Minicomputer: a computer that has greater memory capacity and networking capability than a microcomputer but is generally less powerful than a mainframe. It is usually used for specialized purposes.

Modem: a device enabling computers to communicate with each other via telephone lines. You can hook up your microcomputer with the mainframe at school or with another microcomputer in order to receive and transfer information. In fact, with the right software, your micro can act as a remote terminal to a mainframe.

Monitor: see *CRT.*

Network: computers interconnected for communications purposes. Networks can be highly complex systems linking distant computers. The term can also be used as a verb to indicate the process of using a network. Examples of academic networks include Bitnet (linking IBM mainframes) and Usenet (linking primarily UNIX systems). Networks make possible electronic mail and the transfer of files from one location to another. Sometimes they have bulletin boards. See Appendix I.

On-Line: direct communication between a computer and a terminal. An electronic data base is said to be available on-line if a researcher, using the proper communications hardware and software, may dial in and gain access to it.

Operating System: the master program that gives instructions to the computer about how to handle other programs. The operating system permanently resides in ROM and on disks and normally cannot be changed.

Optical Scanner: a piece of equipment that can take typed or printed text and read it into a computer so that it can be either stored in memory or, with the aid of a speech synthesizer, read aloud. The earliest optical scanners were developed as an aid to the blind. Their principal use in scholarship is to help build data bases and to collate literary texts.

Output: information from a computer that can be read either by a user or by another computer. Output devices include printers, CRTs, speech synthesizers, and modems. The term is sometimes (alas) used as a verb to indicate the process of communicating the noun.

Pascal: a programming language.

Peripheral: a piece of equipment used with a computer—for example, a printer or a modem.

PILOT: acronym for "programmed instruction learning or teaching." A programming language especially designed for writing CAI.

Pitch: the number of characters to the inch. If your printer has microspacing, you can vary the pitch of your printouts.

PLATO: acronym for "programmed logic for automatic teaching operation," a programming language developed at the University of Illinois for implementing CAI in various fields.

Printer: computer-driven machinery that produces on paper information from the computer. See *hard copy, dot-matrix printer, letter-quality printer, laser printer,* and *daisy wheel.*

Printout: see *hard copy.*

Program: the set of sequenced directions telling the computer what to do. As a verb, the act of writing instructions to the computer, using a programming language.

Programmable Key: a key that will operate according to your instructions. It can store text to be inserted into a document with only a few key strokes. Also referred to as a *user-defined key.* See also *function keys.*

Programming Language: a system of rules and symbols used to communicate with the computer for programming purposes. Examples of such languages, which have syntax and other properties similar to those of the languages we speak, include BASIC, COBOL, PL-1, SNOBOL, and FORTRAN. Also called *computer language.*

Proportional Spacing: a formatting feature that allots only the necessary space to each character. For example, an *l* takes up less space than an *m.* Without proportional spacing and microjustification, right-justified text is difficult to read.

RAM: acronym for "random access memory." This memory is easily retrieved but is temporary and is erased when the power is turned off. You can save RAM by writing it to a disk or tape or printing it out.

Random Access: the ability to go straight to a specific part of a file without having to read through the file from the beginning.

Read/Write Head: the mechanism in the disk drive that moves over the spinning disk to store or retrieve information. It is mounted at the end of a short arm, like the needle on a record player.

Reforming Text: in word processing, as a result of the adding, deleting, and moving of text during revision of a document, large gaps may be left in the text, or some parts of the text may exceed the margins. Reforming reduces unnecessary spaces and puts text within the bounds of the margins. Some word processing programs do this automatically; others require the user to do it as part of the editing process.

ROM: acronym for "read only memory." This memory is permanent; that is, what it stores is always in the machine. ROM contains permanent operating instructions for the computer that tell it what to do with the programs you run.

Run: a command that tells the computer to start executing a program or set of instructions. Also used as a verb to mean a program that is operating.

Save: to transfer data in memory to a storage device such as a disk.

Screen: see *CRT*.

Scrolling: moving the cursor so that previously undisplayed text is visible. Because a monitor can usually display only 20 to 24 lines of text, in order to view the preceding or succeeding text in a longer document, the user must scroll.

Simulation: CAI that goes beyond drill-and-practice exercises by encouraging the creative application and manipulation of ideas.

Software: a computer program—a set of instructions telling the computer what to do. Unlike the computer's hardware, which you can see and touch, you cannot see or touch the software, only the storage device that holds it, such as a disk.

Speech Recognition: also called *voice recognition.* The computer's ability to accept human speech as input and respond to it.

Speech Synthesizer: a device that transforms computer output into sounds resembling human speech.

System: the software that directs the computer's internal operation.

Telecommunications: the electronic transmission of information. Radio and television transmissions are a familiar form of telecommunications. Computers networked through telephone lines make possible another form of telecommunications.

Terminal: a piece of equipment, consisting of a keyboard and a monitor, through which a user enters into, and retrieves information from, a mainframe computer. Terminals, sometimes called *work stations* or *dumb terminals,* look something like microcomputers, but they are not autonomous, have no microprocessor, and must be hooked up to a mainframe. With the use of a modem and the communications software, a microcomputer can serve, however, as a remote terminal to a mainframe.

Timesharing: takes place when several people at separate terminals all use the same mainframe computer at the same time.

Toggle Key: in word processing, a key that turns a function on or off. If the function is off, pressing the key will turn it on. If the function is on, pressing the key will turn it off. Functions such as insertion, right justification, underlining, and boldfacing are sometimes controlled with toggle keys.

Transportability: see *compatibility*.

Tutorial: a type of CAI.

User Friendly: said of a computer program that is relatively easy for someone who is not a computer specialist to learn to use.

Videodisc: a device for storing visual information.

Word Processing Software: a program designed to allow the user to manipulate text.

Word Processor: a machine that is strictly dedicated to word processing functions and cannot run other types of software. This type of equipment should not be confused with a microcomputer running word processing software.

Word Wrap: the word processing feature that automatically moves text to a new line when text on the previous line grows too long to fit within the right margin.

INDEX

ACKNOWLEDGMENTS

Permission to reprint materials on the following pages is gratefully acknowledged:

Pages 80, 86, and 87: Excerpted from *A Concordance to the Poems of Alexander Pope*, compiled by Emmett G. Bedford and Robert J. Dilligan (copyright 1974 by Gale Research Company; reprinted by permission of the publisher), Gale Research, 1974.

Page 82: Excerpted from *A Concordance to F. Scott Fitzgerald's The Great Gatsby*, compiled by Andrew T. Crosland (copyright © 1975 by Matthew J. Brucolli and C.E. Frazer Clark, Jr.; reprinted by permission of Gale Research Company), Gale Research, 1975.

Page 83: Excerpted from A Concordance to the Plays and Prefaces of Bernard Shaw, compiled by E. Dean Bevan (copyright © 1971 by Gale Research Company; reprinted by permission of the publisher), Gale Research, 1971.

Page 81: From Linda D. Misek, *Context Concordance to John Milton's "Paradise Lost,"* (Case Western Reserve, 1971), p. 158.

Pages 84 and 85: Reprinted from Bryant C. Freeman (ed.): *Concordance du Théâtre et de Poésies de Jean Racine.* Programmed by Alan Batson. Copyright © 1968 by Cornell University. Used by permission of the publisher, Cornell University Press.

Page 87: From Roy A. Wisbey, *A Complete Concordance to the Vorau and Straussburg "Alexander,"* 1968, pp. 425, 445. Reprinted by permission of W.S. Maney & Son Limited.

Page 89: From John B. Smith, "A New Environment for Literary Analysis," in *Perspectives in Computing 4*, No. 2/3 (1984), p. 25. Reprinted by permission of John B. Smith.

Page 105: From Barron Brainerd, "An Exploratory Study of Pronouns and Articles as Indices of Genre in English," in *Language and Style*, Vol. 5, No. 4, (1972). Reprinted by permission.

Page 109: From J. Joyce, "Networks of Sound: Graph Theory Applied to Studying Rhymes," in *Computing in the Humanities, Proceedings of the Third International Conference on Computing in the Humanities*, ed. Lusigan and North, 1977, p. 310.

Page 111: From Wendy Rosslyn, "COCOA as a Tool for the Analysis of Poetry," in *ALLC Bulletin 3* (1975), pp. 15–16. Reprinted by permission of the ALLC.

Page 115: Reprinted by permission of the publisher, from *Computing in the Humanities*, edited by Peter C. Patton and Renee A. Holoien. (Lexington, Mass.: Lexington Books, D.C. Heath and Company, Copyright 1981, D.C. Heath and Company).

Page 119: From G.L.M. Berry-Rogghe, "The Computation of Collocations and Their Relevance in Lexical Studies," in *The Computer and Literary Study*, ed., Aitken, Bailey, and Hamilton-Smith, 1973, p. 108.

Page 121: Reprinted from *Sixth International Conference on Computers and the Humanities*, edited by Burton and Short, from the article, "Themes, Statistics, and the French Novel" by Paul Bratley and Paul A. Fortier, copyright © 1983, with the permission of the publisher, Computer Science Press, Inc., 1803 Research Boulevard, Rockville, Maryland, U.S.A.

Page 134: Ruth A. Widman, "The Computer in Historical Collation: Use of the IBM 360/75 in Collating Multiple Editions of *A Midsummer Nights Dream,*" in Wisbey, R. A., ed., *The Computer in Literary and Linguistic Research* (New York: Cambridge University Press, 1971), p. 61. Copyrighted by and reprinted by permission of the Cambridge University Press.

Pages 135, 136, and 137: From CNRS (Centre National de la Recherche Scientifique), from Penny Gilbert, "The Preparation of Prose-Text Editions with the COLLATE System," in *La Pratique des ordinateurs dans la critique des textes* (1979). Reprinted by the permission of CNRS (Centre National de la Recherche Scientifique), pp. 246, 250, 252.

Page 140: From Hans W. Gabler's 1984 edition of Joyce's *Ulysses,* p. 1414. Reprinted by permission of Garland Publishers.

ABOUT THE AUTHORS

PAULA FELDMAN has a B.A. from Bucknell University and an M.A. and Ph.D. in English literature from Northwestern University. She is co-editor of *The Journals of Mary Shelley* (Oxford University Press) and author of various articles on Byron, the Shelleys, and their literary circle. Her current project is another scholarly edition, *The Collected Letters of Edward John Trelawny.* A textbook she co-authored, *The Microcomputer and Business Writing* (Random House), is widely used in college business writing classes. She is an associate professor of English at the University of South Carolina, where she has taught for the last twelve years.

BUFORD NORMAN is associate professor of French at the University of South Carolina. He received his B.A. from Davidson College and his Ph.D. from Yale University, with a specialization in seventeenth-century French literature. He has published articles on Pascal, Racine, La Rochefoucauld, Cyrano, and Flaubert, and has recently completed a book on styles and methods in Pascal. His current project is a study of the opera libretto in seventeenth-century France and its relationship to Racinian tragedy. He uses a computer constantly in both his teaching and research, and also in compiling stats for his softball team.